Utilizing Embeddings to Learn a Universal Customer Behavior Representation in E-Commerce

Miguel Alves Gomes

Utilizing Embeddings to Learn a Universal Customer Behavior Representation in E-Commerce

Springer Vieweg

Miguel Alves Gomes
Bergische Universität Wuppertal
Wuppertal, Germany

This work was accepted as a dissertation by the School of Electrical, Information and Media Engineering at the University of Wuppertal in fulfillment of the requirements for the degree Doctor of Engineering (Dr.-Ing.).

ISBN 978-3-658-50780-0 ISBN 978-3-658-50781-7 (eBook)
https://doi.org/10.1007/978-3-658-50781-7

This Springer Vieweg imprint is published by the registered company Springer Fachmedien Wiesbaden GmbH, part of Springer Nature.
The registered company address is: Abraham-Lincoln-Str. 46, 65189 Wiesbaden, Germany

Acknowledgments A dissertation is never accomplished alone. It represents the culmination of countless moments of support, inspiration, and encouragement from many people to whom I am deeply and sincerely grateful.

First and foremost, I wish to express my eternal gratitude to my parents, Julieta and Horacio, who have made my education and academic journey possible. Their unwavering support, constant presence, and belief in me have laid the foundation for everything I have achieved. This dissertation would never have come into existence without their love and encouragement.

I am profoundly thankful to Tobias for his invaluable mentorship. His ideas are always inspiring, his feedback consistently insightful, and his energy genuinely motivating. He is not only a mentor but also a true role model. I am especially grateful for his support during the final weeks of the dissertation. Despite the intense pace, he always made time to provide thoughtful feedback and guidance.

I would also like to express my sincere appreciation to my group leaders. André, who guided me during the final phase of this dissertation, supported me with his precise and constructive feedback during the writing process. His attentive supervision helped sharpen the quality of the final work. Richard, who served as my group leader for over four years, has had a lasting influence on my academic and professional development. He shaped the way I approach research, solve problems, and think critically, his mentorship has left a deep imprint on my working style and intellectual growth.

My gratitude also extends to all my colleagues, whose thoughtful discussions and camaraderie have made this journey more enriching and enjoyable.

Special thanks to Philipp, who, together with Breinify, generously provided the data that formed the empirical foundation of this research.

Finally, I am deeply thankful to my fiancée Nhu and my son Hy. Their presence during the final, most demanding phase of this dissertation has been both grounding and uplifting. In particular, the birth of my son during the time of writing gave me an extraordinary source of strength and motivation. Despite the emotional and physical demands of that period, they filled my life with love and purpose. Their unwavering support and joy made even the most challenging moments meaningful and worthwhile.

Competing Interests The author has no competing interests to declare that are relevant to the content of this manuscript.

Abstract

E-commerce is a highly dynamic and competitive market, in which customer satisfaction plays a central role in determining commercial success. To deliver personalized experiences at scale, systems must be able to model individual customer behavior reliably. This requires a universal customer representation that supports diverse marketing strategies without repeated redesign. However, one major challenge in real-world personalization systems is restricted access to personal data due to customer anonymity and stringent data protection regulations, such as the GDPR. Additionally, these representations should be computationally efficient and capable of real-time inference to enable timely and context-aware customer engagement, which can significantly enhance customer experience and conversion outcomes.

Existing approaches typically fall into two categories: manual feature engineering, which is interpretable but lacks flexibility and generalization, and end-to-end deep learning models, which offer adaptability but are resource-intensive and personal-data-based. Although many recent methods rely on embedding-based representations, these embeddings are typically static by design. Therefore, they are incapable of integrating new products or interactions without full retraining. To date, there is no established solution that addresses these trade-offs while enabling dynamic, privacy-aware personalization.

This thesis responds these gaps by proposing a universal customer representation that is privacy-compliant, task-agnostic, and incrementally adaptable. A decoupled three-stage approach is introduced, in which customer embeddings are learned in a self-supervised manner from behavioral interaction sequences alone, without requiring customer-specific features. These embeddings are then combined with down-stream models for task-specific customer intention prediction. To capture temporal dynamics, the embedding representation is further extended with structured time in-formation derived from the interaction context. To support continuous model adaptation, a lifelong learning embedding approach is developed that enables the incremental integration of new tokens, such as products, without requiring full retraining. This approach also supports dynamic adjustment of the embedding dimensionality to accommodate evolving interaction spaces and employs regularization strategies to prevent the forgetting of previously learned representations.

The effectiveness of the proposed approaches is demonstrated by empirical evaluations across multiple real-world e-commerce datasets and tasks, including purchase prediction, churn prediction, and click prediction. The decoupled three-stage approach consistently outperforms state-of-the-art baselines, which highlights the strength of combining self-supervised representation learning with flexible downstream models. The time-extended embedding significantly improves performance in all datasets, especially under sparse data conditions. Finally, the lifelong learning embedding approach outperforms static retraining in dynamic environments.

By decoupling personalization from personal data, the proposed approach offers a viable path for building data privacy-compliant personalization systems.

Kurzfassung

Der Onlinehandel ist ein hochdynamischer und wettbewerbsintensiver Markt, in dem die Kundenzufriedenheit eine zentrale Rolle für den kommerziellen Erfolg spielt. Um personalisierte Erlebnisse zu ermöglichen, müssen Systeme in der Lage sein, das in-dividuelle Kundenverhalten zuverlässig zu modellieren. Dies erfordert eine universel-le Kundenrepräsentation, die vielfältige Marketingstrategien unterstützt, ohne dass diese neu entwickelt werden müssen. Eine wesentliche Herausforderung von Personalisierungssystemen ist dabei die Einschränkung auf personenbezogene Daten, die durch Kundenanonymität und strenge Datenschutzvorschriften wie die DSGVO bedingt ist. Darüber hinaus sollten diese Repräsentationen echtzeitfähig sein, um eine positive, kontextbezogene Kundenerfahrung in Echtzeit zu gewährleisten.

Die bestehenden Ansätze lassen sich typischerweise in Expertensysteme und End-to-End-Deep-Learning-Modelle unterteilen. Expertensysteme basieren auf manueller Merkmalsentwicklung. Diese ist zwar interpretierbar, jedoch wenig flexibel und generalisierbar. End-to-End-Modelle sind zwar anpassungsfähig, jedoch ressourcenin-tensiv und basieren auf personenbezogenen Daten. Diese Ansätze verwenden häufig Embedding-basierte Repräsentationen, die jedoch in der Regel statisch sind und keine Integration neuer Produkte oder Interaktionen ohne vollständiges Neutraining erlauben. Bis heute existiert keine etablierte Lösung, die diese Zielkonflikte adressiert und gleichzeitig eine dynamische, datenschutzfreundliche Personalisierung ermöglicht.

Diese Arbeit schließt diese Lücke, indem sie eine universelle Kundenrepräsentation einführt, die datenschutzkonform, aufgabenunabhängig und inkrementell anpass-bar ist. Es wird ein entkoppelter, dreistufiger Ansatz vorgestellt, bei dem Kunden-Embeddings ohne die Nutzung kunden-spezifischer Merkmale self-supervised aus Verhaltensinteraktionssequenzen gelernt werden. Diese Embeddings werden anschlie-ßend mit nachgelagerten Lernmodellen zur aufgabenspezifischen Erkennung von Kundenintentionen kombiniert. Zur Erfassung zeitlicher Dynamiken im Kundenver-halten wird die Embedding-Repräsentation durch strukturierte Zeitinformationen aus dem Interaktionskontext ergänzt. Zur kontinuierlichen Modellanpassung wird ein Mechanismus für kontinuierliches Lernen entwickelt, der die inkrementelle Integration neuer Tokens (z. B. Produkte) ohne vollständiges Neutraining ermöglicht. Dieser Mechanismus erlaubt zudem die dynamische Anpassung der Embeddings und nutzt Regularisierungsstrategien, um das Vergessen bereits gelernter Repräsentatio-nen zu verhindern.

Empirische Auswertungen auf mehreren realen Datensätzen und Vorhersageaufgaben, darunter Kauf-, Abwanderungs- und Klickvorhersage, zeigen die Wirksamkeit des Ansatzes. Der dreistufige Ansatz übertrifft durchweg moderne Verfahren und verdeutlicht die Stärke der Kombination aus Repräsentationslernen und Aufgaben-modellen. Das zeiterweiterte Embedding verbessert die Leistung in allen Datensätzen signifikant, insbesondere in solchen mit wenigen Informationen. Schließlich ist der Ansatz des kontinuierlichen Lernens dem statischen Neutraining in dynamischen Umgebungen überlegen.

Durch die Entkopplung der Personalisierung von personenbezogenen Daten bietet der vorgeschlagene Ansatz einen gangbaren Weg zur Entwicklung von Personalisierungssystemen, die den Datenschutz berücksichtigen.

Publications

During my time as a scientific researcher at the Chair of Technologies and Management of Digital Transformation of the University of Wuppertal, the following peer-reviewed publications have been published.

Conference Papers Related to Dissertation

ALVES GOMES, M., TERCAN, H., BODNAR, T., MEISEN, P., AND MEISEN, T. A filter is better than none: Improving deep learning-based product recommendation models by using a user preference filter. In *2021 IEEE 23rd Int Conf on High Performance Computing & Communications; 7th Int Conf on Data Science & Systems; 19th Int Conf on Smart City; 7th Int Conf on Dependability in Sensor, Cloud & Big Data Systems & Application (HPCC/DSS/SmartCity/DependSys)* (2021), pp. 1278–1285. https://doi.org/10.1109/HPCC-DSS-SmartCity-DependSys53884.2021.00195

ALVES GOMES, M., MEYES, R., MEISEN, P., AND MEISEN, T. Will this online shopping session succeed? predicting customer's purchase intention using embeddings. In *Proceedings of the 31st ACM International Conference on Information and Knowledge Management* (New York, NY, USA, 2022), CIKM'22, Association for Computing Machinery, pp. 2873–2882. https://doi.org/10.1145/3511808.3557127

Conference Workshop Papers Related to Dissertation

ALVES GOMES, M., MEISEN, P., AND MEISEN, T. Towards lifelong learning embeddings: An algorithmic approach to dynamically extend embeddings. In *3rd Workshop on End-End Customer Journey Optimization at KDD2024* (2024). https://arxiv.org/abs/2408.14118

Submitted Conference Papers Related to Dissertation

Alves Gomes, M., Meslem, D., Meisen, P., and Meisen, T. Lifelong-learning embeddings: Continual representation learning for dynamic e-commerce trends. In *Submitted to 34st ACM International Conference on Information and Knowledge Management* (2025)

Journal Papers Related to Dissertation

Alves Gomes, M., and Meisen, T. A review on customer segmentation methods for personalized customer targeting in e-commerce use cases. *Information Systems and e-Business Management 21*, 3 (2023), 527–570

Alves Gomes, M., Wönkhaus, M., Meisen, P., and Meisen, T. Tee: Real-time purchase prediction using time extended embeddings for representing customer behavior. *Journal of Theoretical and Applied Electronic Commerce Research 18*, 3 (2023), 1404–1418. https://www.mdpi.com/0718-1876/18/3/70

Alves Gomes, M., Meyes, R., Meisen, P., and Meisen, T. It's not always about wide and deep models: Click-through rate prediction with a customer behavior-embedding representation. *Journal of Theoretical and Applied Electronic Commerce Research 19*, 1 (2024), 135–151. https://www.mdpi.com/0718-1876/19/1/8

Alves Gomes, M., Meisen, P., and Meisen, T. Efficient personalization in e-commerce: Leveraging universal customer representations with embeddings. *Journal of Theoretical and Applied Electronic Commerce Research 20*, 1 (2025). https://www.mdpi.com/0718-1876/20/1/12

Other Publications

Hütten, N., Alves Gomes, M., Hölken, F., Andricevic, K., Meyes, R., and Meisen, T. Deep learning for automated visual inspection in manufacturing and maintenance: A survey of open- access papers. *Applied System Innovation 7*, 1 (2024). https://www.mdpi.com/2571-5577/7/1/11

Contents

Abbreviations

Ad	Advertisement
ANN	Artificial Neural Network
AUC	Area Under the Receiver Operating Characteristic Curve
CBOW	Continuous Bag of Words
CL	Continual Learning
CNN	Convolutional Neural Network
CTR	Click-Through Rate
DIEN	Deep Interest Evolution Network
DIN	Deep Interest Network
DL	Deep Learning
DNN	Deep Neural Network
DT	Decision Tree
DUPN	Deep User Perception Network
EWC	Elastic Weight Consolidation
FN	False Negative
FP	False Positive
FPR	False Positive Rate
GB	Gradient Boosting
GDPR	General Data Protection Regulation
LLE	Lifelong Learning Embedding
LLM	Large Language Model
LR	Logistic Regression
LSTM	Long Short-Term Memory
LwF	Learning without Forgetting

MAS	Memory Aware Synapses
ML	Machine Learning
MLP	Multi-Layer Perceptron
NLP	Natural Language Processing
RF	Random Forest
RFM	Recency, Frequency, and Monetary
RNN	Recurrent Neural Network
ROC	Receiver Operating Characteristic
SMOTE	Synthetic Minority Oversampling Technique
TEE	Time Extended Embedding
TN	True Negative
TP	True Positive
TPR	True Positive Rate
UCR	Universal Customer Representation

List of Figures

List of Tables

Introduction

1

The easiest way to stop piracy is not by putting antipiracy technology to work. It's by giving those people a service that's better than what they're receiving from the pirates.

– Gabe Newell

1.1 Motivation

The current century has been defined by the digitalisation of society, facilitated by the proliferation of mobile devices and the connectivity and utilisation of the Internet. This development has led to a notable simplification in the use of online services and online shopping for the customer. For instance, the advent of one-click purchasing has made it significantly easier for customers to find and purchase products online without navigating through multiple pages or performing extensive searches. This unprecedented accessibility is made possible by search engines and recommendation systems playing a particularly pivotal role in the operations of e-commerce companies [34, 72, 172, 279]. Concurrently, these advancements have created a multitude of opportunities for online businesses to engage with their customers, give them a personalized experience, and increase their revenue [80, 190]. The global e-commerce market reflects this growth, with revenue projected to reach 4,117 billion US dollars in 2024, and is expected to experience an annual growth rate of 9.49% between 2024 and 2029, culminating in a market volume of 6,478 billion US dollars by 2029 [216]. According to market analysis, the number of e-commerce users is projected to rise to 3.6 billion by 2029 [216]. This makes e-commerce a highly competitive and rapidly evolving environment, offering a range of potential opportunities but also posing significant challenges. As highlighted by studies from Leeflang et al. [134], Li et al. [137], and Xiang et al. [140], one possibility for online

M. Alves Gomes, *Utilizing Embeddings to Learn a Universal Customer Behavior Representation in E-Commerce*, https://doi.org/10.1007/978-3-658-50781-7_1

companies is that they must adapt their strategies to align with the evolving needs of their customers in order to maintain a competitive advantage.

The importance of personalization in e-commerce was already recognized in the early 2000s, for example, by Kim and Anh [124], which had led to a paradigm shift in online marketing. Specifically, as a result of the increasing prevalence of the internet and data-driven technologies, the limitations of mass marketing were recognized and opened the potential for more personalized marketing approaches which remains a pertinent issue for both business and academia alike [14, 44, 56, 170, 212]. As shown by studies from Mulhern [166], Zeithaml et al. [266], and Kumar et al. [132], personalization is profitable for companies, and having knowledge about customer behavior is a decisive factor for their success.

In contrast to traditional brick-and-mortar retail, personalization is a privilege of e-commerce which provides a vast array of possibilities for tailoring the shopping experience of customers to align with their preferences and needs. Personalized marketing is made possible by the data gathered from customer interaction, such as browsing history, purchase behavior, or customer feedback. As time progresses, this results in the accumulation of a considerable amount of interaction data, which is a crucial component for the implementation of customization strategies in e-commerce. An additional prerequisite for this customization is the analysis of customer interactions with the objective of obtaining an appropriate behavioral representation model. Such information and representations are fundamental for companies when planning resources, inventories, or marketing strategies [7, 105, 124, 132, 166, 266]. However, even with the data available modeling customer and predicting future customer behavior and intention is a non-trivial challenge as stated by Lin et al. [146] and Martinez et al. [156]. Customer behavior is subject to constant change as it is highly dependent on a variety of factors such as season, inflation, and local as well as global developments.

Achieving personalization requires the development of a robust customer representation capable of capturing intricate customer behavior patterns and performing predictive analyses. Customer representation is a fundamental step in the personalized customer targeting process. Traditionally, this endeavor has demanded substantial manual effort and domain expertise, often involving feature engineering following extensive data analysis processes [7, 67, 105, 146, 156]. Thereby, the Recency, Frequency, and Monetary (RFM)-analysis is one of the most used feature extraction methods in the e-commerce context as shown by Alves Gomes and Meisen [7]. However, the rapid advancements in Machine Learning (ML) and Deep Learning (DL) have transformed this landscape, reducing both the data analysis process and model reengineering, thus allowing for more scalable and automated approaches to personalization. These approaches allow businesses to accurately predict future customer behavior leading to improved customer satisfaction and engagement and therefore, provide tailored customer experiences [59, 130, 192]. Thereby, DL models gained popularity in general due to their ability to rapidly recognize patterns in vast amounts of data swiftly visualize analytics, and provide in-depth insights [48, 82, 213]. Especially, with the ongoing development, deep-attention-based networks for predicting customer click behavior like DIEN [279] or transformer-based models [237] like Bert4Rec [221] for product recommendations are gaining huge popularity in e-commerce. To extract information from the available data and represent customer behavior, these DL approaches use embeddings to project discrete information, such as product IDs, into a latent vector space, as shown by many researchers in the last years [9, 11, 12, 41, 111, 206, 214, 226, 236, 268, 278].

Despite significant advancements in DL and the increasing availability of vast datasets in the e-commerce sector, accurately predicting future customer behavior remains a challenging task. Unlike data in other domains, which often exhibit recurring and stable patterns, customer behavior is inherently dynamic and subject to constant change. Additionally, the data collected is often both use case- and customer-specific, which limits its generalizability and sharing across organizations.

Current methods often necessitate substantial labor-intensive feature engineering that is customized for specific campaigns and use cases to represent their customers. This process must be repeated for different scenarios, as customer representations are narrowly designed for particular contexts. To address this issue, there is a growing need for a more Universal Customer Representation (UCR) as stated by Ni et al. [172] and Yang et al. [261]. In this context, "universal" refers to the development of representations that are applicable across a wide range of use cases and tasks, without the need for reengineering for each specific instance within an online service. For instance, a company only needs to learn a single representation of a customer that can be used for different marketing campaigns such as product recommendations, personalized offers, and customer behavior analysis.

In addition to the technical challenges of data-driven personalization and customer modeling, companies must carefully balance their marketing ambitions with the obligation to adhere to strict data protection laws and privacy regulations. The collection, processing, and storage of customer interaction data must comply with regulation such as the General Data Protection Regulation (GDPR) [69] and similar regional rules [215], which limit the ways in which personal or identifiable information can be tracked, stored, and reused over time. This legal landscape makes it increasingly challenging to build persistent and highly personalized customer profiles without risking non-compliance or violating trust. Consequently, any viable UCR must be designed from the outset to operate within these legal and ethical boundaries, relying wherever possible on anonymous, session-based interaction signals instead of getting the customer's consent. By doing so, companies can ensure that behavioral insights remain actionable while respecting privacy principles and minimizing data exposure. Successfully balancing these obligations with the technical demands of scalability, segmentation, and real-time targeting defines a core challenge for modern e-commerce personalization [7, 105, 124].

1.2 Research Goals

Motivated by the need of personalization considering real-world constraints, the goal of this thesis is to develop a data-driven method for modeling customer behavior that enables accurate predictions of future customer actions. Specifically, the core objective is to create a UCR that is applicable across various use cases within an e-commerce company, including different forecasting tasks such as purchase intention prediction or Click-Through Rate (CTR) but also considering real-world constraints such as limitation of customer data that can be gathered and stored, the need for data privacy, and the requirement for real-time performance. Therefore, the UCR aims to represent each customer in a way that can be consistently applied to different marketing and operational tasks. Thus it optimizes the customer experience across the board which emphasizes the growing importance of automated methods in analyzing customer behavior to anticipate needs and deliver targeted experiences.

In order to be broadly applicable, the proposed method must be transferable, i.e., it should work across diverse e-commerce platforms, regardless of company size or sector. Given the highly dynamic nature of e-commerce, the model must also be designed to be automated and scalable, minimizing the need for human intervention. This requirement eliminates the need for permanent feature engineering, which is often a time-consuming process and may not keep up with rapidly changing customer preferences and behaviors.

In addition, the method must adhere to additional requirements, such as ensuring data privacy and resource conservation as well as real-time capable. Compliance with data protection regulations is essential when handling sensitive customer data. Furthermore, in a landscape where customers are often anonymous and not logged in, it is advantageous to handle data without personal information. Moreover, resource efficiency is crucial, as e-commerce platforms must manage large volumes of data while maintaining optimal performance.

To fulfill the research goal outlined above, this thesis aims to answer three research questions, each addressing specific aspects of customer behavior modeling in the e-commerce domain. The questions are designed to explore both the theoretical and practical implications of developing UCR while considering real-world constraints.

RQ 1

How can customer behavior be represented in the context of e-commerce considering real-world requirements to predict future customer behavior for different tasks and use cases and can interaction data alone be effectively used to learn these representations?

The first research question focuses on the representation of customer behavior in a way that can be effectively utilized across various e-commerce tasks to predict future customer behavior. A key focus here is determining how to develop a UCR that can handle the diverse data sources and the dynamic nature of customer interactions, while considering practical constraints such as data privacy. By addressing this, the thesis explores whether a single, flexible representation can be learned from diverse data sources to optimize customer experiences across a range of e-commerce platforms.

RQ 2

What impact does integrating additional customer behavior data have on self-supervised learned embeddings and how can this integration be practically implemented in e-commerce?

The second research question examines the effect of incorporating additional customer behavior data into self-supervised learning models, which have shown great promise in developing meaningful representations without requiring extensive labeled data. As data in e-commerce can be highly variable, ranging from product views and purchases to browsing patterns and time on page, this question explores how diverse behavioral data sources can improve the quality of learned embeddings and whether these richer representations can enhance the accuracy of predictions. Practical implementation in real-world e-commerce settings, in which companies often have limited resources and strict privacy regulations, is also considered. This research question aims to identify the most effective way to combine different types of customer data for improved performance.

RQ 3

How can self-supervised customer behavior embeddings be improved to adapt to the dynamics of real-world e-commerce applications?

The third research question focuses on solving the limitation of embeddings regarding their missing capability to encode new information after initialization, which is necessary for real-world applications. E-commerce is a highly dynamic environment, in which the broad range of products and services are changing rapidly and furthermore, customer behavior is constantly evolving. In practice, e-commerce platforms face rapidly changing trends, customer preferences, and even external factors, such as seasonality or market shifts. This question investigates methods for ensuring that self-supervised embeddings remain relevant and accurate over time, without requiring extensive retraining or manual intervention. It also explores how embeddings can be refined in real time to account for new patterns in customer behavior, ensuring the model remains aligned with real-world requirements. This question contributes to the development of more robust and flexible models capable of long-term utility in dynamic settings.

Open RQ

Can the proposed three-stage approach using self-supervised learning embedding representation be used on other application domains outside of e-commerce?

In addition to the primary research questions, this thesis explores the generalizability of self-supervised learned customer behavior embeddings to other domains. While the focus is on e-commerce, the underlying principles of behavior modeling, self-supervised learning, and universal representations may have broader applications. For instance, domains such as healthcare, finance, and entertainment also rely heavily on understanding and predicting customer behavior. This open research question investigates whether the techniques and insights derived from this thesis can be extended to other industries, contributing to a wider field of study in ML and representation learning.

By addressing these research questions, this thesis not only develops a practical solution for e-commerce customer behavior modeling but also contributes to the broader understanding of self-supervised learning, representation learning, and their applicability to real-world, resource-constrained environments.

1.3 Thesis Structure

Fig. 1.1 illustrates the structure of the thesis to answer the stated research questions. Chap. 2 lays the theoretical groundwork and provides a detailed exploration of the object of investigation. It begins by offering a comprehensive explanation of customer targeting in e-commerce, including how customers are targeted, the concept itself, and the necessary steps involved in the process. The chapter also defines the specific scope of the investigation by outlining which part of the customer journey is covered and what conditions are considered to address the research questions. Furthermore, foundational knowledge of customer representation is introduced, followed by an overview of ML basics, particularly focusing on sequential models and relevant evaluation metrics within the e-commerce domain. Special attention is given to learning embeddings. Chap. 3 reviews related work, summarizing the state-of-the-art approaches currently used to model customers and predict future behavior. The emphasis here is on the feature engineering and learning models employed in these methodologies. Chap. 4 presents potential use cases and datasets for e-commerce. This includes both freely available datasets as well as a proprietary industrial dataset that is provided for the research. Furthermore, requirements for the use cases are outlined, including the challenges and constraints that must be considered when developing a customer behavior representations. Chap. 5 focuses on how customer behavior can be learned using embeddings. It starts with a formal description of the proposed approach as well as the experimental design and all necessary steps to evaluate the approach. This chapter aims to answer Research Question 1. Chap. 6 investigates how the learned embeddings can be enhanced by integrating additional customer behavior data. It begins with laying the theoretical foundation for time encoding. Based on this foundation, the chapter explores how time encoding can be applied to customer behavior embeddings and examines its effectiveness, thereby answering Research Question 2. Chap. 7 delves into the concept of Lifelong Learning Embedding (LLE). It begins by discussing the motivation for lifelong learning in this context, highlighting why this remains an unsolved problem regarding embeddings in e-commerce. The chapter then introduces the proposed approach and the corresponding results, thereby answering research question 3. Chap. 8 investigates the transferability of the proposed behavioral embeddings

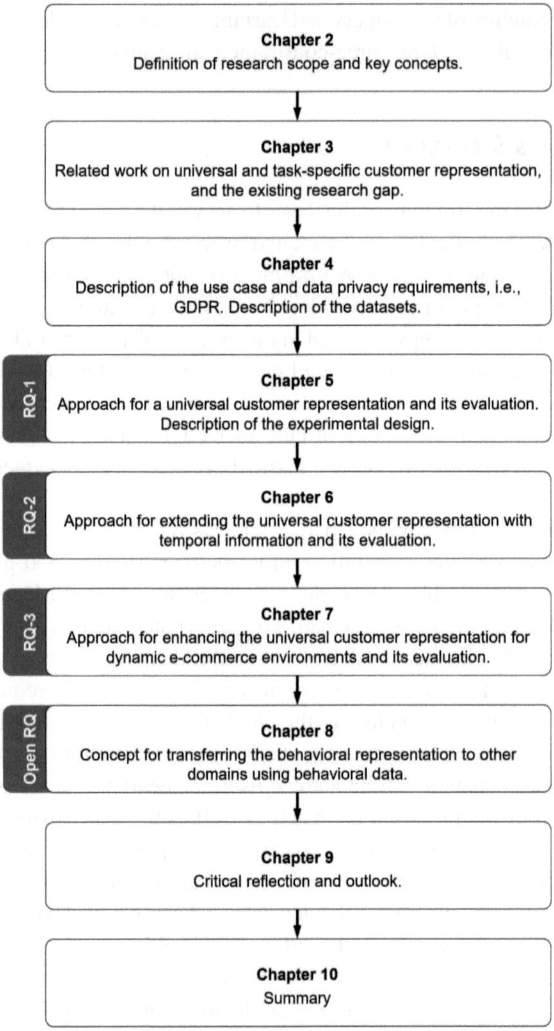

Fig. 1.1 Structure of the thesis and assignment of the research questions

beyond the e-commerce domain. This chapter addresses an open research question regarding how these behavior representation embeddings can be applied to other areas with behavior data. Chap. 9 provides a critical discussion of the results obtained throughout the thesis, identifying potential limitations and offering suggestions for future research. Finally, Chap. 10 concludes the thesis with a summary of the key findings and contributions.

Fundamentals and Research Scope 2

In this chapter, the fundamental concepts and methodologies relevant for answering the research questions are established. This includes the core principles of e-commerce analytics such as the customer journey and customer targeting, and the ML techniques necessary to create a customer representation as well as predicting future customer behavior in e-commerce.

Sect. 2.1 provides a comprehensive definition of customer targeting in e-commerce, explaining the customer journey, how it is typically approached, and highlighting the relationship between customer targeting and the prediction of future customer behavior. Additionally, this section defines the research scope, specifying the areas in which the investigation of this thesis is conducted. Sect. 2.2 examines the various types of customer representations in detail, focusing on how customers and their behavior can be modeled. This includes an exploration of the data-driven approaches crucial for understanding the scope and direction of the research. Sect. 2.3 introduces key ML concepts often used in literature and applications for predicting customer behavior. Special attention is given to the methodologies employed in this research and the corresponding evaluation techniques. Following the introduction of ML fundamentals, Sect. 2.4 explains the concept of embeddings, detailing how they can be learned and applied in the scope to predict future customer behavior.

2.1 Customer Targeting in E-Commerce—Definition and Scope

As outlined in the motivation section of Chap. 1, e-commerce represents a multi-billion-dollar industry with numerous opportunities for research across a variety of use cases and challenges. In this thesis, the focus is on researching and applying

M. Alves Gomes, *Utilizing Embeddings to Learn a Universal Customer Behavior Representation in E-Commerce*, https://doi.org/10.1007/978-3-658-50781-7_2

UCR, with the two goals of enhancing the customer experience through personalization and enabling companies to leverage data in the digital age. Therefore, it is necessary to establish a comprehensive understanding of customer targeting in e-commerce, including the customer journey, personalized customer targeting, and the scope of the research.

2.1.1 Customer Journey

A key concept in both business and academic research is the customer journey, which refers to the entire process a customer undergoes, from the initial interest in a product or service to the completion of the purchase and the after-sales. Nguyen et al. [234] and Santos and Gonçalves [201] highlight that the customer journey is not static; it is a dynamic, highly individualized process that varies from customer to customer and is defined by their individual behavior. Thereby, the customer is an individual who engages in a transaction with a brand by purchasing a product or service as defined by Lemon and Verhoef [135]. Nguyen et al. [234] adds that customers contribute direct monetary value to a company, either through one-time purchases, subscriptions, or repeat transactions.

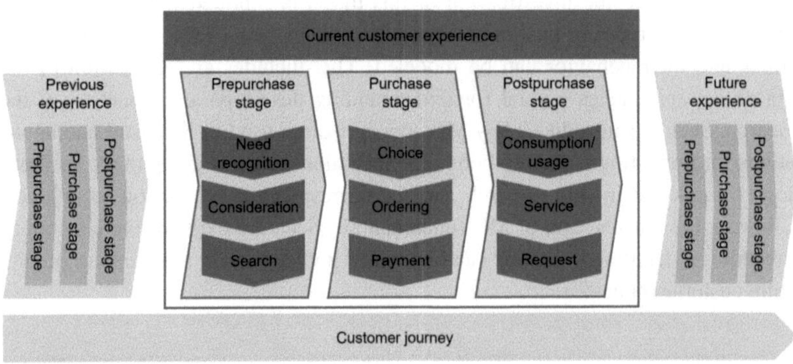

Fig. 2.1 Stages of customer experience within the customer journey adopted from Lemon et al. [135]

Fig. 2.1 illustrates the customer journey, highlighting how each stage is influenced by previous experiences and, in turn, shapes future interactions. This makes customer experience management a dynamic, iterative process. Specifically, Holmlund et al. [103], Homburg et al. [104], and Lemon et al. [135] emphasize that the customer journey is a cyclical process, with each interaction influencing future decisions and experiences. By understanding and optimizing each touchpoint, businesses can better address customer needs throughout the entire journey, from discovery to advocacy. Touchpoints refer to the various interactions that occur between a customer and a brand, business, or retailer throughout the entire customer journey [103, 104, 135, 201, 234]. These touchpoints can be brand-owned, partner-owned, customer-owned, or social/external, and occur across the prepurchase, purchase, and postpurchase stages of the customer journey. Each touchpoint plays a critical role in shaping the customer's experience and decision-making process [103, 104, 135, 201, 234].

Each customer journey begins with the customer's previous experiences, which encompass their past journeys, i.e., interactions with the brand or similar products or services. These experiences shape expectations, perceptions, and behaviors at every stage of the journey.

The first stage of the customer journey is the prepurchase stage. This stage marks the beginning of the customer journey, encompassing the recognition of needs, exploration of options, and information search. As stated by Nguyen et al., customers engage with brands through various touchpoints, which influence their decision-making and perception of value [234]. Brand-owned touchpoints mean they are directly controlled by the brand, such as official websites, mobile apps, online Advertisement (Ad)s, and in-store experiences. For example, a customer researching a smartphone may visit Apple's official website to explore product specifications and promotional offers. Partner-owned touchpoints are managed by third parties or affiliations, such as retailers, distributors, or resellers. These touchpoints include online marketplaces, physical stores, and partner websites. For instance, a customer may visit Amazon or a local electronics store to compare the prices of different smartphone models. Customer-owned touchpoints refer to self-driven interactions, including independent research, personal criteria evaluation, and previous brand experiences. For instance, a customer evaluating a smartphone purchase may rely on personal preferences, reviews, or past experiences with the brand or similar products. Social/external touchpoints are influenced by external sources, such as word-of-mouth recommendations, influencer reviews, social media discussions, and third-party review platforms. Pires et al. [181] emphasize that customers often consult YouTube unboxing videos, Trustpilot reviews, or Reddit discussions before making a purchase decision. In regard to the smartphone example, a customer may seek advice from friends, read online reviews, or watch YouTube videos to gather insights and recommendations.

The second stage, the purchase stage, follows once the customer has considered their options. At this point, interactions with the brand's or partner's platforms, such as websites or physical stores, are regarded as critical touchpoints. Actions such as product selection, ordering, and payment are central to this stage, as customers finalize their decisions and complete the transaction [135, 181, 199, 234].

The postpurchase stage is the third stage of the customer journey. Here, interactions continue through various touchpoints, including brand-owned and partner-provided after-sales services such as customer support, product guides, or engagement through customer feedback channels. Key activities during this phase include product consumption, ongoing usage, service requests, and customer engagement. Positive post-purchase experiences are crucial to customer satisfaction. Lemon and Verhoef [135] highlight the importance of post-purchase interactions in fostering brand loyalty as satisfied customers are more likely to recommend the brand to others and make repeat purchases.

The customer journey is cyclical in nature, with the future customer experience being shaped by the outcomes of the current journey. Positive experiences during and after the purchase phase foster brand loyalty, repeat purchases, and advocacy, while negative experiences can lead to dissatisfaction, customer churn, or switching to competitors [135, 234].

Rosenbloom points out that each stage often requires different marketing channels to effectively engage and guide the customer [199]. As shown by Pires et al., marketing channels are the means through which brands communicate with customers, deliver messages, and facilitate transactions. These channels can be physical or digital, direct or indirect, and play a crucial role in guiding customers through the customer journey. For example, a brand may use social media, email marketing, or online advertising to attract customers during the prepurchase stage, while employing customer service, loyalty programs, or personalized recommendations to enhance the purchase and postpurchase experience [181].

2.1.2 Personalized Customer Targeting

This section is based on a previous publication that reviewed the literature on personalized customer targeting in e-commerce [7]. One contribution of this work was the identification of a customer targeting process that is found in many publications reviewed.

Mass marketing represents one of the most straightforward forms of customer targeting, typically achieved through outdoor or television Ads. However, already in the early 2000s, this approach is increasingly regarded as lacking in personalisation and effectiveness as highlighted by Beaumont et al. [20] and Kim and Anh [124],. Therefore, more personalized approaches are required. Personalized customer targeting refers to the process of tailoring marketing and customer engagement strategies based on the specific preferences, behaviors, and characteristics of individual customers. As highlighted by Lemon and Verhoef [135], Dzulfikar et al. [64], and Zanker et al. [265], in e-commerce, this involves leveraging customer data to deliver personalized experiences at each stage of the customer journey, from pre-purchase interactions to post-purchase engagement.

By analyzing data from previous interactions, brands craft personalized recommendations, offers, and communications that align with each customer's journey stage. For instance, during the pre-purchase phase, personalized targeting might involve recommending products based on the customer's browsing history or prior purchases. In the purchase phase, targeted discounts or promotions can incentivize immediate action, while in the post-purchase phase, personalized follow-ups such as tailored product guides or support services can enhance satisfaction and encourage repeat purchases [36, 181].

Personalized customer targeting relies on extensive data collection and analysis. In previous work, a four-stage model for customer targeting is identified, where data is collected, customer profiles are built, customer analysis is conducted, and targeted marketing is applied [7], as illustrated in Fig. 2.2. Each stage plays a crucial role in transforming raw customer data into actionable insights for targeted marketing.

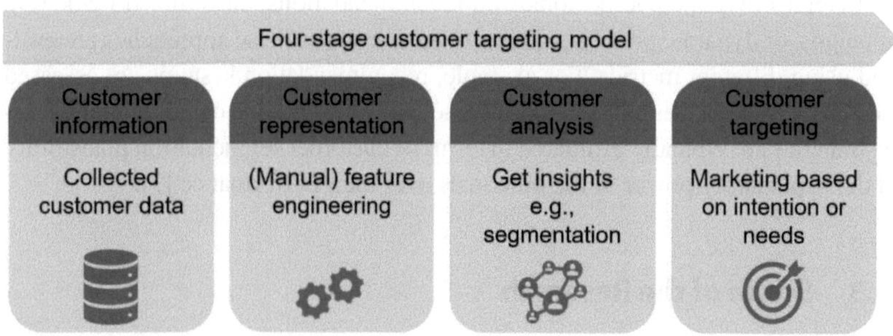

Fig. 2.2 The four-stage customer targeting process adopted from Alves Gomes and Meisen [7]

The process begins with the collection and storage of customer information. This data can be explicitly gathered, as demonstrated in the studies of Hong and Kim [105], Nakano and Kondo [168], and Wu [251], where customer are asked, e.g., via survey, or implicitly tracked, such as clickstream data from website interactions as shown in numerous works [18, 138, 155, 156, 163, 177, 198]. This raw data forms the foundation for the subsequent stages of the customer targeting process.

In the second stage, the data collected is used to build a comprehensive customer representation. This is achieved through feature selection methods, which help identify the most relevant data points that describe customer behavior. Feature selection can be done manually, where marketers and data scientists choose features such as purchase history, click events, or product categories based on their relevance. Alternatively, automated methods can be applied to extract features with the highest information content and remove those that contribute little to the overall understanding of the customer [7]. As this stage is fundamental to the research in this thesis, more details on the feature engineering customer representation will be taken up again explicitly in Sect. 2.2 and 2.3 of this chapter.

The third stage, customer analysis, involves applying analytical methods to extract actionable insights from the customer representations. A common approach in this phase is customer segmentation, where customers are divided into more homogeneous groups based on shared characteristics or behaviors. Segmentation methods often rely on clustering algorithms or other statistical techniques that compare customer profiles and partition them into distinct groups [7].

In the final stage, customer targeting, the insights from customer analysis are used to make informed marketing decisions. Depending on the business objectives, targeting strategies may include personalized recommendations, customized marketing campaigns, or dynamic pricing policies. In the literature, these approaches are evaluated using different metrics. For example, recommendation systems are assessed based on metrics such as hit-rate and accuracy, while marketing campaigns and pricing strategies are typically evaluated in terms of customer segmentation plausibility and the explanatory power of the outcomes over their performance [7].

2.1.3 Scope of the Research

After establishing an understanding of the customer journey and methods for personalized customer targeting, the scope of this research is defined which allows it to address the aforementioned research questions.

Derived from the customer journey where different stages consist of different actors and touchpoints, it is evident that data cannot be implicitly collected at every stage of the customer journey, especially when interactions involve multiple actors. For example, a customer's online search history outside of a company's website or app is typically unknown to the business itself. Technologies like cookies and tracking pixels can help companies gather and share information about customer behavior with other actors, but these methods also raise privacy concerns, as customers may not be aware of how their data is being collected and shared as concerned by Farayola et al. [74]. Therefore, to answer the aforementioned research questions in this research, the focus lies exclusively on stages and customer touchpoints that can be collected by an actor, i.e., brand owner or retail partner. Within the customer journey, the scope includes touchpoints in the prepurchase and purchase stages as illustrated in Fig. 2.3. Specifically, with these touchpoints, the aim is to predict future customer interactions and behaviors. This thesis does not assess the effectiveness of specific targeting strategies in achieving business objectives. Instead, it focuses on analyzing data patterns of customer behavior within these stages and evaluating their predictive potential.

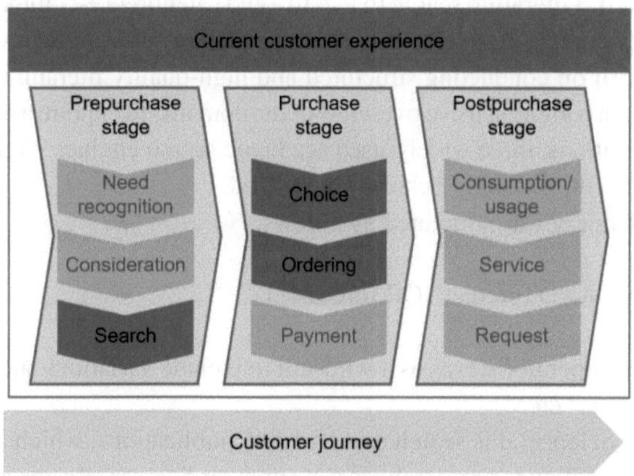

Fig. 2.3 Scope of the research, which focuses on the prepurchase and purchase stages of the customer journey

2.1.4 Forecasting Tasks in E-Commerce

The study of customer behavior has a long history in business. Already in 2002, Wiedermann et al. [246] stated that it is essential for companies success to maintain connections between their customers, especially those with long-term, high-revenue potential. Prediction in e-commerce empowers online retailers to anticipate and respond to customer behaviors [70], market trends [228], and operational challenges. Leveraging the power of data-driven insights and ML algorithms, e-commerce businesses can forecast product demand [87, 191, 219, 241], personalize recommendations [209, 248], help identify customer churn [22, 54, 139, 187], optimize pricing [75, 230], and enhance the overall shopping experience. In the competitive landscape of online retail, prediction in e-commerce is not just about forecasting. According to Wiedermann et al. [246] and Fabra et al. [70], it is a strategic tool for businesses to thrive by delivering better customer experiences and optimizing their operations.

To enable effective and targeted customer engagement, a customer representation must be developed that reflects real-world standards. A critical aspect of this process involves the prediction of future customer behavior. Therefore, forecasting tasks in e-commerce must be identified and categorized based on their relevance to targeted marketing. This ensures that predictive methods are aligned with specific marketing objectives.

In this regard, a literature search to identify and categorize e-commerce forecasting tasks is conducted. Following the recommendations of Vom Brocke et al. [238] and Cooper [50] on conducting structured and high-quality literature reviews, the aim is to obtain a comprehensive overview of the domain. To capture a broad range of relevant publications, three widely-used academic search engines: Web of Science, Dimensions.ai, and Semantic Scholar are utilized.

The search query was structured as follows:

- e-commerce AND (predict* OR forecast*)

The asterisk (*) operator serves as a wildcard to include variations such as "prediction," "predicting," etc.

On Web of Science, this search returns 1,848 publications, which are filtered to include only the following research areas: Computer Science, Business Economics, Engineering, Information Science & Library Science, Operations Research & Management Science, Science & Technology, and Mathematics. The search on Dimensions.ai yields 3,207 publications. On Semantic Scholar, approximately 69,000 publications are found, which are narrowed by restricting the search to fields of study in Business, Computer Science, Economics, Engineering, and Mathematics. Given the high volume of results on Semantic Scholar, the screening is stopped after reviewing around 260 publications, which are sorted by relevance, as the relevance to e-commerce declined with subsequent results, and the suggestions are no longer related to e-commerce. For categorizing e-commerce forecasting tasks, the titles and abstracts of relevant papers are examined to identify the primary forecasting tasks they address. As a result of this literature search, e-commerce forecasting tasks can be broadly divided into two categories:

1. Customer Behavior-Related Forecasting Tasks: These involve predicting customer actions, intentions, or characteristics. Key tasks include:

    - Purchase intention prediction
    - Churn prediction
    - Return prediction
    - Customer lifetime value prediction
    - CTR prediction
    - Next action or next touchpoint prediction
    - Willingness-to-pay prediction
    - Customer demographics prediction

2. Product-Related Forecasting Tasks: These tasks focus on predicting aspects of products or product-related metrics. Key tasks include:

    - Sales and demand forecasting
    - Product return prediction
    - Product price prediction
    - Product property prediction

It is worth noting that the distinction between customer behavior-related and product-related tasks is not always clear-cut. For example, sales prediction and product return forecasting are closely tied to customer behaviors, while product price prediction may overlap with willingness-to-pay prediction.

For this research, the focus lies exclusively on the three most popular customer behavior forecasting tasks which are purchase prediction, churn prediction, and CTR prediction. Purchase prediction is by far the most researched topic followed by churn prediction and CTR prediction.

A purchase prediction model is at the forefront of data-driven decision-making in the retail and e-commerce sectors. By studying this abundance of data, purchase prediction algorithms reveal detailed patterns and linkages that allow businesses to make accurate projections about what items or services a customer is likely to acquire in the future as highlighted by Huang et al. [110]. These forecasts have far-reaching repercussions. Beyari and Garamoun [25] state, marketing efforts may be more efficiently targeted, giving individualized incentives and product recommendations that appeal to particular clients. This level of personalization improves the whole purchasing experience, promoting consumer loyalty and increasing sales income. Purchase prediction model research has grown in importance in the domains of retail, e-commerce, and marketing [165, 211]. The culmination of these research efforts fosters a deeper understanding of purchase prediction, contributing to more accurate models and enhanced decision-making processes in the ever-changing retail and e-commerce industry.

Customer churn prediction is a crucial application in e-commerce as stated by Pfeifer [179], where retaining existing customers is often more cost-effective than acquiring new ones. Churn prediction models analyze customer behaviors, such as purchase frequency, transaction history, and browsing patterns, to estimate the likelihood that a customer will disengage or discontinue their relationship with a company's product or service [22, 28, 178, 187]. By identifying customers at high risk of churning, businesses can take proactive steps to retain them, such as offering personalized retention strategies, exclusive discounts, or improved customer service. This not only helps to stabilize revenue streams but also enhances customer satisfaction, reduces acquisition costs, and promotes long-term business sustainability. Furthermore, churn prediction models provide valuable insights into the drivers of customer disengagement, allowing companies to address specific issues that may be affecting customer loyalty as remarked by Fridrich and Dostal [83]. For instance, understanding the reasons behind customer churn enables businesses to tailor their retention efforts to address customer pain points, ultimately improving the overall customer experience and increasing profitability. As customer retention is a critical factor in sustaining growth, churn prediction has become a central focus for companies aiming to maintain strong, long-lasting relationships with their customers in a competitive e-commerce environment.

CTR prediction has emerged as a core task in the field of online advertising and digital marketing [140, 254]. This is largely due to the increasing importance of search engines and recommender systems in e-commerce, where these tools are integral to customer engagement and conversion as highlighted by numerous studies [34, 72, 172, 279]. CTR serves as a key metric for evaluating the effectiveness of digital Ad. It is calculated by dividing the number of clicks by the number of impressions, where impressions refer to the number of times an Ad is displayed to customers. It directly impacts revenue from sponsored search content, as Ad platforms typically use CTR estimates to determine which Ads to display and at what price [137, 176, 196]. Accurate CTR prediction can significantly enhance the customer experience, as it allows for more relevant and personalized content, ultimately driving higher engagement and business effectiveness [137, 140]. CTR has become an essential tool for optimizing customer engagement and enhancing the profitability of digital content and Ads. Accurate CTR prediction supports better decision-making in the design and placement of Ads, benefiting both consumers and businesses in the competitive e-commerce market.

2.2 Customer Behavior Representation

Customer behavior representation refers to the process of translating customer actions, decisions, and preferences into measurable and analyzable information and it is a fundamental step in the customer targeting process [7]. Creating these is crucial for understanding and addressing customer needs in product development, marketing, and service design. Specifically, customer behavior representation methods encompass various approaches to understand, analyze, and predict consumer actions and preferences. These methods are crucial for businesses to improve customer satisfaction, optimize marketing strategies, and enhance overall performance as highlighted by Cai [32]. Raza [193] states that customer behavior encompasses the actions, decisions, and emotional responses of individuals or groups in their roles as consumers. These behaviors are influenced by a combination of psychological, social, cultural, and economic factors. Representing customer behavior involves translating the interactions within a customer journey into measurable and analyzable data to uncover patterns and insights. In the literature, different approaches to represent customer behavior exist, e.g., data-driven approaches [1, 7, 115], Psychographic Profiling or segmentation [147, 245], Empathy Mapping [210], Journey Mapping [109] and others, whereby the boundaries of the approaches flow into each other. This thesis deals with the data-driven approaches of customer behavior representation, assuming implicitly collected data as previously defined. Unlike qualitative methods such as empathy mapping or psychographic profiling, data-driven techniques offer measurable, objective insights derived from actual customer interactions and behaviors. This empirical foundation ensures a higher level of accuracy and scalability when modeling customer behavior, making data-driven approaches particularly suitable for large-scale e-commerce applications. While human-centered techniques provide valuable perspectives, they are often subjective and harder to validate at scale.

In previous work, data-driven customer behavior representations are categorized further into two primary approaches: expert-modeled and mathematically modeled [7]. Expert-modeled customer representations rely on predefined patterns or features derived from domain knowledge and extensive analysis. These expert models incorporate demographic information such as age, gender, or income, and touchpoint information such as session length, number of clicks, or interactions as well as time information. These representations aim to structure customer interactions in a way that directly supports analysis and decision-making.

Mathematically modeled representations utilize heuristics, statistical, and ML techniques to derive meaningful features from the raw data. Based on the results of the previously conducted literature review, the RFM analysis is by far the most popular feature selection method to model a customer representation [7]. The RFM analysis describes customers based on RFM features. Recency relates to the time of the last customer activity, like a purchase. Frequency describes how often a customer interacts in a given period and monetary measures how much money a customer spends in that period [112]. Extensions of RFM, such as adding customer lifetime value or product preferences, are used to enhance its insights [37, 218].

2.3 Machine Learning Principles

In this section, the technical principles required for the development of customer representations and the prediction of future customer behavior are described. Thereby, the learning principles that allow models to learn from the context of data are the key feature for the customer representation approach proposed in this thesis. Data-driven approaches increasingly rely on ML techniques. Learning, in its essence, is the process of mapping experiences onto behavior [53]. It extends to computational systems that aim to extract patterns and insights from data. ML focuses on utilizing data to model relationships and predict outcomes, enabling systems to improve performance over time through the assimilation of past experiences [116, 283]. The core idea is to enhance data-driven decision-making and predictive capabilities [58] by analyzing structured or unstructured data. Hereby, ML systems identify patterns and relationships that can be applied to new and unseen data distributions. The field encompasses several approaches, categorized by the manner in which the system learns: supervised [51, 173], unsupervised [13], self-supervised [97], and reinforcement learning [223]. In this thesis, the focus is on supervised and self-supervised learning, which are imperative for the development of customer representations and the prediction of future customer behavior.

2.3.1 Supervised and Self-Supervised Learning Principles

An Artificial Neural Network (ANN) is a mathematical model motivated by the neural network of the brain of a living being and has been studied for over 50 years [167]. The two main components of a neural network are neurons that are connected and the activation of these neurons. Mathematically, an ANN can be formulated as a sequence of matrix operations. Each neuron processes an input $x \in \mathbb{R}^n$ through a weighted sum and applies a non-linear activation function σ, yielding an output $y = \sigma(Wx + b)$, where W is the weight matrix, b is the bias [100, 205]. These networks are split into layers, where each layer has several neurons that are densely connected to each neuron of the next layer as illustrated in Fig. 2.4.

ANNs are the basis for all modern DL approaches [277] of which the simplest form of such networks is the feed-forward network.

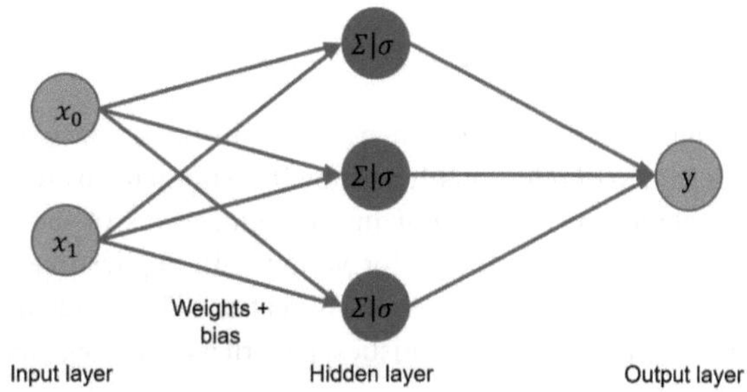

Fig. 2.4 A basic feed-forward neural network with two input neurons, one hidden layer of three neurons, and a single output neuron. Each connection has weights and biases. The sum and activation function σ are applied at each neuron

Supervised learning is an approach where the goal is to identify and classify patterns based on labeled training data. This method has proven effective across various applications, including image recognition, system identification, and time series analysis [51, 89, 194]. However, numerous real-world data mining and ML applications face a common challenge where an abundance of unlabeled training instances coexists with a limited number of labeled ones. The acquisition of labeled examples is frequently costly, arduous, or time-consuming due to the requirement of skilled human annotators with sufficient domain expertise [160, 270]. For instance, in an e-commerce setting, the task is to classify whether a customer is profitable or unprofitable based on their purchase history. A substantial amount of data can be readily collected. However, the labeling of non-profitable or profitable customers necessitates thorough scrutiny, judgment, and sometimes even time-intensive tracing tasks performed by experienced human assessors, resulting in significant expenses. To address the aforementioned limitations of supervised learning, self-supervised learning has emerged as a promising alternative which do not require labeled data. Self-supervised learning is an advanced ML technique that enables models to learn meaningful representations from unlabeled data. It bridges the gap between supervised and unsupervised learning by creating artificial supervisory signals from the data itself [47, 97, 202, 225]. Which means, the model is trained on a task that does not require explicit human labeling. For instance, it might involve predicting masked or distorted portions of the input data. This approach allows the model to learn rich, contextual representations of the data without the need for expensive and time-consuming manual annotations [97, 237].

2.3.2 Feature Engineering

Feature engineering is a critical component of ML, involving the extraction, transformation, and selection of relevant information from raw data to create meaningful features for ML algorithms. By optimizing the dimensions of the feature space, it reduces complexity and tailors data for various ML applications, such as process prediction, detection accuracy, and classification. This fundamental task has been a central research focus within statistics, pattern recognition, and ML since its inception [127, 131].

Effective feature engineering ensures that the raw data contains the essential information required for ML to yield accurate and reliable results. In e-commerce, this process is pivotal for representing customers and their shopping behaviors. Selecting appropriate features determines the efficiency and accuracy of ML algorithms by providing a concise and representative presentation of data objects [61]. Moreover, Chen et al. [42] emphasize that well-curated features not only enhance model performance but also exhibit a high degree of generalizability and reusability across various domains and tasks, thereby amplifying their overall value and applicability. However, achieving generalizable and reusable feature representations remains a fundamental challenge. Identifying and extracting such features necessitates substantial effort, as it requires a deep understanding of both the domain-specific data characteristics and the underlying learning models [21]. The ability to systematically discover and construct features that maintain their effectiveness across different applications is, therefore, a critical aspect of advancing feature engineering methodologies.

Feature transferability and generalization are pivotal concepts that enhance the adaptability and efficiency of ML algorithms as well as signifying a model's ability to apply learned patterns to unseen data. A model that generalizes well can maintain robust and consistent performance in real-world scenarios, demonstrating an understanding of the underlying data structures rather than merely memorizing training examples. By reusing features extracted for one task in another, ML models can generalize knowledge across tasks, reducing the need for extensive data collection and training. This approach is particularly beneficial when data is scarce or expensive to acquire. By leveraging prior work, models can quickly adapt to new challenges, improving performance and reducing computational overhead. Recent advancements in pre-trained models, such as BERT [60] in Natural Language Processing

(NLP) and deep convolutional networks in computer vision, exemplify the strides made in feature generalization [145, 197]. These models leverage large datasets to capture intricate patterns and semantics, enabling fine-tuning for specific tasks. This capability has transformed ML workflows, improving performance, reducing data requirements, and accelerating deployment.

The transition from traditional feature engineering to representation learning has played a crucial role in improving feature transferability [21]. Representation learning automates feature extraction by leveraging data-driven techniques, enabling the model to learn hierarchical representations directly from raw data. Self-supervised learning methods such as contrastive learning [260, 261] and reconstruction-based learning [24, 267] have further enhanced generalization by capturing intrinsic structures and patterns within data. However, challenges remain, particularly in adapting features across tasks with differing requirements. Addressing these challenges is a vital area of ongoing research, with significant implications for the scalability and versatility of ML applications. As advancements continue, feature generalization is poised to unlock new opportunities across diverse domains, reinforcing its status as a cornerstone of ML development, especially in the dynamic nature of e-commerce.

2.3.3 Sequential Learning Models

Customer behavior data is inherently sequential, reflecting the temporal nature of customer interactions. To model these customer behavior sequences effectively, sequential learning models can be employed, enabling the capture of dependencies and patterns within the customer behavior over time. Recurrent Neural Networks (RNNs) are a class of neural networks designed to process sequential data by maintaining a hidden state that evolves over time. The hidden state acts as a memory that captures information from previous time steps, allowing the network to retain context and learn dependencies within the sequence. At each time step t, $t \in \mathbb{N}$, the hidden state h_t is computed as:

$$h_t = f(W_h h_{t-1} + W_x x_t + b), \tag{2.1}$$

where:

- h_{t-1} is the hidden state from the previous time step,
- x_t is the input at the current time step,
- W_h, W_x, and b are trainable weights and biases,
- $f(\cdot)$ is a nonlinear activation function.

The output y_t at each step is typically given by:

$$y_t = g(W_y h_t + b_y), \tag{2.2}$$

where W_y and b_y are output weights and biases, and $g(\cdot)$ is a function such as softmax for classification tasks. RNNs are effective for modeling sequences but suffer from limitations in capturing long-range dependencies due to issues such as vanishing or exploding gradients. [271]

To address the shortcomings of standard RNNs, Hochreiter and Schmidhuber [102] introduced the Long Short-Term Memory (LSTM) architecture, which incorporates a gated mechanism designed to preserve information over extended sequences. This mechanism is realized through a set of learnable gates that modulate the internal memory cell, denoted as c_t, allowing the network to learn both short-term and long-term temporal dependencies more effectively.

An LSTM unit at time step t receives the input x_t, the previous hidden state h_{t-1}, and the previous cell state c_{t-1}. The internal dynamics are governed by three gating functions, namely the input gate i_t, forget gate f_t, and output gate o_t. These gates are computed as follows:

$$f_t = \sigma(W_f x_t + U_f h_{t-1} + b_f) \tag{2.3}$$
$$i_t = \sigma(W_i x_t + U_i h_{t-1} + b_i) \tag{2.4}$$
$$o_t = \sigma(W_o x_t + U_o h_{t-1} + b_o) \tag{2.5}$$

where $\sigma(\cdot)$ is the sigmoid activation function, and W, U, and b are learnable weights and biases for each gate. The candidate memory cell $\tilde{c}_t$ is computed as:

$$\tilde{c}t = \tanh(W_c x_t + U_c ht - 1 + b_c), \tag{2.6}$$

which is subsequently combined with the previous cell state to produce the updated memory cell:

$$c_t = f_t \odot c_{t-1} + i_t \odot \tilde{c}_t, \tag{2.7}$$

and the new hidden state is obtained via:

$$h_t = o_t \odot \tanh(c_t), \tag{2.8}$$

where $\odot$ denotes element-wise multiplication. The gating mechanisms allow LSTMs to selectively retain and discard information, thereby mitigating the vanishing gradient problem commonly encountered in standard RNNs.

LSTMs have been widely used in various sequence modeling tasks, but they have certain limitations such as computational complexity, particularly in handling long-range dependencies and parallelization [273] which have led to the development of Transformer models which were proposed by Vaswani et al. [237]. Transformers represent a paradigm shift in sequence modeling, eliminating the recurrence in favor of self-attention mechanisms. A Transformer model processes sequences in parallel, making it highly efficient and scalable. The core component of a Transformer is the self-attention mechanism, defined as:

$$\text{Attention}(Q, K, V) = \text{softmax}\left(\frac{QK^\top}{\sqrt{d_k}}\right) V, \tag{2.9}$$

where Q, K, and V are the query, key, and value matrices derived from the input embeddings and d_k is the dimensionality of the key vectors. The input embeddings themselves are vector representations of tokens in a given sequence, typically obtained using pre-trained embeddings or learned jointly with the Transformer model in an end-to-end fashion. To capture diverse relationships within the data, Transformers use multi-head attention where each attention head is calculated independently and then concatenated. Since Transformers lack inherent sequential ordering, positional encodings are added to the input embeddings to incorporate order information. Summarizing, a Transformer consists of an encoder and decoder block of which a Transformer encoder consists of multiple layers, each with Multi-head self-attention, feedforward neural network, residual connection, and layer normalization. The Transformer decoder includes similar components, with additional cross-attention mechanisms to attend to encoder outputs. Transformers are the basis for state-of-the-art models like BERT [60] and GPT family [29, 188, 189] as well as Large Language Models (LLMs), excelling in NLP and computer vision tasks.

Table 2.1 summarizes the advantages and disadvantages of RNNs, LSTMs, and Transformers. RNNs are simple and efficient for modeling short sequences, making them suitable for small datasets with limited dependency lengths. However, they struggle with capturing long-range dependencies due to the vanishing gradient problem and are limited in their ability to process sequences efficiently because of their sequential computation. LSTMs address the vanishing gradient issue by introducing gating mechanisms, enabling them to capture moderate-length dependencies effectively. Despite their improved performance, LSTMs are computationally more expensive than RNNs, as the gating mechanisms significantly increase the number of parameters, and their sequential nature still limits parallelization. Transformers, on the other hand, leverage self-attention mechanisms to capture long-range dependencies and parallelize computation, making them exceptionally powerful for large

Table 2.1 Overview of the advantages and disadvantages provided by RNNs, LSTMs, and Transformers

Model	Strengths	Weaknesses	Best For
RNNs	Simple, efficient for short sequences	Vanishing gradients, limited long-range memory	Small datasets, short sequences
LSTMs	Handles moderate-length dependencies well	Slower training, limited scalability	Medium-length sequences, moderate datasets
Transformers	Parallelizable, excellent on long-range tasks	Expensive, requires large datasets	Large datasets, long sequences, state-of-the-art NLP and computer vision

datasets and long sequences. This scalability and efficiency come at the cost of computational expense, as Transformers have a large number of parameters and require substantial resources to train effectively. Additionally, for tasks involving very short sequences, Transformers may be more complex compared to simpler models like RNNs and LSTM.

2.3.4 Evaluation of Machine Learning Models

In order to evaluate the quality of an ML model, different evaluation metrics exist, determining the performance and effectiveness. In complex systems, a lack of transparency in these evaluations can lead to severe consequences, such as poor resource allocation in decision-making [281]. Evaluation metrics provide quantitative measures of a model's learning capability and its ability to make accurate predictions or classifications. Selecting appropriate metrics depends on the specific ML task, classification, regression, or clustering, and the dataset characteristics. Properly chosen metrics guide model development, fine-tuning, and ensure that ML solutions meet their intended goals [107].

For classification tasks, as used in this thesis, metrics such as accuracy, precision, recall, F1-score, and Area Under the Receiver Operating Characteristic Curve (AUC) are commonly employed. Each has strengths and weaknesses, and the choice depends on the problem objectives and data characteristics. Therefore, it is crucial to understand the four basic components of classification performance metrics [164, 174, 185].

- True Positive (TP): The model correctly predicts a positive class when the actual class is positive.
- True Negative (TN): The model correctly predicts a negative class when the actual class is negative.
- False Positive (FP): The model incorrectly predicts a positive class when the actual class is negative.
- False Negative (FN): The model incorrectly predicts a negative class when the actual class is positive.

Precision measures the proportion of correctly predicted positive instances out of all instances predicted as positive. It evaluates how many of the model's positive predictions are actually correct. Mathematically, precision is defined as:

$$Precision = \frac{TP}{TP + FP} \tag{2.10}$$

A high precision score indicates that the model has a low rate of false positives, making it especially useful in scenarios where false positives are costly [185].

Recall (also known as sensitivity or True Positive Rate (TPR)) measures the proportion of correctly predicted positive instances out of all actual positive instances in the dataset. It evaluates the model's ability to capture all relevant positive cases. Recall is defined as:

$$Recall = \frac{TP}{TP + FN} \tag{2.11}$$

A high recall score indicates that the model captures most of the relevant instances, making it critical in scenarios where false negatives are more problematic, such as fraud detection or identifying rare diseases [185].

Accuracy evaluates the proportion of correct predictions to the total number of predictions:

$$Accuracy = \frac{TP + TN}{TP + TN + FP + FN} \tag{2.12}$$

While accuracy is straightforward and provides an overall success rate, it is insufficient for imbalanced datasets where one class dominates. In such cases, accuracy may mask poor performance in minority class predictions [158].

Imbalanced datasets and unequal costs of different types of errors make metrics like F1-score and AUC more informative than accuracy alone. In general, real-world datasets are often imbalanced, with one class significantly outnumbering the other [23, 93, 164, 185].

The F1-score is the harmonic mean of precision and recall, offering a balanced metric that captures the trade-off between these two measures. It is particularly useful when the costs of FP and FN differ [235].

$$F1 = \frac{2 \cdot Precision \cdot Recall}{Precision + Recall} = \frac{2 \cdot TP}{2 \cdot TP + FP + FN} \tag{2.13}$$

High F1-scores indicate that precision and recall are both high, ensuring that the model performs well in both capturing relevant instances (recall) and minimizing irrelevant ones (precision) [93]. Models with high F1-scores are particularly valuable when identifying minority classes in imbalanced datasets. That is especially where false negatives are critical because the F1-score ensures that the balance between precision and recall is explicitly addressed. A high F1-score implies fewer missed detections and fewer false alarms, which is essential for reliable decision-making.

The Receiver Operating Characteristic (ROC) curve illustrates the trade-off between the TPR and the False Positive Rate (FPR) as the decision threshold varies. Whereby the TPR is the y-value and the FPR is the x-value on the diagram. The AUC quantifies the model's ability to discriminate between classes [76]. The FPR is defined as:

$$FPR = \frac{FP}{FP + TN} \tag{2.14}$$

The AUC is the integral of the ROC curve:

$$AUC = \int_0^1 TPR(FPR^{-1}(x))\,dx \tag{2.15}$$

An AUC of 0.5 indicates no discriminative ability (random guessing), while an AUC of 1.0 represents perfect discrimination [106]. AUC is particularly suited for imbalanced datasets because it remains unbiased by the proportion of class distributions [81]. Specifically, AUC provides an overall view of model performance across various thresholds, making it robust to class imbalances and shifts in data distribution. It is particularly valuable in scenarios where operational thresholds may change, such as adjusting sensitivity in spam filters or credit risk models.

2.4 Learning Embeddings

Learning embeddings is considered a core problem of representation learning, where raw observations are mapped into latent vectors that capture the underlying explanatory factors of variation [21]. In contrast to manual feature engineering, such representations are learned directly from data and are used as inputs for a wide range of downstream models. Embeddings are therefore treated as dense, low-dimensional vectors that encode semantic or structural information about entities such as words, images, or customers.

Different paradigms for embedding learning are distinguished in the literature. A first family is reconstruction-based methods, where an encoder maps an input to a latent code and a decoder reconstructs the input from this code, as in classical autoencoders and their variants [21, 230]. A second family is predictive or context-based methods, in which embeddings are trained to predict parts of the data from other parts, such as neighboring tokens in text. A third family is contrastive methods, where representations are optimized so that similar inputs are mapped to nearby points in the embedding space, while dissimilar inputs are pushed apart [43].

In this thesis, the focus is placed on context-based embedding learning for customer behavior representations, enabling intricate behavioral patterns and relationships within the data to be captured. Context-based embeddings are chosen because the meaning of an entity is observed to emerge primarily from its surrounding context, a principle established in distributional semantics and verified across multiple domains [201]. In contrast to reconstruction-based objectives, in which similarities in the raw input signal are brought into relation and low-level patterns are primarily preserved [230], context-based methods encourage the representation space to reflect co-occurrence structure, temporal proximity, and behavioral similarity. This property is shown to be particularly advantageous for customer modeling, where interactions, sequential events, and usage patterns carry the dominant semantic signal [226, 236, 278]. One of the foundations for context-based embeddings were brought by Mikolov et al., they proposed word vectors named Skip-Gram and Continuous Bag of Words (CBOW) [161]. Fig. 2.5 illustrates the architecture and fundamental idea of both word embedding approaches.

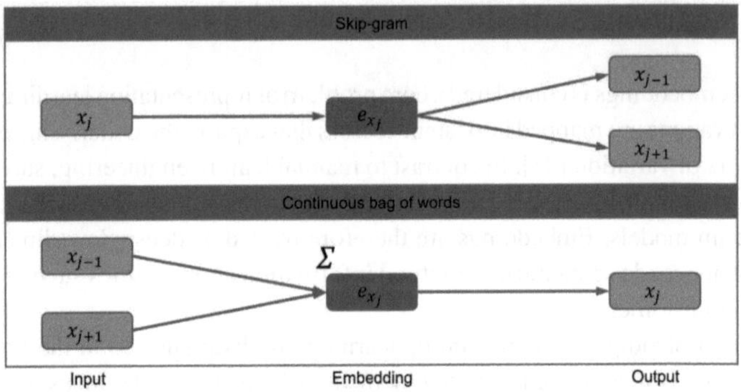

Fig. 2.5 Skip-Gram and CBOW embedding architecture as proposed by Mikolov et al. [161]

Both approaches utilize a single-layer neural network with weight parameters θ to model the relationships between an input word $x_j \in X$, $j \in \mathbb{N}$ and its surrounding context $k_j = \{x_{j+m}, x_{j+m-1}, ..., x_{j-m+1}, x_{j-m}\} \setminus x_j$ with context window size $M = 2 \times m$, $m \in \mathbb{N}$. The Skip-Gram model aims to predict the context words $x_{j+\alpha}$ given a central word x_j. Formally, it maximizes the likelihood:

$$L(\theta) = \prod_{j=1}^{n} \prod_{\alpha=-m,\alpha\neq 0}^{m} P(x_{j+\alpha}|x_j;\theta) \tag{2.16}$$

where $P(x_{j+\alpha}|x_j;\theta)$ is the conditional probability of a context word given the central word. This probability is typically modeled as a softmax over the output layer of the neural network:

$$P(x_{j+\alpha}|x_j;\theta) = \frac{\exp(e_{x_{j+\alpha}}^{\top} e_{x_j})}{\sum_{w\in V} \exp(e_w^{\top} e_{x_j})}. \tag{2.17}$$

Here, e_{x_j} is the D-dimensional embedding vector for the input word x_j, $e_{x_{j+\alpha}}$ is the embedding for a context word, and V is the vocabulary. Training involves adjusting θ to maximize $L(\theta)$. The embedding e_{x_j} can be directly linked to the weights θ of the neural network. Specifically, in a single-layer neural network for word embedding, the input layer is a one-hot encoded vector x_j, which is a sparse vector of size $|V|$, where $|V|$ is the vocabulary size. Hereby, the embedding vector e_{x_j} is derived from the weights $\theta \in \mathbb{R}^{|V|\times D}$ as

$$e_{x_j} = \theta^T x_j. \tag{2.18}$$

In contrast, the CBOW model predicts the central word x_j based on its surrounding context $x_{j+\alpha}$. The likelihood function for CBOW is defined as:

$$L(\theta) = \prod_{j=1}^{n} \prod_{\alpha=-m,\alpha\neq 0}^{m} P(x_j|\{x_{j+\alpha}\};\theta), \tag{2.19}$$

where the conditional probability is:

$$P(x_j|\{x_{j+\alpha}\};\theta) = \frac{\exp(e_{x_j}^\top h_j)}{\sum_{w\in V}\exp(e_w^\top h_j)}. \tag{2.20}$$

The hidden representation h_j is typically the average or sum of the embeddings of the context words:

$$h_j = \frac{1}{2m} \sum_{\alpha=-m,\alpha\neq 0}^{m} e_{x_{j+\alpha}}. \tag{2.21}$$

Both models rely on the hypothesis that words with similar contexts are closer in a D-dimensional vector space. The cosine similarity between two embeddings, e_{x_a} and e_{x_b}, quantifies their contextual similarity:

$$\text{sim}(x_a, x_b) = \frac{e_{x_a}^\top e_{x_b}}{\|e_{x_a}\|\|e_{x_b}\|}. \tag{2.22}$$

2.5 Summary

This chapter lays the theoretical groundwork necessary to address the research questions posed in this thesis and presents the underlying concepts and methodologies, by defining key concepts of customer journey and personalized customer targeting, the scope of investigation, exploring necessary ML methodologies, and establishing evaluation metrics.

Customer targeting in e-commerce revolves around understanding and enhancing the interactions between customers and brands. The customer journey is a pivotal concept for personalization which allows personalized targeting. In the targeting process customer behavior representation is required. Customer behavior representation transforms raw data from customer interactions into structured, analyzable formats.

For the investigation conducted in this thesis, ML principles are necessary, particularly supervised and self-supervised learning. Self-supervised learning is highlighted for its capability to extract meaningful patterns from unlabeled data, making it ideal for modeling dynamic and diverse customer behavior, especially with embeddings and supervised learning techniques. For task prediction, the focus is on learning models that can process sequential information. The evaluation of predictive models is based on metrics that address the challenges of imbalanced datasets common in e-commerce. Metrics such as precision, recall, F1-score, and AUC are employed to assess the performance and reliability of the models. Embeddings are employed as a method for representing customer behaviors in a dense, low-dimensional vector space. Techniques like Skip-Gram and CBOW are foundational in embedding learning, capturing semantic and contextual relationships within data.

State-of-the-Art

3

As introduced in Chap. 1, the primary objective of this thesis is to explore methodologies for constructing a UCR to enable personalized customer targeting. Consequently, this chapter provides an overview of state-of-the-art approaches for representing customer behavior. Sect. 3.1 presents general methodologies for developing and utilizing UCR, as outlined in Chap. 2. Sect. 3.2 examines approaches that focus on task-specific customer representation, highlighting techniques tailored to distinct applications. Subsequently, the limitations of the current state-of-the-art approaches in UCR approaches and task-specific customer representation are highlighted and analyzed in Sect. 3.3, identifying potential research gaps and opportunities for further advancements. Finally, Sect. 3.4 introduces a two-stage end-to-end modeling paradigm inspired by existing literature, illustrating its relevance to personalized customer targeting.

3.1 Universal Customer Representation Approaches

In the context of e-commerce, UCR encodes customer behavior into a representation that can be reused across different domains and tasks [24, 172, 248]. According to Ni et al. [172] most research on customer representation focuses on predictive models for specific tasks, and only a few studies investigate learning a UCR despite its potential for improving personalization. Nevertheless, interest in this research area is increasing, as evidenced by a growing number of publications as shown in table 3.1 which provides an overview of various approaches for constructing UCR.

In regard to related work in UCR research, studies utilize text-based representations, tables combined with text-based representations, and activity-based representations to model customer behavior. Thereby, most of the proposed UCR approaches rely on text-based representations, which utilize product name, category, descrip-

M. Alves Gomes, *Utilizing Embeddings to Learn a Universal Customer Behavior Representation in E-Commerce*, https://doi.org/10.1007/978-3-658-50781-7_3

Table 3.1 Overview of related work UCR research approaches with information about how the representations are build and what prediction model is used to solve e-commerce prediction tasks

Representation Based On	Representation Learning	Prediction Approach	Prediction Task	Reference & Year
Text	Contrastive Learning	Transformer-based	User safety Churn prediction	[73] (2024)
		Attention-Network	Demography prediction Preference prediction	[260, 261] (2021, 2023)
	Contrastive & Multi-Task Learning	Transformer-based	Recommendation CTR prediction	[209] (2023)
	Self-Supervised Pretraining	Transformer-based	Next-item prediction	[108] (2022)
			CTR prediction Demography prediction	[248] (2020)
		Attention-Network	Demography prediction Preference prediction	[95] (2021)
Table & Text	Reconstruction	Autoencoder	Recommendation Churn prediction	[24] (2024)
Activity	Reconstruction	Transformer-based with CNN-based Encoder	Demography prediction Recommendation	[267] (2024)
	Multi-Task Learning	LSTM Attention-Network	CTR prediction Price preference	[172] (2018)

tion, or search queries [108, 260, 261]. Furthermore, the learning methods for UCR across the studies can be categorized into four approaches, self-supervised pretraining, contrastive learning, reconstruction, and multi-task learning. Self-supervised pretraining includes methods that train customer representation without labeled data as aforementioned in Chap. 2.3 by learning patterns in raw behavior logs using self-supervised objectives such as masked prediction or next-event prediction [108, 248]. Thereby, contrastive learning and reconstruction are a special form of self-supervised learning. Contrastive methods learn vector representations, i.e., embeddings by maximizing similarity between positive pairs while minimizing similarity between negative pairs, leading to task-agnostic, transferable representations [260, 261]. A positive pair typically consists of two semantically similar samples, such as two different representations of the same product (e.g., descriptions, images, or customer interactions with it), while a negative pair consists of semantically dissimilar samples, such as representations of different products with distinct attributes or customer preferences. In reconstruction approaches, the representation is learned by compressing the data into a latent vector space and then reconstructing the input, ensuring that important features are retained [24, 267]. The fourth way to learn UCR is by multi-task learning, where the customer representation is trained jointly on multiple tasks (e.g., CTR prediction, recommendation, demographic classification) to ensure generalization of the representation and adaptability across different domains [172, 209].

The generalizability of the customer representation is usually evaluated on various downstream tasks, such as CTR prediction, recommendation, demographic classification, and price preference modeling. The evaluation of the representation is done by measuring the performance of the downstream tasks, where the representation is used as input to the prediction model. For instance, Fang et al. [73] focus on learning UCR with a Transformer-based architecture using behavioral logs and chat data from Snapchat. To create domain-agnostic representations, they introduce Masked Behavior Prediction and User Contrastive Learning, where customer sequences are masked to force the model to infer missing behaviors while maintaining long-range dependencies between customer interactions. The resulting embeddings from the Transformer output are fine-tuned on multiple downstream tasks, including customer safety classification and churn analysis.

Shin et al. [209] presented a Contrastive Learning User Encoder, a scalable pretraining framework that learns UCR from 50 billion behavior tokens. They employ multi-modal contrastive learning, where behavior data such as product descriptions or search queries is transformed into natural language descriptions to bridge semantic gaps across domains.

Hou et al. [108] proposed a UCR learning framework that eliminates reliance on explicit item IDs to improve transferability across recommendation tasks in different domains. Their approach utilizes a Transformer-encoder (BERT [60]) to represent customers by their items based on their textual descriptions. This method enables cross-domain adaptability by training on multiple recommendation scenarios using multi-domain negatives to learn generalizable sequential patterns. They show the transferability to different domains in next-item prediction.

In the first work of Yang et al. [261], they introduced the Lifelong User Representation Model (LURM), which encodes customer behaviors across their entire lifetime of interactions in a self-supervised manner and fine-tune that model for customer gender, age, and preference prediction. Their approach consists of two core modules: the Bag-of-Interests model, which clusters customer interactions into high-dimensional sparse vectors, and the Self-Supervised Multi-anchor Encoder Network, which maps these representations to low-dimensional universal embeddings using the title of reviewed products. They construct customer representations by processing millions of customer interactions across various time periods, ensuring that the learned embeddings capture both short-term and long-term preferences while maintaining task-agnostic properties. In their second work Yang et al. [260], extend their previous work on UCR by developing a full-lifecycle customer representation approach that models long-term behavioral evolution. Their methodology integrates the Bag-of-Interests encoding with hierarchical time-aware modeling, allowing the representation to adapt to shifting customer preferences over time. Furthermore, they include search queries, purchases, and content interactions to generate the customer representations.

Gu et al. [95] introduce the Self-Supervised User Modeling Network, which constructs UCR by leveraging long-term behavioral consistency in customer interactions. Their approach is based on the hypothesis that customer behaviors are influenced by stable attributes such as demographics, age, and interests, leading to persistent interaction patterns. To capture these consistencies, the authors propose behavioral consistency loss, where the model is trained to predict future customer behaviors based on past actions. The model which uses an attention-based mechanism is trained on large-scale e-commerce logs and social media datasets, using product titles, search logs, or customer tweets and demonstrating that the learned representations can be seamlessly transferred to various downstream tasks such as customer gender, age, preference prediction, and category classification without requiring task-specific training.

Wu et al. [248] introduced Pre-training User Model which learns UCR from large-scale unlabeled behavioral data by using two self-supervised learning tasks: Masked Behavior Prediction, where parts of the customer behavior sequence are hidden and must be reconstructed, and Next-K Behavior Prediction which forces the model to anticipate future interactions. They train their model on web browsing and Ad impression text data which is based on the title of the webpage or Ad, allowing it to generalize effectively to CTR prediction and demographic classification tasks.

Bertrand et al. [24] propose an autoencoder-based framework for learning UCR embeddings from tabular data, designed to provide plug-and-play representations for downstream ML tasks such as churn prediction, anomaly detection, and personalized recommendations. Their approach leverages Contractive Autoencoders to enhance reconstruction accuracy and representation robustness. The model processes tabular data, including customer metadata, financial transactions, and textual descriptions. Like Hou et al. [108] they use a pre-trained language model for text processing.

Only two UCR approaches use activity data instead of text. Zeng et al. [267] propose DDHCN, a dual-decoder transformer-based network designed for mobile app usage modeling. Their approach learns UCR with reconstruction by using a convolutional encoder with a Transformer, allowing the model to extract both global and local behavioral patterns from mobile usage logs. They construct customer representations by processing large-scale mobile app interaction datasets and enhance adaptability through a fine-tuning strategy that incorporates hypernetworks for flexible adaptation to multiple downstream tasks such as age prediction, gender classification, and personalized app recommendations.

Ni et al. [172] propose the Deep User Perception Network (DUPN) a multi-task learning approach designed to learn UCR by integrating diverse e-commerce tasks such as search ranking, recommendation, and price preference modeling. Instead of training separate models for each task, their model learns a shared representation that encodes short-term interactions using LSTMs and long-term preferences via attention-based pooling. Their approach differentiates behavior types (e.g., clicks, purchases) from item features, allowing the model to effectively learn time-aware dependencies. Additionally, a multi-task objective ensures the representations are robust across multiple domains, leading to improved transferability. In their experiments, their model is trained on billions of customer interactions from Taobao and deployed in real-time personalization systems, where it consistently improves CTR prediction, ranking accuracy, and customer engagement by leveraging the shared knowledge across tasks.

It is emphasized that the effectiveness of UCR is primarily demonstrated through their performance on a range of downstream prediction tasks, e.g., CTR prediction, and demographic classification. The quality of a UCR is measured by how well the learned representations generalize to these tasks, indicating their ability to capture essential customer behavior patterns and preferences. Thereby, task-specific metrics such as AUC, and F1 score, are used as proxies for representation quality. This indirect evaluation strategy highlights the capacity of UCRs to capture high-level behavioral abstractions that are transferable across domains, thereby validating their universality and practical applicability in real-world e-commerce systems.

The reviewed UCR approaches demonstrate significant advancements in modeling customer behavior by leveraging DL architectures, such as attention networks and transformer-based models, to jointly learn reusable customer representations and optimize performance across multiple prediction tasks in an end-to-end manner. These methods primarily rely on textual data as the basis for representation learning, with self-supervised objectives like contrastive learning, masked behavior prediction, and reconstruction employed to enhance generalizability and cross-domain transferability. While promising results have been reported in downstream tasks including CTR prediction, recommendation, and demographic classification, the literature remains largely focused on text-based modalities. Only a minority of studies explore activity-based representations, limiting applicability in domains where textual information is sparse or unavailable. Overall, current UCR research underscores the potential of UCR modeling but also reveals a strong dependency on data modalities and architectural design choices which is further discussed in Sect. 5.6.

3.2 E-commerce Task-Specific Customer Representation Approaches

Compared to UCR, the majority of related work focuses on task-specific customer representation approaches, optimizing models for distinct e-commerce prediction tasks, such as CTR prediction, purchase prediction, and churn prediction are more common approaches in the literature. Table 3.2 provides a comparative overview of task-specific customer representation methods. While UCR approaches prioritize generalization and transferability, task-specific models optimize predictive accuracy for specialized e-commerce tasks. Recent advances in task-specific customer representation approaches can be categorized, similarly to the UCR approach, based on the type the representations are based on, namely activity-based, text-based, multi-modal (activity and text, image and text). Thereby, most approaches are based on activity data which differs from the observation made for UCR approaches. Within each category, different representation learning strategies are employed, including end-to-end learning, graph-based learning, contrastive learning, and multi-task learning. However, many representations are created by feature engineering. The prediction approaches for each task encompass traditional ML-based, DL architectures such as LSTM, Deep Neural Networks (DNNs), Convolutional Neural Networks (CNNs), attention-based networks, and Transformer models. The number of different approaches highlights the diversity of methodologies and their respective applications. Furthermore, it underscores the difference in approaches within the prediction task, where purchase and churn prediction relay on customer representation based on feature engineering and ML models for prediction and CTR prediction approaches tend to use more sophisticated end-to-end learning approaches with attention-based models for improving predictive performance by learning patterns directly from the data.

Table 3.2 Comparison of the state-of-the-art approaches for task-specific customer representation learning across different input modalities, representation learning strategies, and prediction approaches

Representation Based On	Representation Learning	Prediction Approach	Prediction Task	Reference
Activity	None, Feature Engineering	ML-based	Purchase prediction	[18, 39, 66–68, 138, 156, 163, 177, 198, 220, 269]
				[146, 155]
	End-to-End	LSTM		[206]
	Graph			[282]
	None, Feature Engineering	ML-based	Churn prediction	[22, 54, 65, 83, 133, 139, 154, 178, 187, 255]
	None, Feature Engineering	ML-based	CTR prediction	[176, 196]
	End-to-End	Attention-based		[45, 72, 117, 136, 180, 242, 243, 256, 257, 268, 272, 276, 279, 280]
		Transformer-based		[41, 142, 264, 275]
		DNN		[111]
	Contrastive Learning	CNN + DNN		[98]
		Attention-based		[85]
	End-to-End	Hybrid		[153, 254]
	Graph	DNN		[137, 247]
		Attention-based		[79]
	Feature Engineering + Multi-Task Learning	Transformer-based	CTR prediction Purchase prediction	[244]
Text	None	LLM	CTR prediction	[90]
Activity & Text	Feature Engineering + End-to-End	Hybrid	CTR prediction	[15]
	End-to-End	Attention-based	CTR prediction	[262]
Image & Text	End-to-End	CNN	CTR prediction	[240]
		Attention-based		[88, 140, 148, 258]

As highlighted in Sect. 2.1, purchase prediction is an essential task in e-commerce and retail analytics, aiming to anticipate customer purchasing decisions based on historical and real-time interactions. Various methodologies have been explored in the literature, leveraging ML, DL, and hybrid approaches to enhance prediction accuracy. Traditional purchase prediction models have primarily relied on feature engineering techniques to construct customer representations and it is the most common approach in the purchase prediction literature. These methods involve manually selecting and engineering features from customer attributes, browsing behavior, and transaction history. For instance, Park et al. [177] and Romov et al. [198] use a Gradient Boosting (GB) method mainly on categorical features. Li et al. [138] utilize a linear regression model for purchase prediction. Martinez et al. [156] apply different models like logistic lasso regression, extreme learning machine (single-layer Multi-Layer Perceptron (MLP)), and GB to make the classification, if a customer will purchase or not in a given month. Balyemah et al. [18] employed Logistic Regression (LR) and Random Forest (RF) classifiers using clickstream data, including session duration and search queries, to predict purchases. Similarly, Sudirman et al. [220] utilized an optimized Decision Tree (DT) model with Particle Swarm Optimization to enhance prediction accuracy by leveraging customer demographics and purchase history. A notable challenge in purchase prediction is transitioning from post-event analysis to real-time inference [67]. Esmeli et al. [67] addressed this gap by developing an early purchase prediction framework that extracts session-related features to make just-in-time predictions while customers are actively browsing. Lin et al. [146] compared LR with LSTM for real-time purchase prediction. Also, Malik et al. [155] and Sheil et al. [206] use LSTM for purchase prediction. Thereby, Malik et al. introduced an enhanced LSTM model incorporating Recursive Feature Elimination for feature selection, focusing on clickstream interactions and digital coupon usage. Sheil et al. proposed a three-layered LSTM architecture with an embedding layer to simultaneously represent and predict purchase intentions in an end-to-end manner. Recent advances have integrated graph neural networks and hybrid architectures to improve prediction robustness. Zhou and Hudin [282] combined time-series attention mechanisms with event-based timestamp encoding, enhancing their customer representation through graph neural networks.

Similar to purchase prediction, customer churn prediction is a fundamental challenge in e-commerce, as businesses seek to retain valuable customers and reduce revenue loss. Churn prediction models aim to identify customers at risk of discontinuing engagement with a platform by analyzing historical interactions, transactional behavior, and various engagement metrics. The literature has explored diverse approaches using ML. Thereby, the studies have employed feature engineering techniques to construct customer representations for churn prediction. Xiahou and

Harada [255] extracted features based on customer activity and the time of the day and leveraged K-Means clustering for customer segmentation, followed by Support Vector Machines for classification, demonstrating that customer segmentation improves prediction accuracy. Friedrich and Dostal [83], Perišić and Pahor [178], and Rachid et al. [187] extracted RFM-related features to represent the customer. Thereby, Perišić and Pahor [178] expanded the traditional RFM model by incorporating Lifetime, Intensity, and Rewards features to better predict churn in the mobile gaming sector. Their study demonstrated that frequency-related behavioral features were the strongest predictors of customer attrition. Similarly, Rachid et al. applied K-Means clustering in combination with Length-Recency-Frequency-Monetary modeling, followed by DT Ensemble and ANNs for classification. This approach effectively differentiated between total and partial churners, improving prediction granularity. Li and Li [139] proposed a ML-model combining LR and Extreme GB, identifying over 20 critical features related to order history, customer profiles, and after-sales interactions. Their study highlighted the effectiveness of combining simple and complex models to enhance prediction performance. Berger et al. [22] use a combination of transactional and behavioral/usage features such as number of sessions, session length, and conversion rate over all historical sessions and emphasized the importance of interaction-based feature extraction, demonstrating that purchase history and session frequency serve as strong churn indicators. Their study found that behavior-driven models outperform static demographic features in predicting customer disengagement.

CTR prediction plays a crucial role in optimizing search results, Ads, and recommendation systems. The literature presents a range of approaches whereby a substantial number of studies explored end-to-end DL architectures to improve CTR prediction accuracy. Here, customer representation is learned end-to-end while learning to solve the task. Notably, Deep Interest Network (DIN) [280] and Deep Interest Evolution Network (DIEN) [279] leverage customer interest modeling based on historical click behavior. These approaches utilize attention mechanisms to dynamically adjust customer representations based on evolving interests. Similarly, the Deep & Cross Network [242] introduces explicit feature crossing, enabling efficient representation learning for sparse and dense features. This approach has been widely adopted in large-scale online advertising systems. Beyond standard DL models, recent studies have introduced advanced architectures, such as Transformer-based models. For instance, Feature-Interaction-Enhanced Sequential Transformer) [264] integrates sequential modeling with self-attention layers to capture customer behavior patterns more effectively. Additionally, Externality Transformer [41] incorporates externality modeling to account for contextual Ad placements in sponsored search.

Contrastive learning has emerged as a powerful technique for CTR prediction. Multi-Interest Self-Supervised Learning approach [98] applies interest-level contrastive learning to refine customer behavior embeddings. Similarly, the Collaborative Contrastive Network [85] enhances CTR prediction by distinguishing customer preferences through co-click and co-non-click relationships. Hybrid models that combine different ML paradigms have also reported strong performance. The model proposed by Xia et al. [254] integrates LightGBM with DL-based representations to optimize feature interactions. Moreover, hybrid approaches incorporating multimodal data sources, such as image and text-based features, have been explored. For example, CNN-based models have been used to extract visual cues from Ads, as demonstrated by Furong Wang et al. [240]. Graph-based neural networks have also been employed to model customer intent and behavioral relationships. The Graph Intention Network [137] leverages co-occurrence graphs to enhance customer preference modeling. Similarly, the Recurrent Attention over Contextualized Page sequence [72] refines CTR prediction by incorporating page-wise customer interaction sequences. Another notable direction is session-aware CTR prediction, which distinguishes between homogeneous and heterogeneous customer sessions. The Deep Session Heterogeneity-Aware Network [275] introduces a session-filtering mechanism to remove noise from customer activity logs, improving overall prediction accuracy. The recent surge in LLM has influenced CTR prediction research. Binzong Geng et al. [90] propose an LLM-enhanced approach that utilizes hierarchical encoding to process long-sequence textual customer behaviors efficiently.

Task-specific customer representation in e-commerce exhibit a wide methodological diversity, with models tailored to optimize predictive accuracy for individual tasks such as purchase prediction, churn detection, and CTR prediction. In contrast to UCR research, the majority of these methods rely on activity-based data and employ traditional ML pipelines grounded in manual feature engineering, particularly in purchase and churn prediction, underscoring a preference for interpretable and computationally efficient solutions. However, CTR prediction has increasingly adopted advanced DL strategies, including end-to-end architectures with attention mechanisms, transformers, contrastive learning, and graph-based models, to enable real-time inference and capture nuanced behavioral patterns. Multimodal fusion strategies and hybrid models further enrich customer representations by incorporating heterogeneous data sources such as images, text, and sequential interactions. Overall, the literature reflects a trade-off between interpretability and modeling complexity, with task-specific approaches offering specialized solutions at the cost of limited generalizability and increased reliance on handcrafted features in less mature domains.

3.3 Limitations of State-of-the-Art Customer Representation Approaches

Despite the promising advancements in UCR approaches several limitations persist among the proposed approaches. As highlighted in Sect. 3.1, a predominant reliance on text-based representations is observed, which may not be fully applicable to all e-commerce use cases where such text data is unavailable or limited. For instance, most approaches in task-specific customer representation rely on activity data (cf. Sect. 3.2). Current literature on UCR approaches exhibits limited generalizability to activity-based environments, where representations must be learned directly from behavioral patterns rather than annotated content.

Regarding task-specific customer representation approaches, most of the approaches rely on feature engineering to construct customer representations, which is a common practice in purchase and churn prediction tasks as shown in the literature review in Sect. 3.2. However, feature engineering-based approaches come with several drawbacks, e.g., the need for domain expertise, manual preprocessing, and limited adaptability to dynamic customer interactions, as the success of the model heavily relies on identifying meaningful features from raw data and continuous analysis of the performance. These limitations hinder the scalability and generalization of the model, as the engineered features may not capture the full complexity of customer behavior. Manually engineered features are often specific to a particular dataset or task, making them difficult to generalize across domains. For example, studies such as those by Park et al. [177] and Romov et al. [198] rely on manually selecting categorical features to predict purchases which is not always given. Furthermore, the manual feature engineering process is time-consuming and requires continuous maintenance to adapt to changing customer preferences and behaviors. In contrast, end-to-end learning methods offer a more flexible and scalable alternative by learning customer representations directly from raw data, eliminating the need for manual feature engineering. This approach enables the model to capture complex patterns and adapt to dynamic customer interactions, enhancing prediction accuracy and generalization across different domains as underlined by Wu et al. [248] which show that self-supervised representation learning significantly outperforms feature-engineered models in large-scale behavioral analysis. Additionally, this is highlighted by the fact that no UCR approach in the literature uses feature engineering but learning approaches for customer representation as shown by the reviewed literature in Sect. 3.1.

While end-to-end approaches offer several advantages, such as eliminating manual feature engineering, there are several downsides and challenges to consider. Many DL models require extensive computational resources for training making them less practical for real-time applications. For instance, Transformer-based models, such as those used by Hou et al. [108] and Wu et al. [248], demand high GPU power to process large behavioral datasets, making them costly to build in the first place. Zhou et al. [279, 280] demonstrated that attention-based models significantly improve CTR prediction, but the computational overhead is much higher than traditional ML-based methods. Another issue to consider is the need for large-scale data for training, as end-to-end models require substantial amounts of data to learn meaningful representations effectively. For instance, the study by Shin et al. [209] trained their model on 50 billion behavior tokens to learn UCR, highlighting the importance of large-scale data for effective representation learning. Ni et al. [172] proposed a DL approach for UCR, but the effectiveness of their model decreases when dealing with cold-start customers with limited interaction history.

Besides methodical limitations, further challenges arise from the underlying data requirements of current representation approaches. As data privacy becomes an increasingly critical concern, the demand for privacy-preserving methods intensifies [69]. However, end-to-end models often require access to demographic and personal customer data, raising privacy concerns and making it challenging to comply with data protection regulations. This is a widespread issue in the customer representation research, including feature engineering and end-to-end learning approaches alike. For instance, the studies from Xiahou and Harada [255], Li and Li [139], Balyemah et al. [18], and Sudirman et al. [220] rely on customer demographics to predict customer purchase intention and churn.

In summary, while feature engineering-based models are interpretable and computationally efficient, they suffer from limited adaptability, require extensive domain expertise, and are challenging to scale across dynamic and heterogeneous e-commerce environments. End-to-end learning models, in contrast, automate feature extraction and offer greater generalization across tasks and domains, yet they introduce several critical drawbacks, including high computational demands, personal information, and the need for large-scale training data. Moreover, a major limitation across nearly all current UCR approaches is their predominant reliance on textual data as the primary input modality for representations. This design choice restricts applicability in real-world scenarios where textual metadata is sparse, incomplete, or entirely absent, such as anonymous browsing contexts, where only behavioral signals are available. In addition, neither feature engineering nor end-to-end methods adequately addresses the growing need for data protection and privacy compliance. Most state-of-the-art approaches either rely directly on demographic and personal customer data or omit mechanisms to ensure compliance with legal frameworks such as the European Union's GDPR [69], which mandates customer consent, limits data storage, and governs profiling practices. To address these critical limitations, the UCR approach proposed in this work introduces a privacy-conscious, domain-adaptable, and computationally efficient representation learning approach. The technical design and methodology of this approach will be presented in detail in Chap. 5.

3.4 End-to-End Customer Representation Learning

From the current literature, it is evident that various approaches exist for constructing customer representations and predicting customer behavior. In purchase and churn prediction tasks, customer representations are traditionally engineered through domain expertise, relying on feature engineering and manual preprocessing. This conventional approach follows the four-stage approach introduced in Chap. 2, which consists of data collection, feature engineering for customer representation creation, customer analysis, and customer targeting or customer behavior prediction. However, as previously shown in Sect. 3.1 and Sect. 3.2, advancements in DL have led to the emergence of end-to-end learning methods that streamline this process by learning customer representations in conjunction with the predictive task within a unified system.

To align with these advancements, a two-stage end-to-end customer targeting approach is proposed in this thesis, as illustrated in Fig. 3.1. This approach integrates customer representation learning and prediction into a single learning process. By integrating representation learning and prediction within a single approach, end-to-end approaches leverage the full potential of DL techniques to enhance customer targeting effectiveness. This two-step paradigm not only simplifies model development but also enables adaptive learning from dynamic customer interactions,

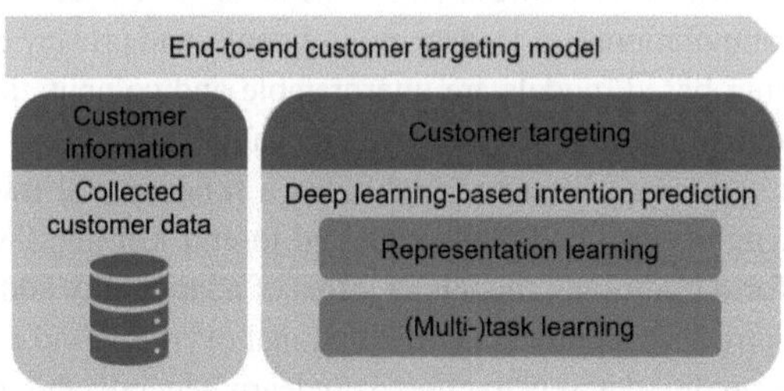

Fig. 3.1 End-to-end customer targeting process using DL. The customer representation stage is omitted, as the representation is learned jointly with the predictive task in an end-to-end manner

indicating robust and scalable customer representation learning without the need for manual feature engineering and therefore, improves the model adaptability.

3.5 Summary

This chapter provides an overview of contemporary methodologies for customer representation learning, particularly in the context of personalized customer targeting. UCR aims to construct reusable customer representations applicable across multiple tasks. Various methodologies have been proposed, primarily categorized based on input type (e.g., text-based, activity-based, multimodal) and learning techniques. Most studies leverage text-based representations and self-supervised learning, including contrastive learning, multi-task learning, and reconstruction-based approaches. Transformer-based models dominate the field, enhancing generalization across domains. The representations are evaluated on different downstream tasks demonstrating the transferability and adaptability of the customer representation.

In contrast to UCR, task-specific representations are optimized for distinct prediction tasks such as CTR prediction, purchase prediction, and churn prediction. While UCR methods emphasize transferability, task-specific models prioritize predictive accuracy within specific domains. These methods rely on diverse architectures and representation approaches, including feature engineering, end-to-end learning, graph-based learning, and contrastive learning. Notably, CTR prediction studies have explored advanced architectures such as attention networks and transformer models to improve prediction accuracy.

End-to-end learning methods have emerged as a promising alternative to traditional feature engineering-based approaches, offering automated feature extraction and improved generalization. However, these methods come with several challenges, including high computational costs, data requirements, and privacy concerns. While feature engineering-based models are interpretable and computationally efficient, they lack adaptability and require extensive manual effort.

All in all, the reviewed literature highlights a fundamental trade-off between manual feature engineering and automated end-to-end learning. While DL-based methods outperform traditional models in terms of adaptability and predictive performance, they introduce significant computational overhead and require access to large-scale, high-quality datasets to effectively learn generalizable representations.

Use Cases and Data

4

As highlighted in Chap. 1, modern e-commerce platforms must offer personalized experiences to retain customers. This necessity demands the implementation of diverse and adaptable marketing strategies tailored to individual customers. However, achieving personalization at scale requires knowledge about the customers and their intentions, which can be challenging due to the dynamic nature of customer interactions.

This chapter introduces the practical use case and the data foundations employed in this work to investigate and validate the proposed UCR concept. Specifically, it first introduces the use case within the scope of the research as described in Chap. 2.1. In Sect. 4.2, a data model is presented that abstracts customer interactions in a privacy-preserving and regulation-compliant manner. Then, the datasets used in this thesis are introduced, including a real-world dataset provided by Breinify Inc. and three publicly available benchmark datasets to showcase the transferability, robustness, and reproducibility of the proposed UCR approach across diverse e-commerce environments. Additionally, the characteristics of the datasets are presented. This statistical overview serves as both a descriptive and preparatory component of this thesis, laying the foundation for understanding the preprocessing steps detailed in Sect. 5.4.1. Additionally, the differences between the datasets are highlighted, emphasizing their suitability for evaluating the proposed UCR approach in various e-commerce contexts.

M. Alves Gomes, *Utilizing Embeddings to Learn a Universal Customer Behavior Representation in E-Commerce*, https://doi.org/10.1007/978-3-658-50781-7_4

4.1 Use Case—Customer Behavior Prediction Along the Customer Journey

In the domain of e-commerce, customer journeys are typically composed of sequential interactions spanning various phases, from initial exploration to evaluation, intent formation, and eventual purchase (cf. Chap. 2). Some of these phases generate interaction data that reflects customer preferences, intentions, and engagement levels. The ability to accurately interpret and predict customer behavior throughout this journey is crucial for delivering timely and relevant personalization, which has been shown to enhance customer satisfaction and increase business outcomes.

As defined in Chap. 2.1, the use case investigated in this thesis takes place in the pre-purchase and purchase phase of the customer journey for an arbitrary e-commerce company. In this scenario, customers interact with an online shop, and the company's goal is to target each individual with personalized marketing strategies so that the outcome of the interaction is maximized. From the company's perspective, maximizing the outcome typically involves increasing key performance indicators such as conversion rates, average order value, and customer lifetime value, while simultaneously reducing churn and acquisition costs. From the customer's perspective, outcome maximization translates into receiving timely, relevant, and context-aware product suggestions or offers that align with their preferences and intent, ultimately enhancing satisfaction, reducing search friction, and improving the overall customer shopping experience [224].

A typical e-commerce use case involves a customer browsing the platform, viewing products, and potentially adding items to a shopping cart. Throughout this process, a personalized targeting system must determine the probability of key behavioral outcomes, such as whether the customer is likely to make a purchase, churn, or click on a recommended item. For instance, if a high purchase likelihood is predicted, targeted strategies such as dynamic pricing, limited-time offers, or product bundling can be deployed to accelerate the decision and increase the average order value. Additionally, retargeting ads or personalized upselling prompts may be shown to encourage checkout completion. When a churn risk is identified, such as when a customer shows declining engagement or long inter-session times, retention-focused interventions can be applied, including loyalty incentives, or customized offers to recapture interest. Lastly, when the targeting system predicts a high click-through probability for certain content or product categories, personalized recommendations or featured banners can be prioritized in real time to increase interaction depth and guide the customer toward conversion paths with higher expected value. These are example strategies, that are designed to optimize both short-term transactional outcomes and long-term customer satisfaction, aligning predictive signals with context-aware marketing decisions that respect the customer's inferred intent and current stage in the journey.

To support such real-time, personalized decision-making, real-time responsiveness is critical. As highlighted by Esmeli et al. [67], in e-commerce, the ability to deliver personalized customer experiences in real time is essential for maintaining engagement and improving conversion rates. If a company fails to respond while the customer's interest is still active, the opportunity to influence decision-making is often lost. Real-time interactions are particularly important in high-intent phases, such as when a customer is actively browsing or comparing products, as delays in personalized content, such as recommendations, promotions, or cart reminders can result in abandonment or disengagement.

According to foundational research in human-computer interaction, system responsiveness is perceived as real-time if feedback is delivered within approximately 0.1 seconds [33, 162]. When system responses exceed this threshold, customers begin to perceive latency, which can diminish trust, interrupt cognitive flow, and reduce the overall usability of the platform. Overall, real-time capability serves as both a technological requirement and a competitive differentiator. It enables platforms to respond dynamically to customer behavior, maximize relevance, and execute timely marketing strategies, all of which are essential in a fast-paced digital environment where attention spans are short and customer expectations for immediacy are high.

Moreover, such personalized targeting systems must operate efficiently within resource-constrained environments. E-commerce platforms can experience high traffic volumes and must adapt to varying customer behaviors across time, while also ensuring minimal use of computational resources and memory. These resource-constrained environments are further complicated by strict data privacy regulations, e.g., GDPR. Therefore, companies must ensure data privacy and compliance with regulations across different jurisdictions [31, 69, 215, 233], which often prohibit the persistent collection of personal data or limits its storage duration. Additionally, as many customers browse anonymously without logging in, accurately modeling behavior becomes particularly challenging without violating privacy laws. Therefore, behavior prediction strategies must be designed to maximize personalization while ensuring lawful and ethical handling of sensitive customer data.

To support such a personalized targeting system in such a use case, the UCR must satisfy several essential properties to ensure that real-time customer behavior can be modeled effectively and responsibly. Specifically, the UCR must:

- Be **task-agnostic**, enabling reuse across multiple prediction tasks such as purchase prediction, churn prediction, and CTR prediction, without requiring task-specific retraining. Not only are these three prediction tasks the most prominent in e-commerce research, as highlighted in Sect. 2.1, but the acquisition of ground truth labels for these tasks requires only interaction data, such as purchase events for purchase prediction.
- Be **privacy-preserving**, ensuring that meaningful behavioral patterns are captured exclusively from non-personal interaction data, without requiring persistent customer identifiers or invasive profiling. This ensures full alignment with strict data privacy regulations (e.g., GDPR) and supports anonymous or session-based personalization.
- Be **computationally efficient** and lightweight, allowing high-throughput inference within strict latency thresholds of approximately 0.1 seconds to support real-time personalized decision-making at scale.
- Be **scalable and generalizable**, performing robustly across different datasets, use cases, and customer interaction scenarios, as demonstrated in this thesis by its evaluation on diverse tasks and datasets.

4.2 Data

Understanding customer behavior in e-commerce environments requires the collection and processing of detailed interaction data. However, this necessity must be balanced with strict adherence to data privacy regulations and ethical principles. This section therefore introduces the data governance and infrastructure underlying this thesis, beginning with an overview of the key data protection laws, most notably the GDPR, that regulates how customer data can be collected, processed, and retained in e-commerce contexts. Building on these regulatory foundations, a formalized data model is presented that abstracts customer interactions in a privacy-preserving and compliant manner. The subsequent sections describe how this data model enables the generation of lawful customer representations and detail the real-world dataset used to empirically evaluate the proposed UCR approach for the use case. Furthermore, three publicly available benchmark datasets are introduced to demonstrate the transferability, robustness, and reproducibility of the proposed UCR approach across diverse e-commerce environments.

4.2.1 Data Privacy Regulations

There exist multiple legal frameworks worldwide that regulate the collection, storage, and processing of personal data [69, 215, 233]. Thereby, the GDPR, as it is the most comprehensive, strict, and widely adopted data privacy regulation to date. Recent estimates indicate that the EU accounts for roughly 450 million internet users and approximately 15-20% of global e-commerce sales by value [217]. This underscores that any company operating internationally or serving EU customers must ensure compliance with the GDPR. Therefore, basing this thesis on GDPR principles guarantees that the developed customer representation is aligned with some of the strictest privacy standards globally, making it adaptable to other jurisdictions with similar or emerging regulations.

The GDPR has been enforced since 2018 and governs how organizations must handle the personal data of individuals within the EU, and it applies extraterritorially to any company offering goods or services to EU residents, regardless of where that company is based. It defines personal data broadly as any information that can directly or indirectly identify a natural person. This includes obvious identifiers such as names, addresses, or email addresses, but also less direct identifiers such as IP addresses, cookies, or device fingerprints.

At its core, the GDPR is structured around several fundamental principles: lawfulness, fairness, transparency, purpose limitation, data minimization, storage limitation, integrity and confidentiality, and accountability [69]. Organizations must clearly define and limit the purposes for which they collect personal data and must not process it further in ways that are incompatible with those original purposes. Moreover, the principle of data minimization requires that only the minimum necessary data is collected to fulfill a specific purpose.

For e-commerce platforms, these requirements are especially relevant because online services routinely handle a large volume of personal information for tasks like customer authentication, payment processing, and behavioral targeting. Such activities typically require a clear legal basis (e.g., contractual necessity or explicit consent) and come with strict obligations for informing customers, managing data subject rights, and implementing robust technical and organizational safeguards.

A key implication of the GDPR is that personal data must not be retained longer than necessary for its intended purpose, and it must be secured through measures like pseudonymization, encryption, and contractual safeguards for third-party processing [69].

However, the GDPR does not apply to information that has been rendered truly anonymous. Recital 26 clarifies that data is outside the scope of the GDPR if it can no longer be attributed to an identifiable individual, whether directly or indirectly [69]. As such, building customer representations based solely on aggregated, session-based, or fully anonymized interaction data can significantly reduce legal burdens and align with the principles of data minimization and privacy by design.

4.2.2 Data Model

Given the stringent requirements introduced by data protection laws such as the GDPR, it is essential to design a data model that reconciles analytical expressiveness with strict legal constraints. Building on the principles discussed above, the data model developed in this thesis is intentionally structured to abstract customer journeys and behavioral trajectories in a way that maximizes predictive utility while minimizing the processing of personally identifiable information. This privacy-first approach ensures that the proposed UCR operates fully within the boundaries of modern data governance requirements.

In response, this thesis proposes a minimalistic, i.e., without personal information, regulation-compliant data model that should enable robust behavioral inference while maintaining a privacy-preserving structure. This data model is designed to be broadly applicable across e-commerce platforms, particularly in scenarios where customer authentication is optional or unavailable. For instance, many customers interact with e-commerce platforms anonymously, without logging in or granting tracking consent, making long-term identification and behavior linkage infeasible.

Specifically, customer behavior is represented as a time-ordered sequence of discrete interaction events. Each event corresponds to a single customer interaction with a functional unit of the platform, modeled as a tuple:

$$\text{InteractionEvent} = (\text{touchpoint}, \text{timestamp}, \text{sequenceId})$$

The components of this tuple are defined as follows:

- `touchpoint`: A symbolic identifier indicating the feature or interface element engaged by the customer (e.g., product view, search query, category visit). This abstract labeling enables the encoding of intent signals without exposing semantic or personal content.
- `timestamp`: A time marker specifying when the interaction occurred. Temporal information is necessary for capturing event order.
- `sequenceId`: A session-level identifier used to group temporally proximal events from the same customer. This identifier allows the system to reconstruct the sequence of events within a session, enabling the analysis of behavioral patterns and transitions.

A dataset $\mathcal{D}$ of customer interactions is then defined as a collection of interaction events:

$$\mathcal{D} = \{(\text{touchpoint}_i, \text{timestamp}_i, \text{sequenceId}_i) \mid i = 1, 2, \ldots, N\}$$

where N is the total number of interaction events in the dataset. The proposed data model should be suitable for contemporary e-commerce environments. For instance, it excludes personally identifiable information, such as persistent identifiers, demographic metadata, or device-level tracking information, and uses only anonymized sequence identifiers instead, which should enable behavior modeling even when customers are unauthenticated, making it robust in settings where login rates are low or explicit consent is limited. Furthermore, the data model is platform-agnostic ensuring applicability across a wide range of digital commerce systems, regardless of backend complexity or customer data maturity.

This data model should form the foundation for constructing customer representations that are transferable, regulation-compliant, and usable in real-time personalization pipelines.

4.2.3 Breinify Dataset

To evaluate the conducted experiments in this thesis, a real-world dataset has been provided by Breinify Inc., a San Francisco-based company specializing in AI-powered personalization. Breinify enables enterprise clients, such as retail and consumer goods brands, to implement personalized marketing strategies across various channels, including web, email, SMS, and others [114, 182].

For this thesis, Breinify has contributed a dataset obtained from a U.S.-based retailer. The dataset captures rich interaction-level information, covering over 53 million customer events recorded between January 1, 2020, and May 8, 2020. These events represent engagement with the retailer's online store and provide the basis for modeling customer behavior throughout the pre-purchase and purchase phases of the customer journey, as defined in Chap. 2.1.

Each event in the dataset contains both contextual and behavioral attributes, including:

- Customer information: customer ID (where available), IP address, device type, session ID, and estimated geographic location.
- Interaction details: URL of the visited page, referrer URL, event timestamp, and event type. All events include URLs, though some are customer-specific (e.g.,

personalized carts or checkout links). Additionally, referrer URLs are recorded to trace navigation paths, including from external search engines.

- Event type categories: page-visit, product-view, add-to-cart, remove-from-cart, check-out, click-recommendation, and others.
- Product metadata: product ID and associated information, such as categories or product price. Applicable only for certain event types. Product interactions appear only in events categorized as product-view, add-to-cart, remove-from-cart, and check-out. Notably, product-view events always involve a single product, while add-to-cart and remove-from-cart events may involve multiple products.

All events include URLs, of which some are customer-specific (e.g., personalized carts or checkout links). Additionally, referrer URLs are recorded to trace navigation paths, including from external search engines. An example customer event in the dataset might look like the following:


```
{
    "_id": {
        "$oid": "abc"
    },
    "rawDataId": "def",
    "ipAddress": "127.0.0.0",
    "signature": "FUrld2YAFcT4GSdt",
    "apiKey": "54F6-09BB",
    "unixTimestamp": 1514764800,
    "user": {
        "sessionId": "abcd-0001",
        "email": "user@email.com",
        "additional": {
            "referrer": "https://www.google.com/search?q=xyz",
            "url": "https://www.breinify_dataset.com",
            "timezone": "America/Los_Angeles",
            "localDateTime": "Sun Dec 31 2017 15:59:59 GMT-0800",
        },
        "userId": "12345"
    },
    "activity": {
        "type": "pageVisit",
        "category": "other",
        "tags": {
            "pageId": "https://www.breinify_dataset.com",
            "title": "Breinify Dataset"
        }
    }
}
```

Each customer action is recorded as a discrete event and includes all components required by the formal data model: a session identifier, a timestamp, and a representation of the touchpoint. The provided session ID field allows events to be grouped into temporally bounded interaction sequences, enabling session-level modeling without reliance on persistent customer identification. The timestamp field offers precise temporal resolution necessary for constructing ordered event trajectories, capturing session dynamics, and supporting time-aware modeling. For the touchpoint, the dataset provides multiple alternatives for defining meaningful and privacy-compliant interaction identifiers. One possible encoding leverages the combination of event type and URL, which captures both the nature of the action (e.g., product view, add-to-cart) and the context in which it occurred (e.g., specific product or category page). Alternatively, in cases where product interactions are present, a more abstract representation using event type and product ID can be used. This abstraction omits potentially sensitive or personal-specific URL information while retaining sufficient semantic granularity for behavioral modeling. Both options conform to the symbolic and anonymized nature of the touchpoint as defined in the data model, enabling the construction of customer representation from sequences of interaction events without using personally identifiable information. The event tuple based on the example above would then be represented as:

```
InteractionEvent =
("pageVisit:https://www.breinify_dataset.com",
1514764800,
"abcd-0001")
```

Although the Breinify dataset contains sufficient detail to construct a highly granular customer data model with persistent personal identifiers, doing so would conflict with the requirements of modern privacy regulations such as the GDPR. If an organization wishes to operate within the EU or serve EU-based customers, it must adapt its data handling practices to ensure that personal identifiers are either removed or pseudonymized in line with the principles of data minimization and privacy by design. Therefore, in this thesis, the Breinify raw data is deliberately transformed using the data model. This demonstrates how even data-rich environments can be aligned with strict privacy regulations by designing representations that capture only the essential behavioral context without storing any direct or persistent customer-specific information.

For having a further understanding of the Breinify dataset, it is essential to examine the structural and statistical properties of the dataset in more detail. Table 4.1 provides an overview of key dataset characteristics. Among the 53.8 million inter-

Table 4.1 Key information about the Breinify e-Commerce dataset, including the number of events, sessions, URLs, products, and customers, as well as session statistics and conversion rates

General Information	Total	Page-Visit	Product-View	Add-to-Cart	Remove-From-Cart		Check-Out
Number of Events	53,825,295	41,041,995 (76.25%)	4,537,668 (8.43%)	3,452,637 (6.41%)	700,226 (1.30%)		107,186 (0.20%)
Number of Sessions		**Check-Out**					
	6,195,916	101,401 (1.64%)					
Number of URLs	5,003,592						
Number of Products	36,012						
Number of Product Categories	592						
Number of Customers		**Events**		**Sessions**			
		Known	**Unknown**	**Known**	**Unknown**		
	574,890	21,784,141 (40.47%)	32,041,154 (59.53%)	455,944 (7.36%)	5,739,957 (92.64%)		
Session Statistics	**Mean**	**Std**	**Min**	**25%**	**50%**	**75%**	**Max**
Events per Session	8.687	57.725	1	2	3	8	49,499
Products per Session	3.186	35.981	1	1	1	3	24,679
Session Duration in min.	27.775	144.443	0	0	0.6333	4.650	1,439.983
Conversion Rates	**Rate**						
Customers with Purchase	78,470 (13.65%)						
Viewed-Product-to-Purchase	2.36%						
Add-to-Cart- to-Purchase	3.10%						

action events, the majority are page visits (76.25%), followed by product views (8.43%), add-to-cart events (6.41%), remove-from-cart events (1.30%), and checkout events (0.20%). The dataset includes 6.2 million unique sessions, of which 1.64% result in a checkout. It also includes over 5 million unique URLs, 36,012 distinct products, and 592 product categories. Customer identification is partial: approximately 40.47% of the events and only 7.36% of the sessions are attributable to known customers. The remaining majority are associated with anonymous customers, a typical constraint in real-world e-commerce platforms operating under privacy-aware settings. In terms of behavior, the average session includes 8.687 events, involves 3.186 products, and spans approximately 27.8 minutes. Conversion rates from product view to purchase (2.36%) and add-to-cart to purchase (3.10%) reflect expected drop-offs along the conversion funnel. Notably, only 13.65% of customers purchased during the recorded period, confirming a class imbalance relevant for downstream predictive modeling tasks. Furthermore, the dataset exhibits a strong skew in session length and interaction volume: most sessions are short, while a small number contain thousands of events. This long-tail distribution is typical in e-commerce traffic and underscores the need for robust, generalized representations.

The presentation of detailed dataset statistics serves as both a descriptive and preparatory component of this thesis. On the one hand, it offers essential insight into the nature and scope of the behavioral data used for modeling customer interactions. The distributions of event types, session lengths, product interactions, and conversion rates reflect the operational realities of e-commerce platforms and highlight the variability and sparsity inherent in real-world customer behavior. On the other hand, this statistical overview lays the foundation for understanding the subsequent preprocessing steps detailed in Sect. 5.4.1. Characteristics such as the skewed frequency of interaction types, the imbalance between known and anonymous customers, and the long-tail distribution of session activity directly influence the data transformation procedures applied prior to customer behavior prediction. For example, sparsity in purchase events and uneven session lengths necessitate normalization techniques and session segmentation strategies. The presence of customer-specific URLs and complex interaction metadata calls for filtering and abstraction mechanisms to preserve privacy and semantic consistency. Moreover, the high proportion of anonymous customers underscores the importance of designing representations that are robust to missing or partial customer identifiers. Thus, the statistical analysis presented here not only contextualizes the dataset's representational challenges but also motivates the architectural and algorithmic choices made in the preprocessing pipeline. This ensures that the behavioral signals fed into the customer representation are both clean, semantically meaningful, and compliant with privacy-preserving constraints.

In summary, the Breinify dataset provides a rich testbed for evaluating the proposed UCR approach. Its combination of diverse interaction types, partial customer observability, and temporal sequence data aligns well with the formal data model previously described. It enables experimentation across key prediction tasks, purchase likelihood, churn, and CTR prediction, using real-world, anonymized behavioral data. Additionally, the presence of anonymous customers, varied session lengths, and detailed interaction metadata allows for evaluating the scalability, transferability, and robustness of learned representations under realistic operational constraints.

4.2.4 Benchmark Datasets

To rigorously evaluate the transferability and generalizability of the proposed UCR approach, three publicly available benchmark datasets, YooChoose, RetailRocket, and OpenCDP are employed alongside the proprietary Breinify dataset. Each of these benchmarks has been selected not only for its prevalence in the academic literature but also for its unique characteristics that test different dimensions of representational transfer. Their inclusion ensures that the UCR approach is validated across varying e-commerce use cases, behavioral prediction tasks, and data regimes, reflecting the diversity and complexity of real-world online retail environments. Other large-scale e-commerce datasets, such as the Amazon Review Dataset [171] or the Criteo Display Advertising Challenge Dataset [227], are not considered because they primarily focus on static customer-item ratings or impression logs of viewed Ads which only cover one touchpoint of the customer journey but not a sequence of touchpoints which is the focus of this thesis. More details on the datasets and their choice are provided in the following.

YooChoose E-Commerce Benchmark Dataset

The YooChoose e-Commerce benchmark dataset was introduced in 2015 for the RecSys Challenge and is widely utilized as a benchmark for purchase prediction [67, 146, 163, 177, 198]. It contains click and purchase event data from a European online retailer, including session information for purchased products, along with corresponding price and quantity details. The dataset comprises approximately 9.2 million sessions and 33 million customer interactions collected over a six-month period from April to September 2014. Each event is characterized by session ID, event timestamp, product information, and product category. Notably, customer identification data is not included, and the dataset consists exclusively of view and purchase events.

Table 4.2 provides an overview of the YooChoose dataset. The dataset contains 34.15 million events, with 96.63% of the events being product views and 3.37% check-out events. The dataset includes 52,739 unique products from 340 categories and 9.2 million sessions. The conversion rate observed in the dataset is 3.49% from viewed-product to purchase. Of all sessions, 5.51% end in a check-out event. On average, a session consists of 3.69 events and has a duration of 6.739 minutes. The dataset exhibits a skewed distribution of events per session, with most sessions containing only a few events which is highlighted by the quantiles.

Table 4.2 Key information about the Yoochoose e-commerce benchmark dataset, including the number of events, sessions, and products, as well as session statistics and conversion rates

General Information	Total	Product-View	Check-Out				
Number of Events	34,154,697	33,003,944 (96.63%)	1,150,753 (3.37%)				
Number of Sessions		**Check-Out**					
	9,249,729	509,696 (5.51%)					
Number of Products	52,739						
Number of Product Categories	340						
Session Statistics	**Mean**	**Std**	**Min**	**25%**	**50%**	**75%**	**Max**
Events per Session	3.69	4.04	1	2	2	4	262
Duration in min	6.739	12.906	0	0.550	2.233	6.950	1,218.950
Conversion Rates	**Rate**						
Viewed-Product-to-Purchase	3.49%						

In the context of transferability, the dataset serves as a representative use case distinct from the proprietary Breinify dataset. Its clear focus on session-level behavior, with no persistent customer identification, makes it directly comparable to the real-world data constraints addressed in this thesis. Furthermore, the YooChoose dataset offers explicit purchase labels derived from real checkout events rather than synthetic or proxy constructs, making it a robust benchmark for validating purchase prediction, which is the primary downstream task. Moreover, it poses a deliberate challenge for representation creation because it contains limited event diversity (only product views and purchases) and short interaction sequences, which test whether representation can generalize in low-context scenarios where behavioral signals are sparse. Demonstrating strong performance under these constraints highlights the representation's ability to generalize without relying on rich customer profiles or long behavioral histories, conditions that match many real-world deployment settings where customer anonymity is the norm.

Finally, its wide adoption in the research community as a standard benchmark dataset for purchase prediction ensures that results are comparable and reproducible. Taken together, YooChoose is therefore an essential dataset for demonstrating that tested approaches are portable, robust, and effective across platforms with different behavioral structures and strict privacy limitations.

RetailRocket E-Commerce Benchmark Dataset

The RetailRocket E-Commerce Benchmark Dataset is primarily employed as a benchmark for churn prediction [22, 83]. However, it has also been utilized in purchase prediction tasks [206] and CTR prediction [268]. The dataset was collected from an e-commerce platform over a period of 4.5 months, spanning from May to September 2015, and comprises approximately 2.75 million events recorded from 1.4 million customers. Each event is characterized by five attributes: visitor ID, item ID, timestamp, and event type (view, add-to-cart, or transaction). Additionally, supplementary information, including item prices and categories, is provided. Notably, session-level data is not included.

Table 4.3 provides an overview of the RetailRocket dataset. The dataset contains 2.75 million events, with 96.67% of the events being product views, 2.52% add-to-cart events, and 0.81% check-out events. The dataset includes 235,061 unique products from 1,331 categories and 1.4 million customers. The conversion rates observed in the dataset are 0.84% from viewed-product to purchase, and 32.39% from add-to-cart to purchase. Only 0.83% of all customers completed a purchase.

Although RetailRocket also contains purchase events, it does not provide explicit session identifiers by design, which limits its suitability as a fully consistent session-based transferability benchmark compared to YooChoose. Nevertheless, the dataset remains highly relevant for this thesis because it is the established benchmark for churn prediction, which is one task to show the generalizability of the proposed UCR approach. Unlike YooChoose, this is possible because customer information is available to generate churn labels, which will be detailed in Sect. 5.4.1. Moreover, using RetailRocket allows direct performance comparison with a substantial body of published churn prediction baselines, demonstrating whether a single UCR can generalize effectively to predictive tasks beyond purchase intent, even when the input structure is less than ideal. As such, RetailRocket serves as a critical complement to YooChoose, ensuring that the proposed UCR approach is tested for robustness

Table 4.3 Key information about the RetailRocket e-commerce benchmark dataset, including the number of events, products, customers, and conversion rates

General Information	Total	Product-View	Add-to-Cart	Check-Out
Number of Events	2,756,101	2,664,312 (96.67%)	69,332 (2.52%)	22,457 (0.81%)
Number of Products	235,061			
Number of Product Categories	1,331			
Number of Customers	1,407,580			
Conversion Rates	**Rate**			
Customers with Purchase	11,719 (0.83%)			
Viewed-Product-to-Purchase	0.84%			
Add-to-Cart-to-Purchase	32.39%			

across prediction tasks, input granularities, and practical data constraints found in modern e-commerce environments.

OpenCDP E-Commerce Benchmark Dataset

The OpenCDP e-commerce benchmark dataset was utilized in the 2020 RecSys tutorial and is provided by the REES46 marketing platform [195]. This dataset contains data on customer behavior from a large online store offering multiple categories of products. The data covers the period from October 2019 to April 2020. Each entry in the dataset corresponds to a specific customer event and comprises nine distinct attributes which are session ID, customer ID, event time, event type (view, add-to-cart, or purchase), item ID, product category ID, product brand, product price, and product category brand. It further comprises over 411 million events stemming from approximately 89 million sessions. Not only does this dataset provide rich information, but it is also considerably larger than other datasets, making it to test the scalability of the presented approach.

Table 4.4 provides an overview of the OpenCDP dataset statistics. The dataset contains 411.7 million events, with 93.69% of the events being product views, 4.64% add-to-cart events, and 1.66% check-out events. The dataset includes 386,299 unique products from 1,325 categories and 15.6 million customers. The conversion rates observed in the dataset are 1.78% from viewed-product to purchase, and 35.83%

from add-to-cart to purchase. Only 13.20% of all customers completed a purchase. The session statistics of the OpenCDP dataset show that a session consists of 4.590 events and has a duration of 13.819 minutes.

Table 4.4 Key information about the OpenCDP e-commerce benchmark dataset, including the number of events, sessions, products, and customers, as well as session statistics and conversion rates

General Information	Total	Product-View	Add-to-Cart	Check-Out			
Number of Events	411,709,736	385,746,849 (93.69%)	19,114,063 (4.64%)	6,848,824 (1.66%)			
Number of Sessions		**Check-Out**					
	89,693,595	5,449,934 (6.08%)					
Number of Products	386,299						
Number of Product Categories	1,325						
Number of Customers	15,639,803						
Session Statistics	**Mean**	**Std**	**Min**	**25%**	**50%**	**75%**	**Max**
Events per Session	4.590	11.150	1	1	2	5	34,570
Duration in min	13.819	94.344	0	0	0.700	4.183	1,439.983
Conversion Rates	**Rate**						
Customers with Purchase	2,064,899 (13.20%)						
Viewed-Product-to-Purchase	1.78%						
Add-to-Cart-to-Purchase	35,83%						

Due to its extensive scale and fine-grained structure, OpenCDP is deliberately included to evaluate the scalability and robustness of the tested approach under industrial-scale data volumes. Compared to YooChoose and RetailRocket, OpenCDP offers orders of magnitude more events and a broader product catalog, including detailed brand and category information. This diversity of signals allows testing whether the UCR approach can maintain efficiency, expressiveness, and real-time feasibility when exposed to high-cardinality token spaces and millions of sessions. Additionally, the dataset's explicit session and customer IDs, paired with multi-type events (views, add-to-cart, purchases), make it highly suitable for stress-testing the proposed design under conditions that approximate large-scale, real-world deployment. By validating the method on OpenCDP, this thesis demonstrates that the tested approaches can scale beyond smaller benchmarks to handle the dynamic, data-intensive environments characteristic of modern e-commerce platforms.

Data Model Alignment

All three datasets are structured around interaction-level records and conform to the data model introduced. Each dataset includes timestamped interaction events, product identifiers, and session or customer-level grouping identifiers that make it feasible to construct sequences of customer activity for UCR generation:

- In the RetailRocket dataset, each interaction includes a visitor ID, event type, timestamp, and item ID. While explicit session identifiers are not available, session boundaries can be heuristically derived using temporal segmentation techniques, enabling compliance with the defined session-based interaction model, which is further described in Sect. 5.4.1. Touchpoints are constructed by combining event type and item ID.
- The YooChoose dataset includes explicit session IDs and timestamps along with product ID and event types (view, purchase). This allows direct alignment with the data model, where touchpoints are formed by combining the event type with the product identifier.
- The OpenCDP dataset offers the most comprehensive structure, including session ID, event time, event type, item ID, and extended product metadata. Session ID and timestamp for the data model are directly available and like the other benchmarks, touchpoints are formed from the combination of event type and item ID.

After adapting the data model to all datasets, personally identifiable information is absent, and any identifiers are either anonymized or transient. This ensures that customer representations can be created from data fully aligned with data privacy principles. Furthermore, despite differences in platform architecture, customer visibility, and product taxonomy, each dataset can be uniformly abstracted into sequences of interaction events conforming to the proposed data model, enabling consistent experimental setup and cross-dataset evaluation. This generality is critical for enabling reproducible research and deploying scalable personalization in heterogeneous real-world environments.

4.2.5 Comparative Analysis of Datasets

The four datasets employed in this thesis, Breinify, RetailRocket, YooChoose, and OpenCDP, exhibit substantial differences in scale, structure, customer observability, and interaction behavior. These differences are representative of the heterogeneity commonly encountered in real-world e-commerce platforms and serve as an empirical basis to assess the transferability and generalizability of the proposed UCR approach.

Among the datasets, Breinify is used as the primary source for evaluating the UCR approach under production-like conditions. The remaining benchmark datasets serve to demonstrate the adaptability of the method across varied data conditions, reflecting platforms with distinct instrumentation levels, session logic, and interaction types.

Dataset scale varies significantly. OpenCDP is the largest, with over 411 million events and 15.6 million customers. In contrast, RetailRocket is the smallest, containing 2.75 million events and 1.4 million customers. Breinify and YooChoose represent intermediate cases, with 53.8 million and 34.2 million events respectively. Despite size differences, all datasets offer dense clickstream information that can be used to extract customer behavior patterns.

Breinify provides the richest interaction taxonomy, including page-visit, product-view, add-to-cart, remove-from-cart, and check-out events, with page visits constituting the majority (76.25%). The benchmark datasets, RetailRocket, YooChoose, and OpenCDP, are more concentrated, with over 90% of events being product-views. This variation in event granularity reflects the instrumentation capabilities of the respective platforms and highlights the value of using a uniform, minimal interaction representation across datasets.

The datasets differ not only in structure but also in the visibility of customer and session-level information. Breinify contains a hybrid mix of known and anonymous customers, with only 7.36% of sessions attributed to known identities. OpenCDP and RetailRocket offer consistent customer identifiers, though RetailRocket lacks session information entirely and requires session IDs to be reconstructed using temporal heuristics. Conversely, YooChoose provides full session identifiers but no customer-level identifiers, operating solely at the session granularity. This diversity underscores the need for customer modeling approaches that are robust to missing identifiers and adaptable to different identification schemes, a requirement directly supported by the data model.

Clear differences are also observed in customer behavior across datasets. While all datasets show similar low viewed-product-to-purchase conversion rates (ranging from 0.84% in RetailRocket to 3.49% in YooChoose), substantial variation exists in session-level conversions. Breinify records only 1.64% of sessions ending in a check-out, compared to 5.51% in YooChoose and 6.08% in OpenCDP. Add-to-cart to purchase conversion rates are particularly high in RetailRocket (32.39%) and OpenCDP (35.83%), suggesting strong purchase intent when customers interact with carts. In contrast, Breinify's lower rate (3.10%) may reflect a different product domain, pricing model, or engagement behavior. Session lengths also vary. Breinify sessions are longer and denser, averaging 8.69 events per session, while YooChoose and OpenCDP average 3.69 and 4.59 events, respectively. These variations impact sequence modeling complexity and further motivate the need for generalizable, sequence-agnostic customer embeddings.

4.3 Summary

This chapter introduced the primary use case of this thesis: predicting customer behavior along the e-commerce customer journey with a focus on real-time, personalized marketing interventions. The problem was situated in the pre-purchase and purchase phases of the customer journey, where platforms must identify the likelihood of key behavioral outcomes, such as purchase, churn, or CTR, in order to drive engagement, conversions, and customer satisfaction. Functional goals such as predictive accuracy are coupled with non-functional constraints including low-latency inference, data efficiency, and legal compliance under privacy regulations, i.e., GDPR.

To support these objectives, a regulation-compliant, platform-agnostic data model was proposed. This model represents customer behavior as a sequence of timestamped interaction events identified by symbolic touchpoints and session-level identifiers. It is designed to exclude personal identifiers while preserving behavioral semantics, enabling scalable and privacy-preserving representation learning.

Four datasets with high heterogeneity regarding events, information, and conversion rates were introduced to explore and validate the transferability and generalizability of the proposed UCR approach. The Breinify dataset, used as the primary experimental foundation, contains 53.8 million events and captures a wide spectrum of customer interactions, including page visits, product views, cart actions, and purchases alongside high customer anonymity and long-tailed session distributions. To complement this, three benchmark datasets, RetailRocket, YooChoose, and OpenCDP were selected for their diversity in structure, customer visibility, and session granularity. RetailRocket lacks session-level identifiers and is dominated by product views; YooChoose provides session-based sequences without customer

IDs; and OpenCDP offers rich, large-scale interaction logs with full customer and session information.

A comparative analysis of these datasets revealed notable differences in event types, conversion rates, customer observability, and session statistics, mirroring the heterogeneity found in operational e-commerce systems. Despite these variations, all datasets were successfully mapped to the unified data model using only the minimal required attributes: (1) touchpoint identifiers, (2) timestamps, and (3) session IDs. This demonstrates the model's ability to abstract over platform-specific differences while preserving the behavioral semantics necessary for learning robust and transferable representations.

In conclusion, this chapter laid the empirical and conceptual groundwork for evaluating the UCR approach across multiple use cases and data environments. By defining the essential data properties and validating their availability across structurally diverse datasets, the chapter ensures that the methodology remains scalable, privacy-preserving, and reproducible, preparing the foundation for the representation learning and evaluation pipelines discussed in subsequent chapters.

5 Learning Universal Customer Behavior Representation in E-Commerce with Embeddings

Following the discussion of the theoretical foundations, the limitations of existing approaches, and the goal for applying UCR in a real-world e-commerce scenario, this chapter addresses the first research question:

> **How can customer behavior be represented in the context of e-commerce considering real-world requirements to predict future customer behavior for different tasks and use cases and can interaction data alone be effectively used to learn these representations?**

To answer this question, the chapter begins by critically examining the core challenge of representing customer behavior in a way that is both predictively useful and operationally feasible. The predictive usefulness of the representation is empirically validated using established accuracy metrics (cf. Sect. 2.3). The operational feasibility is ensured by measuring the end-to-end latency of the representation generation and prediction pipeline, in line with real-time system requirements established in prior human-computer interaction studies [33, 162] and discussed in Chap. 4. Therefore, advantages and disadvantages of prior approaches (cf. Chap. 3) are considered in regard of real-world settings, i.e., restrictions of personal information due to data regularization or because customers are not logged in as well as the need for real-time predictions as already highlight in Chap. 4.

Building on this foundation, an approach is proposed that leverages the strengths of both traditional and end-to-end approaches to learn customer behavior representations in a self-supervised manner. Specifically, the approach leverages embedding techniques to learn low-dimensional vector representations of customer behavior that are task-agnostic, compact, and transferable across prediction tasks and datasets. The design is grounded in the previously defined data model, ensuring compatibility with heterogeneous and arbitrary interaction data. The methodological pipeline is

M. Alves Gomes, *Utilizing Embeddings to Learn a Universal Customer Behavior Representation in E-Commerce*, https://doi.org/10.1007/978-3-658-50781-7_5

then introduced, detailing the preprocessing steps, embedding strategies, training regimes, and evaluation protocols used across different datasets.

Finally, the chapter presents and critically discusses the experimental results. The evaluation focuses on the effectiveness of the proposed UCR approach in supporting accurate and scalable behavior prediction under real-world conditions. Insights gained from these experiments are used to answer the first research question.

5.1 Learning Customer Behavior for Targeting in E-Commerce

As aforementioned, traditional approaches, which often rely on the four-phase model and extensive feature engineering, suffer from the major drawback that features for representing customer behavior must be manually identified for each e-commerce task. This process requires substantial domain expertise and time. Moreover, the resulting representations are typically not generalizable, as they are engineered with a specific use case or dataset in mind.

In contrast, end-to-end approaches learn customer representations directly within models, either through task-specific training or pretraining followed by fine-tuning, and therefore, reducing the required feature engineering process. However, these methods encounter two primary challenges as highlighted in the related work in Chap. 3. Firstly, they require large-scale datasets and secondly, the resulting representations are encoded in the learning model as a whole. This means that the learned representations are not reusable for other tasks, which limits their applicability and generalizability as UCR. Moreover, the data requirements often exceed the information available in real-world applications. Attributes such as demographic information of the customers are frequently assumed but are absent in practice. In many cases, these attributes cannot be collected due to privacy regulations as already highlighted in Sect. 4.2.

Therefore, a decoupled three-stage approach for customer targeting in e-commerce is proposed to address the limitations of existing methods and align with real-world operational constraints, particularly data privacy compliance and real-time prediction requirements. This approach integrates the strengths of both traditional feature-based and modern representation learning techniques, while removing the need for manual feature engineering and extensive customer profiling.

As illustrated in Fig. 5.1, the methodology consists of three sequential stages: customer information collection, customer representation learning, and customer targeting.

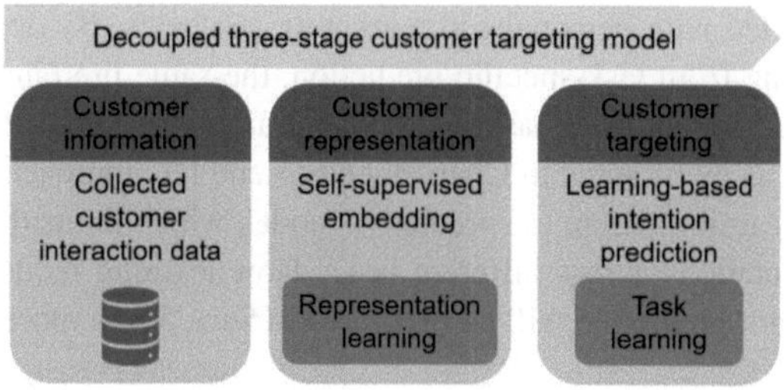

Fig. 5.1 The proposed decoupled three-stage customer targeting approach. It retains the customer representation stage and learns it explicitly from interaction data without manual feature engineering and customer analysis stage

In the first stage, customer information is collected exclusively from arbitrary touchpoints within the customer journey. A touchpoint is defined as an interaction event specific to the application context, such as a page view, a product click, or a URL visit. Unlike other approaches that depend on explicit customer identifiers or enriched personal profiles (cf. Chap. 3), this stage relies solely on implicitly observed behavioral signals, structured according to the unified data model introduced in Sect. 4.2. As a result, the necessary customer interaction data are already defined and captured in the form specified by the data model.

The second stage introduces the central innovation of this proposed approach: the automated learning of a UCR using self-supervised embedding techniques. Unlike traditional feature engineering methods, which are based on the four-stage customer targeting approach (cf. Sect. 2.1), usually requires manual analysis to identify, extract, and validate behaviorally relevant features for each representation, task, and use case. This requires not only the customer representation phase but also the subsequent customer analysis phase, where customer characteristics are manually analyzed. The proposed approach eliminates this manual customer analysis altogether. Instead, customer behavior is learned directly from sequential interaction data by exploiting contextual dependencies among touchpoints. By training self-supervised embeddings inspired by the distributional hypothesis, latent behavioral patterns are captured without the need for labeled supervision or handcrafted feature sets. The goal is that, this results in a compact, generalizable representation that can be reused across prediction tasks and datasets. Technical details of the embedding design are provided in Sect. 5.2.

In the third stage, the learned UCR is used as the input feature set for downstream learning models that forecast customer behavior so that customers can be effectively targeted with personalized marketing strategies. By decoupling representation learning from task-specific prediction, the same pretrained embeddings can be leveraged for multiple tasks without retraining or task-specific modifications. Contrary, as highlighted in Chap. 3, end-to-end DL approaches often embed representation learning within the predictive model, which limits the reusability of learned representations across different tasks. How learning models are used for customer behavior prediction will be presented in Sect. 5.3 in more detail.

5.2 Universal Customer Representation with Embeddings

Building on the three-stage targeting approach introduced in the previous section, this section focuses on the second stage: learning a UCR. In the proposed approach, only behavioral data are utilized to represent each customer, whereby a customer is described by the full sequence of touchpoints generated during their interactions with the e-commerce platform. These touchpoints are ordered chronologically to preserve the temporal flow of the customer journey.

The underlying assumption is that customers with similar intentions behave similarly in their customer journey, i.e., they follow similar sequences of touchpoints. For example, customers intending to purchase an item typically exhibit comparable navigation patterns, such as repeated product views, adding items to the cart, or returning to the checkout page. This behavioral similarity provides the basis for generalizing customer intent without explicit demographic data or personally identifiable information.

To capture these latent behavioral patterns, a representation learning technique inspired by the Skip-Gram model [161] is employed (c.f. Sect. 2.4). Originally developed for NLP to learn word similarities from context, the Skip-Gram approach is adapted here to learn semantic vector representations of touchpoints based on their co-occurrence within a contextual window in the customer sequence. The Skip-Gram approach is chosen over the CBOW approach for two primary reasons. First, Skip-Gram aligns more closely with the nature of the problem, in which a single observed touchpoint is used to predict its surrounding context. In real-world deployments, future customer interactions are typically unavailable at inference time, rendering CBOW less suitable due to its reliance on aggregating future context. Second, prior experiments conducted, reveal that Skip-Gram achieves slightly improved performance over CBOW in capturing behavioral semantics in sequential customer data [12]. As a result, each touchpoint is embedded into a continuous vector space such that those occurring in similar sequential contexts are placed proximally in the latent space. This should ensure that the sequential structure of the entire session is preserved in the learned representation, allowing the aggregated embeddings of all touchpoints to encode the customer's behavioral intent comprehensively. A UCR is derived that can be reused across different prediction tasks and operational domains without requiring additional manual feature engineering.

Formally, each customer $c_i \in C$, where C is the set of all customers, is modeled as a time-ordered sequence of touchpoints $s_i = \{t_0, t_1, ..., t_{n_i}\} \in S$, where n_i is the length of the sequence of customer c_i and S is a set of all Sequences. The similarity between two touchpoints (t_a, t_b) in a given latent vector space is connected to their respective context (k_a, k_b), which is defined as the set of surrounding touchpoints within a specified window size $M = 2 \times m, m \in \mathbb{N}$. Specifically, the context of a touchpoint t_j is defined as $k_j = \{t_{j+m}, t_{j+m-1}, ..., t_{j-m+1}, t_{j-m}\} \setminus t_j$.

To learn meaningful representations, an embedding is learned by a single-layer neural network parameterized by $\theta \in \mathbb{R}^{|T| \times D}$, where $|T|$ is the number of touchpoints and D is the dimensionality of the embedding space, is trained to maximize the likelihood of observing a context k_j given a touchpoint t_j. This yields the objective function, which is defined as the product of the probabilities of observing each touchpoint t_j given its context k_j across all touchpoints in the sequence s_i:

$$\mathcal{L}(\theta) = \prod_{j=0}^{n} \prod_{\alpha=-m,\alpha\neq 0}^{m} P(t_{j+\alpha} \mid t_j; \theta). \tag{5.1}$$

The conditional probability $P(t_{j+\alpha} \mid t_j; \theta)$ is modeled using the softmax function over the learned embeddings:

$$P(t_{j+\alpha} \mid t_j; \theta) = \frac{\exp(e_{t_{j+\alpha}}^{\top} e_{t_j})}{\sum_{t \in T} \exp(e_t^{\top} e_{t_j})}, \tag{5.2}$$

where $e_{t_j} = \theta^T t_j$ is the embedding representation of touchpoint t_j, derived from the network's input weight matrix via the one-hot encoding of the touchpoint. This learning process ensures that touchpoints frequently co-occurring in similar temporal contexts acquire proximal locations in the embedding space.

Once trained, the embedding function $E(t_j)$ maps each touchpoint to a dense, semantic vector $e_{t_j} \in \mathbb{R}^D$, such that touchpoints sharing similar sequential roles across customers are geometrically aligned. To obtain the UCR for a given customer c_i, the set of touchpoint embeddings in the sequence s_i can either be aggregated or concatenated to form a fixed-length input vector, or processed as an ordered sequence where each embedding is fed into a model capable of handling variable-length input. The aggregation or concatenation option enables the entire sequence to be transformed into a single, compact representation suitable for models requiring fixed-size inputs, whereas sequential processing retains the original temporal structure and allows interaction dependencies to be captured in full. This design operationalizes the hypothesis that customers with analogous touchpoint sequences demonstrate similar intentions and behaviors, which can be effectively modeled through the learned embeddings. Empirical evidence supporting this assumption is presented in subsequent sections using real-world interaction data. Table 5.1 summarizes the notation employed in this section.

Table 5.1 Notation and description for the proposed embedding approach

Notation	Description
C, T, S	Set of all customers C, customer touchpoints T, and sequences S
c_i, t_j	A customer $c_i \in C$ and touchpoints $t_j \in T, i, j \in \mathbb{N}$
s_i, n_i	$s_i = \{t_0, t_1, ..., t_{n_i}\}$, $s_i \in S$ is a ascended time-ordered customer behavior sequence with sequence length n_i, $n_i \in \mathbb{N}, n_i > 1, i \in \mathbb{N}$
k_j, M	A interaction t_j of s_i has a context $k_j = \{t_{j+m}, t_{j+m-1}, ..., t_{j-m+1}, t_{j-m}\} \setminus t_j$ with context window size $M = 2 \times m, m \in \mathbb{N}, m \times 2 \leq n_i, i \in \mathbb{N}$
e_{t_j}, D	D-dimensional embedding representation e_{t_j} of interaction t_j, $e_{t_j} \in \mathbb{R}^D$
$E(t_j)$	Embedding function E that uses the trained embedding and maps $t_j \rightarrow e_{t_j}, j \in \mathbb{N}$

5.3 Learning Model Training for Customer Behavior Prediction

Following the generation of dense vector representations for customer touchpoints and sequences, the UCR, as introduced in Sect. 5.2 embeddings are utilized as input features to train task-specific models for predictive future customer behavior, namely purchase prediction, churn prediction, and CTR prediction. The goal is to investigate whether the pretrained UCR embeddings capture sufficient information to support generalized customer behavior modeling.

Specifically, the problem can be formulated as following: Let $s_i = \{t_0, t_1, ..., t_{n_i}\} \in S$ denote the touchpoint sequence of customer $c_i \in C$, with corresponding UCR $E(s_i) = F(\{e_{t_0}, e_{t_1}, ..., e_{t_{n_i}}\})$, where F is the manipulation function for the embedding representationthat converts the sequence of touchpoint embeddings into the required input format, through aggregation or concatenation when a fixed-size vector is needed, or as an identity mapping when models can directly process the ordered sequence. The objective of the learning model is to estimate a mapping function Y that takes the pretrained UCR as input and produces an output y_i representing the predicted outcome for customer c_i. In all three investigated tasks, this output y_i is formulated as a binary classification target, where $y_i \in 0, 1$ indicates the absence or presence of the specific behavior of interest.

For example, in the purchase prediction task, the UCR derived from the customer's sequence of page views and product interactions is used to predict whether a purchase event will occur within a defined time horizon ($y_i = 1$) or not ($y_i = 0$).

This mapping function Y can be modeled by the conditional probability $P(y_i \mid UCR)$. This formulation reduces each task to a supervised learning problem and allows for the application of various learning models, including traditional ML models like LR, DT, RF, and GB, as well as more advanced models like MLP, LSTM, and transformer-based models (cf. Chap. 2).

The models are optimized using an objective function that minimizes the prediction error. In this work, since each prediction task is formulated as a binary classification problem, the binary cross-entropy variant is applied:

$$\mathcal{L}(w) = -\frac{1}{N} \sum_{i=1}^{N} [y_i \log \hat{y}_i + (1 - y_i) \log(1 - \hat{y}_i)], \tag{5.3}$$

where N is the number of samples, y_i is the true label, and $\hat{y}_i = f_w(UCR)$ is the learning model's prediction for the UCR of customer c_i and f_w is the learned function parametrized by w.

However, each model requires the UCR in a specific input format, which is ensured by applying the manipulation function F. Models that operate on fixed-size input vectors depend on F to transform the variable-length sequence of touchpoint embeddings into a consistent format, either by concatenation or aggregation. In the case of concatenation, the embeddings are linked in sequence order, with variable-length sequences standardized through padding or truncation to meet the model's input dimension requirements. Alternatively, aggregation functions, such as mean, maximum, sum, or more advanced pooling operations, are applied to merge the sequence into a single vector of fixed dimensionality. This guarantees that the resulting representation remains consistent in size, independent of the original number of touchpoints. For sequential models, that are capable of processing sequences of arbitrary length, the manipulation function F acts as an identity mapping, passing the ordered embeddings directly without transformation.

5.4 Evaluation Methodology

The primary objective of the experiments conducted in this chapter is to empirically evaluate whether the proposed UCR approach can effectively model customer behavior from different e-commerce interaction data, and whether the learned representations are sufficiently general to support multiple downstream prediction tasks without retraining or task-specific adaptation.

In particular, the experiments aim to demonstrate the feasibility of learning reusable, behavior-based representations from heterogeneous, privacy-compliant data, and applying them to three core prediction tasks commonly encountered in e-commerce: purchase prediction, churn (return) prediction, and CTR prediction.

The experimental pipeline is structured into four sequential stages, as illustrated in Fig. 5.2:

1. Data preprocessing,
2. Embedding training,
3. Task-specific model training, and
4. Evaluation.

The first stage involves preparing raw interaction data for embedding training and downstream prediction. This includes data cleaning, transformation, and structur-

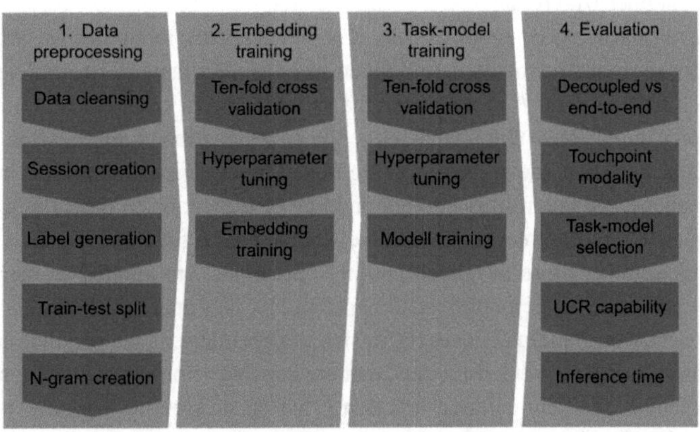

Fig. 5.2 Experimental process for learning customer behavior representations in e-commerce for evaluating the proposed three-stage approach, including the steps of data preprocessing, embedding training, task-specific model training, and the conducted evaluation

ing customer interactions into sequences of touchpoints according to the unified data model introduced in Chap. 4. To ensure comparability and reproducibility, all datasets are preprocessed using a consistent methodology. This includes session segmentation, touchpoint abstraction, and label generation tailored to each predictive task.

In the second stage, embedding training is conducted to learn the UCR from interaction sequences. As described in Sect. 5.2, this involves training a self-supervised Skip-Gram-inspired model to embed touchpoints based on their temporal context. The goal is to capture latent behavioral patterns in a dense, fixed-size vector representation that generalizes across tasks, customer types, and interaction patterns, while remaining agnostic to explicit customer identifiers or sensitive attributes.

In the third stage, the learning models for the downstream tasks are trained using the pretrained UCR embeddings as input features. Therefore, for each task, a learning model is trained independently, ensuring that performance reflects the quality of the learned representation rather than benefits from task-specific tuning. As inherent to the proposed decoupled approach, no fine-tuning of the embedding layer is performed during downstream training; instead, the embeddings remain fixed once learned in the self-supervised stage. More details about the model selection is provided in Sect. 5.6.

In the final stage, the effectiveness of the proposed UCR approach is evaluated by assessing predictive accuracy and real-time feasibility on the downstream tasks. Thereby, various aspects are investigated, including the impact of using a pretrained versus an end-to-end representation, the influence of different touchpoint modalities, the suitability of alternative learning models, and comparative performance against baseline methods commonly found in the literature. The aim of this evaluation is to determine whether the proposed UCR can demonstrate robustness, task transferability, and operational feasibility under realistic conditions.

A detailed explanation of each processing and evaluation stage is provided in the subsequent sections, which elaborate on the methodological design, implementation specifics, and empirical analysis underpinning the proposed approach.

5.4.1 Data Preprocessing

The data preprocessing stage is crucial for ensuring the quality, consistency, and validity of the experimental results. Consequently, all four datasets are standardized, anomalies are eliminated, and it is ensured that each dataset contained events with identifiable sessions, touchpoints, and timestamps, as defined in the data model (cf. Sect. 4.2).

Session Construction

While the Breinify, YooChoose, and OpenCDP datasets inherently provide session information, the RetailRocket dataset does not. To address this, sessions for RetailRocket are heuristically constructed by grouping events based on timestamps. Herefore, a session is defined as a sequence of events performed by a single customer within a given time window. For this work, this means that if a customer performs an event within 30 minutes, it is considered to be part of the same session. If the customer does not perform any event within 30 minutes, a new session is created. This approach ensures that a continuous customer journey is not arbitrarily divided into multiple sessions if the customer pauses.

Although customer identifiers (e.g., user IDs) are available for three datasets, these identifiers are not considered in the following steps. Instead, only the session itself is analyzed. This decision is motivated by the fact that identifiers require explicit logins, which, for instance, are infrequent in the Breinify dataset as already mentioned in Sect. 4.2. Moreover, for the UCR proposed in this thesis, the use of explicit customer identifiers is deliberately avoided to ensure compliance with data protection regulations.

Session-Level Anomaly Removal

To ensure the quality, consistency, and representativeness of the data, session-level anomalies are removed following session construction. This step is necessary because, as discussed in Sect. 4.2, the number of events per session exhibits a heavy-tailed distribution in all datasets. Such extreme cases can introduce bias, distort model learning, and lead to overfitting on rare, non-representative behaviors. For example, in the Breinify dataset, sessions range from 1 to 49,499 events, with a mean of 8.69, a median of 3, and the 25th and 75th percentiles at 2 and 8 events, respectively (cf. Table 4.1). To systematically identify and exclude these outliers, the 99.5th percentile is used as a robust cutoff, as it effectively filters the extreme tail while preserving the vast majority of typical customer sessions. In this case, approximately 0.5% of sessions contain more than 100 interactions and are therefore removed from the dataset. The same percentile-based criterion is applied to all other datasets to maintain methodological consistency. For instance, YooChoose sessions range from 1 to 262 events, while OpenCDP sessions reach up to 34,570 events, both exhibiting similarly skewed distributions that justify the same threshold. Additionally, sessions containing fewer than three events are discarded, as sequences of such short length are considered insufficient for modeling meaningful customer behavior. In practice, tasks such as purchase prediction generally require at least a view event and a subsequent action, such as adding an item to a cart, to infer intent reliably.

Touchpoint Construction

Subsequently, touchpoints are constructed from the raw events to represent customer interactions in a structured, processable format suitable for embedding using the data model. As described in Chap. 2, a touchpoint in the context of a customer journey is defined as an interaction between a customer and the touchpoint owner, in this case, the online shop. To create a distinct and interpretable representation, each touchpoint is generated by combining the interaction type (e.g., view, add-to-cart, checkout) with the associated item or element (e.g., product identifier or, for Breinify, a URL). Specifically, the event type and event element are concatenated into a single string in the format "eventTypeString:EventElementString", so that each interaction is uniquely and unambiguously represented as a distinct touchpoint. This ensures that different actions on the same item (e.g., viewing versus adding to cart) are treated as separate behavioral signals within the sequence, thereby preserving the semantic detail needed for meaningful representation learning. For example, if a customer views Product "A"and then adds the same product to the cart, the resulting touchpoint sequence is represented as ("view:A", "addtocart:A"). Each sequence is defined as a time-ordered list of touchpoints belonging to a single session and implicitly linked to the customer who generated it. However, the proposed approach deliberately avoids the use of explicit customer identifiers beyond this session linkage. This design ensures that while sequences reflect customer-specific behavior, no persistent cross-session customer tracking is required, supporting compliance with data protection constraints.

Label Generation

Following the construction of touchpoint sequences, target labels are derived for the three predictive tasks: purchase prediction, churn prediction, and CTR prediction. For purchase prediction, each session is labeled based on the presence or absence of a checkout event. If a checkout action occurs within the session, it is labeled as a purchase otherwise, it is labeled as no purchase. For example, if a session includes the touchpoints "view:ProductA", "addtocart:ProductA", and "checkout:ProductA" the label for purchase prediction is positive.

For churn prediction, labels are generated based on whether a follow-up session by the same customer exists in the dataset. In the literature, various approaches have been proposed, such as monitoring customer activity within the final month of the available data to infer churn status [22, 83] or requiring clear evidence of transactional behavior to distinguish returning from lost customers [46, 54, 139]. Based on these related studies, a simplified heuristic is derived in this work. To apply this heuristic, the customer identifiers provided in the datasets are temporarily used to detect whether a follow-up session by the same customer exists. If no subsequent session is found, the current session is labeled as churned. If at least one later session exists, it is labeled as not churned. This rule avoids dependence on strict time windows and preserves more data for training. Continuing the example, if the session described above is the last recorded for that customer, it is labeled as churned. For the YooChoose dataset, churn labels cannot be assigned due to the lack of persistent customer identifiers.

For CTR prediction, labels are created to indicate whether a recommended item was clicked within a session. In the Breinify dataset, this information is directly available through explicit recommendation click events; therefore, positive and negative click labels can be assigned by annotating each session according to whether a recommendation was actually clicked. For the other datasets, where explicit click feedback is unavailable, a negative sampling strategy is applied that is directly derived from established literature [141, 172, 196, 278–280]. In line with these studies, 50% of sessions are randomly augmented with an item that the customer did not click, thereby generating realistic negative examples while preserving all positive labels from the original data. This procedure ensures that the resulting dataset reflects both observed click behavior and plausible non-click scenarios as guided by prior research practice.

Train and Test Data Partitioning

The datasets are subsequently partitioned into training and testing subsets. To reflect realistic deployment conditions and mitigate feature leakage, the final month of data for each dataset is designated as the testing period. This temporal holdout strategy is preferred over random sampling to better model future unseen interactions. Table 5.2 summarizes the key statistics of the datasets following the data preprocessing steps described above. Specifically, the table reports the number of sessions, the number of unique touchpoints, and the statistical information about the number of touchpoints per session. Touchpoint statistics are further distinguished for datasets such as Breinify, where both product- and URL-based interactions are used. In addition, it presents the distribution of labels for the three predictive tasks, purchase prediction, churn prediction, and CTR prediction.

The label statistics highlight a significant class imbalance in several datasets, particularly for the purchase and churn prediction tasks, where positive labels constitute only a small fraction of the total sessions. This imbalance underscores the necessity for appropriate handling during model training and evaluation. To address this imbalance during model training, different sampling strategies are employed. Specifically, random undersampling of the majority class is applied to reduce its dominance, and Synthetic Minority Oversampling Technique (SMOTE) [40] is utilized to synthetically generate additional samples for the minority class. These

Table 5.2 Statistics of the four datasets after preprocessing and splitting into training and test sets

Dataset		Num. Sessions	Touchpoints					Purchase	Churn	Click
			Unique	Mean	Std	Min	Max			
Breinify	train	1,288,795	(URL) 66,205	11.19	14.03	3	99	82,710	1,212,607	17,632
			(Products) 35,499	7.57	5.62	3	33	(6.4%)	(94.1%)	(1.3%)
	test	119,513	(URL) 20,051	12.91	13.58	3	85	7,594	117,119	1,447
			(Products) 15,871	6.89	4.69	3	28	(6.4%)	(97.8%)	(1.4%)
YooChoose	train	3,731,708	44,435	5.46	3.76	3	31	310,851	✗	1,865,854
								(8.3%)		(50%)
	test	676,286	27,016	5.72	4.08	3	33	59,675	✗	338,143
								(8.8%)		(50%)
RetailRocket	train	165,842	119,702	5.52	4.78	3	52	7,818	149,810	82,921
								(4.7%)	(90.3%)	(50%)
	test	19,741	32,270	5.20	4.22	3	48	896	18,980	9,870
								(4.5%)	(96.1%)	(50%)
OpenCDP	train	32,930,752	509,286	8.12	7.33	3	58	3,738,748	5,829,219	16,465,376
								(11.3%)	(17.7%)	(50%)
	test	6,121,525	336,587	8.93	8.33	3	65	674,628	2,604,572	3,060,762
								(11%)	(42.5%)	(50%)

techniques are selected to enhance the robustness of the classifiers and to mitigate biases that could arise from skewed class distributions. All sampling operations are performed exclusively on the training sets to prevent information leakage into the evaluation phase. In previously conducted experiments, it has been shown that random undersampling yields the best results for session-based behavior prediction [6]. Therefore, in this thesis, random undersampling is applied to the training data for all three tasks.

N-Gram Generation

To obtain UCR embeddings, n-grams need to be generated from the touchpoint sequences. Therefore, additional data preprocessing steps are required to create overlapping n-grams that explicitly encode the local context in which each interaction occurs. This context provides the basis for training the embeddings in a self-supervised manner, as it enables the model to learn how each touchpoint relates to its immediate predecessors and successors within the customer journey. By doing so, the sequential dependencies that reveal latent behavioral intent should be preserved and captured during training.

For n-gram creation, a context window of size $M = 2$ is employed across all experiments, which balances between capturing meaningful local dependencies and maintaining computational efficiency. Mikolov et al. [161] have shown that immediate neighbors often provide the strongest contextual signals for inferring latent intent without adding additional noise. As a result, overlapping trigrams are generated from the training sequences $s \in S_{\text{train}}$. Specifically, for each touchpoint t_i, a training sample in the form of the tuple (t_i, t_{i-1}, t_{i+1}) is created, wherein t_{i-1} and t_{i+1} represent the immediate historical and future touchpoints of a customer, respectively. In order to handle boundary cases, special "START" and "END" tokens are introduced, where $i = 0$ or $i = n$ with t_n denoting the final interaction in a session. These tokens preserve the structural integrity of the sequences and enable the model to distinguish between initial, intermediate, and terminal interactions. Furthermore, to address the out-of-vocabulary problem arising from novel products or interactions present only in the testing data, an "UNKNOWN" token is incorporated into the vocabulary, following established practices in the sequence modeling literature [9, 222]. The "UNKNOWN" token randomly replace touchpoints of the trigrams in the training process, with a probability equal to the ratio between known and unknown touchpoints derived from the test dataset. Table 5.3 presents the statistics of the used context data.

Through this structured self-supervised training approach, the UCR embeddings are intended to capture semantically rich and contextually grounded representations

Table 5.3 Statistics of the n-gram training datasets utilized to create a customer representation through embedding training

Dataset	Num. Trigrams	Num. Touchpoints	Num. Unknown Touchpoints
Breinify (URLs)	2,812,129	66,205	2,771 (4.19%)
Breinify (products)	1,335,785	35,499	513 (1.45%)
YooChoose	1,719,739	27,016	2,511 (9.29%)
RetailRocket	750,056	119,702	8,071 (6.74%)
OpenCDP	103,881,685	509,286	69,770 (13.7%)

of customer behavior, serving as the foundational building blocks for all downstream predictive tasks explored in this work.

5.4.2 Technical Training Procedure

After constructing n-grams from the touchpoint sequences, the UCR embeddings are learned in a self-supervised manner. As outlined in Sect. 5.2, the embedding model is trained by minimizing the cross-entropy loss for predicting surrounding context touchpoints within each trigram. This training process uses the Adam optimization algorithm [126]. To ensure robust performance and prevent overfitting, hyperparameter tuning is systematically performed for each dataset using ten-fold cross-validation, with the validation folds drawn exclusively from the training partition and the objective defined as minimizing the contextual prediction loss.

The search space for the embedding dimensionality is defined in powers of two, 2^n with $2 \leq n \leq 10$, resulting in an optimal embedding size of 32 for the Breinify, YooChoose, and RetailRocket datasets, and 64 for the OpenCDP dataset due to its greater variety of distinct touchpoints. The number of training epochs is fixed at 100, which empirically corresponds to the point at which the loss converges without further improvement. The batch size is selected from a range defined in powers of two, spanning from 2^4 (16) to 2^{12} (4096), to balance computational efficiency with gradient stability. Larger batches are preferred for stable gradient estimates and hardware efficiency, whereas smaller batches introduce useful stochasticity for generalization. An initial learning rate of 1.000×10^{-3} is used, consistent with best practice for embedding training. To address the computational cost of large output spaces in datasets such as OpenCDP, the Adaptive Log Softmax With Loss technique [94] is employed to approximate the softmax layer efficiently and accelerate convergence.

Hyperparameter optimization is conducted using Optuna [3], which employs asynchronous Tree-structured Parzen Estimator sampling to systematically explore the search space and construct a probabilistic model of the objective function. This enables promising hyperparameter configurations to be selected effectively, balancing exploration and exploitation.

Once the embeddings have been learned, the pretrained UCR embeddings are employed as input features to train models for each downstream prediction task. Thereby, the same pretrained UCR embeddings are used as input for all tasks. This stage is used to evaluate whether the learned representations capture sufficient information to support robust behavioral predictions without task-specific tuning. As previously highlighted, separate models are trained independently for each of the three target tasks, ensuring that performance reflects the quality of the learned representation rather than benefits from task-specific tuning. This single-task training strategy provides a clearer assessment of the UCR embeddings compared to multi-task learning, as it isolates the contribution of the learned representation without introducing additional shared-task inductive biases or auxiliary information that could artificially enhance performance through cross-task parameter sharing from the learning model.

To handle the fact that many models require fixed-size input, session lengths are standardized. For this purpose, training is performed for multiple session sizes within a range of 3 to 20 touchpoints, as this interval covers the majority of session lengths observed in the datasets used in this work. Sequences shorter than the chosen length are zero-padded, while longer sequences are cropped at the end to fit the required fixed length. For models capable of handling variable-length sequences directly, the complete touchpoint sequence is used without truncation or padding. Additionally, different pooling strategies for aggregation were tested to produce fixed-size representations, including mean, max, and sum pooling; however, consistent with the findings previously conducted, it was observed that direct concatenation of embeddings consistently outperformed these aggregation methods for session-based prediction tasks [9].

Hyperparameter tuning and ten-fold cross-validation are again applied to the downstream model training, ensuring that optimal parameters are identified for each task under consistent experimental conditions. During this search, the session length parameter is randomly selected within a normal distribution centered on the mean and standard deviation of the session length for each dataset, further ensuring robust coverage of session variability. For all downstream tasks, the final trained models use the best parameter configurations identified during this search.

5.5 Baseline Approaches

A comparative analysis is conducted using alternative baseline approaches for each prediction task, alongside one strategy for generating an UCR model. For each task, a set of preliminary experiments is carried out to determine the most effective baseline model. While predictive performance served as the primary evaluation metric, additional criteria are considered, including the ability of each method to generate representations based solely on observable customer interactions, without relying on persistent identifiers or historical profiles. For the experiments, the following baseline approaches are adapted to the experimental pipeline described in Sect. 5.4.

5.5.1 Purchase Prediction Baseline

A purchase prediction baseline is included in this thesis to provide a rigorous reference point for evaluating the effectiveness of the proposed UCR approach. Since purchase intention prediction is the central downstream tasks investigated, it is necessary to compare the performance of the UCR embeddings to a well-established task-specific method that represents the state of the art in session-based purchase prediction. This enables the proposed representation to be benchmarked against existing techniques that have demonstrated high performance on real-world e-commerce datasets.

To select an appropriate baseline, the systematic review of recent purchase prediction methods is used (cf. Sect. 3.2). The selection focus on studies that have been evaluated on the YooChoose dataset, which is widely used as a benchmark for session-based purchase behavior. The selection followed three key criteria: (1) the approach must be adaptable across different datasets without extensive modification, (2) the approach must demonstrate strong predictive performance relative to competing methods, and (3) the approach must be feasible for real-time inference, relying solely on session-level information without requiring persistent customer profiles.

Based on this assessment, the method proposed by Esmeli et al. [67] was selected as the primary purchase prediction baseline. Among the reviewed publications, this approach achieved the highest AUC score of 0.69 on the YooChoose benchmark dataset, surpassing comparable methods by Sheil et al. [206] (0.65), Lin et al. [146] (0.66), and Romov and Sokolov [198] (0.66). The feature representation designed by Esmeli et al. is built entirely from session-level behavioral signals, ensuring transferability to other use cases in this thesis and supporting real-time prediction without relying on long-term customer tracking.

In Esmeli et al. proposed method, customers are represented using twelve features extracted from session-level behavior. These include eight session and touchpoint-based metrics, and four temporal features. Specifically:

- Total viewed items: The number of touchpoints observed within a session.
- Number of unique items: The count of unique touchpoints in the session.
- Session duration: The duration of the session, measured in minutes.
- Click rate: The ratio of total viewed items to the session duration.
- Maximum and minimum popularity: The interaction frequency of the most and least popular touchpoints, respectively.
- Average duration per item: The mean time spent on each touchpoint.
- Unique categories: The number of distinct item categories encountered. While product categories are explicitly available in the public datasets, in the closed industrial dataset, the event type is used as a proxy category (e.g., based on URLs).
- Temporal features: Including the hour of day, day of week, weekend indicator (binary), and day of year at the session start.

To solve the prediction task, several classifiers are evaluated, including DT (0.66 AUC), LR (0.66 AUC), Support Vector Machines (0.61 AUC), GB (0.68 AUC), and MLP (0.68 AUC). Ultimately, the RF classifier (0.69 AUC) is employed, as it consistently outperformed all other alternatives. These experiments were conducted using the YooChoose dataset to ensure comparability, and the chosen set of classifiers reflects the same learning models employed by Esmeli et al., aligning this evaluation with established benchmarks in session-based purchase prediction.

5.5.2 Churn Prediction Baseline

Similar to the purchase prediction baseline, a churn prediction baseline is included to provide a robust point of comparison for evaluating the effectiveness of the proposed UCR approach in modeling customer churn probability. Since predicting whether a customer will return is a common and highly relevant use case in session-based e-commerce, it is necessary to benchmark the new representation against an established method that has demonstrated strong performance under real-world conditions.

The selection of the churn baseline is derived from the previously conducted literature review and focuses on methods developed for session-based environments where long-term historical data are limited. The same selection principles applied to the purchase prediction baseline guided this decision. The approach must be usable for short-term behavior, must deliver state-of-the-art predictive performance, and must be adaptable to the constraints of session-level data availability.

However, unlike purchase prediction, related approaches in churn prediction cannot be modeled meaningfully without some form of short-term historical data. As no churn method in the literature is designed to rely exclusively on the current session, selected historical features must be retained to ensure that the baseline remains meaningful and comparable. This makes the churn baseline the only case in this thesis where the strict rule of using only session-local information is deliberately relaxed to maintain a fair benchmark.

Based on this, the method introduced by Berger et al.[22] is selected as the primary churn prediction baseline. The experiments conducted on the RetailRocket dataset show that the approach of Berger et al. has an AUC score of 0.983, outperforming other state-of-the-art churn prediction methods, such as those proposed by Fridrich et al.[83] (0.85 AUC) and Xiahou and Harada [255] (0.87 AUC).

To align the approach of Berger et al. to the experiments conducted throughout this thesis, the original handcrafted feature set is adapted carefully. The full set of 26 features is reduced to 18 by omitting features that are either not feasible to obtain (such as explicit payment records or ratings) or that would introduce feature leakage for purchase prediction tasks (e.g., features that reveal checkout information directly). This ensures that the core logic of the baseline for detecting churn from shifts in recent customer behavior remains intact. Although not all features are retained, the empirical results on the RetailRocket dataset confirm that the predictive performance of the adapted churn baseline remains robust and suitable for comparison.

The retained features are categorized into four major groups: (1) session-level metrics, (2) purchase-proxy signals, (3) behavioral change indicators, and (4) interaction-based attributes.

1. **Session-Based Features**

   - Total number of sessions associated with the customer
   - Duration of the session
   - Number of actions in the session
   - Average time per action
   - Day of the week of the session
   - Day of the month of the session
   - Weekend indicator

2. **Purchase-Proxy Features**

   - Number of add-to-cart events
   - Session-to-add-to-cart ratio
   - View-to-add-to-cart ratio

3. **Behavioral Change Metrics**

   - Change in session duration (last session vs. historical average)
   - Change in number of actions (last session vs. historical average)
   - Change in session gaps (most recent vs. earlier gaps)

4. **Interaction Patterns**

   - Number of sessions since last add-to-cart
   - Time since last add-to-cart
   - Time since last visit
   - Add-to-cart event in the last session (binary)

In parallel to the purchase prediction baseline, multiple classifiers are initially tested, including DT (0.89 AUC), Support Vector Machines (0.84 AUC), LR (0.95 AUC), GB (0.91 AUC), and MLP (0.90 AUC). All churn prediction experiments were conducted using the RetailRocket dataset. Ultimately, the RF classifier (0.93 AUC) is used, as it consistently outperformed alternative models across all tested configurations.

5.5.3 CTR Prediction Baseline

A CTR prediction baseline is included to provide a strong benchmark for evaluating the ability of the proposed UCR approach to model implicit customer engagement signals. To select an appropriate baseline for CTR prediction, the conducted literature review and DeepCTR library [207] are used, which provides an implementation of most leading DL architectures for click prediction. Thereby, the Amazon Review dataset [171] is employed for the selection step, as it is widely recognized in the literature as a standard reference for evaluating CTR prediction systems. The selection focused on identifying an approach that combines high predictive performance with a feature design that can be reasonably adapted to the privacy-preserving, session-based datasets used in this thesis.

Based on this assessment, the DIN introduced by Zhou et al.[280] was chosen as the primary CTR prediction baseline. Unlike the two previously introduced baselines, DIN is an end-to-end architecture specifically designed to capture the relevance of historical customer behaviors in relation to target items by means of an adaptive activation unit and an attention mechanism. Zhou et al. state that this design enables the model to focus on the most relevant parts of the customer interactions when estimating click-through probability, yielding high predictive performance. In benchmarking experiments on the Amazon Review dataset, DIN outperformed alternative CTR approaches such as DIEN[279] (0.77 AUC), TIEN [141] (0.75 AUC), and MARN [140] (0.75 AUC), achieving an AUC of 0.79.

While the original DIN design incorporates four groups of input features, customer profile features, customer behavior features, Ad features, and contextual features, not all of these can be used in the conducted experiments. Due to the privacy requirements and therefore, the absence of personally identifiable information in the available datasets, customer profiles and detailed contextual features cannot be included. As a result, only customer behavior features are used, including click and view event signals and associated product event type information derived from the available session data. This adaptation is necessary because the original profile and context features are not part of the proposed data model.

Although this means the DIN baseline cannot leverage all possible input signals, it remains an important benchmark. Using DIN with the behavior-only feature subset still provides a relevant and realistic comparison for evaluating whether the proposed UCR embeddings can match the predictive power of specialized end-to-end CTR models that directly exploit customer interaction sequences. This ensures that the evaluation remains fair and aligned with practical deployment constraints in real-world e-commerce scenarios where comprehensive customer profiles are not always available.

5.5.4 UCR Baseline

A baseline for UCR is included to benchmark the proposed self-supervised UCR approach against an established state-of-the-art approach that is specifically designed to produce task-agnostic representations of customer behavior. Since the central contribution of this thesis is to demonstrate that a decoupled UCR can capture generalizable behavioral signals, it is necessary to compare its performance to a purpose-built universal representation model from the literature.

Based on the literature review in Sect. 3.1, the DUPN proposed by Ni et al.[172] is selected. As summarized in Table 3.1 in Chap. 3.1, DUPN is one of the only two approaches specifically designed to learn UCR directly from interaction data. The alternative candidate, which is the Dual-Decoder Hierarchical Context Network proposed by Zeng et al. [267], is not considered. This approach relies heavily on extensive long-term historical interaction sequences, which are unavailable in the conducted experiments in this thesis. Consequently, DUPN remains the only viable choice that meets the data availability constraints.

Originally, DUPN is a multi-task learning approach designed to produce universal representations for multiple downstream tasks, including search ranking, recommendation, and price sensitivity modeling. The model encodes sequential customer behaviors using a recurrent encoder and aggregates long-term preference signals through an attention-based pooling mechanism. It also integrates different types of interaction signals (e.g., clicks, purchases) and item attributes, which enables fine-grained modeling of customer intent across tasks. The use of multi-task objectives strengthens the robustness and transferability of the learned embeddings.

However, in the context of this thesis, only the core architecture of DUPN can be adopted, as not all of its input features are available. Due to privacy constraints and the nature of the session-based datasets, customer demographic profiles and persistent long-term customer metadata required by the original design cannot be used. Consequently, only behavior-property tuples derived from interaction logs are retained as inputs. These include the activity type, event type (e.g., view or add-to-cart), and timestamp information available in the clickstream data.

Although this means that DUPN in this thesis cannot leverage the full feature set originally proposed, it remains a valid and important baseline. Using the core sequential encoding and attention-based aggregation of behavioral signals still provides a realistic and rigorous point of comparison for evaluating whether the proposed decoupled, self-supervised UCR can achieve similar or better transferability without relying on multi-task learning or rich customer profiles. This ensures that the evaluation addresses the fundamental research question of whether a universal representation can be learned directly from session-based behavioral signals alone.

5.6 Results and Discussion

This section presents the results of the systematic evaluation of the proposed UCR approach. The experiments are designed to assess whether meaningful customer behavior representations can be learned from arbitrary e-commerce interaction data, and whether these representations generalize across tasks and datasets without task-specific retraining.

All experiments follow a consistent, reproducible protocol and are evaluated using both classification performance metrics and operational feasibility criteria such as real-time inference latency. A random undersampling strategy is applied during training to mitigate class imbalance and has been found to consistently improve model stability and predictive accuracy across training, validation, and test datasets as aforementioned. To ensure robustness against random initialization effects, each experimental configuration is trained ten times using independent random seeds, and the reported results are averaged across these runs.

Due to the availability of explicit checkout events as ground-truth signals, purchase prediction serves as the reference task for most of the evaluations. In contrast to churn and CTR prediction, which depend on heuristic approximations of customer behavior, the purchase labels rely on direct observation of true events. A detailed discussion of this distinction and its implications for evaluation is provided in Chap. 9.

The evaluation is structured around several focused experimental objectives:

1. An investigation is conducted to determine whether the proposed decoupled approach, which relies on a self-supervised pretrained UCR, provides measurable advantages over an end-to-end strategy in which the UCR is learned jointly with the downstream task. This experiment directly addresses whether decoupling representation learning from task-specific model training improves generalizability.
2. An empirical comparison of different touchpoint modalities is carried out for the Breinify use case, where both product identifiers and URL-level information are available to represent customer interactions. This comparison tests whether more granular interaction data yield richer and more predictive UCR embeddings, informing how input data granularity affects representation quality.
3. The evaluation examines the impact of different downstream learning models on predictive performance when using the same pretrained UCR embeddings as input features. By testing a range of models, including both classical ML methods and DL architectures, this experiment identifies which model designs are best

suited to leverage the learned representations and ensures that the proposed approach is not overly reliant on a specific model type.

4. A series of comparative experiments benchmark the proposed UCR approach against baseline methods established in the literature. This includes comparisons to traditional feature engineering pipelines for purchase prediction, churn prediction baselines that rely on handcrafted features, an end-to-end task-specific CTR model, and an existing UCR baseline. This experiment provides a rigorous test of whether the proposed self-supervised UCR can match or exceed the performance of specialized alternatives under realistic constraints.
5. The real-time applicability of the approach is evaluated through dedicated latency benchmarks. Given the demanding speed requirements of practical e-commerce systems, it is imperative that customer representations and predictions can be generated within milliseconds at scale. To assess this, inference times for both representation generation and downstream prediction are measured for varying numbers of sessions, ranging from small batches to millions of sessions, and averaged across 100 repetitions to ensure statistical robustness.

5.6.1 Evaluation of Pretrained versus End-to-End UCR Embedding

One central question in the evaluation of the proposed three-stage customer targeting approach is whether the pretrained, self-supervised UCR embedding offers any practical advantage over a conventional end-to-end trained model, where the customer representation is learned jointly with the downstream prediction task. Hence, a comparative evaluation is performed between a self-supervised pretrained UCR embedding and an end-to-end trained approach. The evaluation employed the two aforementioned performance metrics, namely AUC-score and F1-score. For both approaches, an LSTM-based architecture is employed as the downstream model for predicting purchase and click probability on the Breinify dataset. The LSTM demonstrates the most robust performance among tested models (cf. Table 5.6).

As shown in Table 5.4, the pretrained UCR consistently outperforms the end-to-end approach in purchase prediction on the Breinify dataset. In terms of AUC, the pretrained approach achieved a mean score of 0.943, compared to 0.929 for the end-to-end method. Similarly, the F1-score also improved, rising from 0.909 to 0.922.

Table 5.4 Resulting performance of pretrained UCR and end-to-end UCR using an LSTM on the Breinify Dataset for the purchase prediction task

Approach	AUC		F1	
	Mean	Std	Mean	Std
Pretrained UCR	**0.943**	**0.0028**	**0.922**	**0.0019**
End-to-end UCR	0.929	0.0049	0.909	0.0065

Beyond the absolute performance improvements, the pretrained UCR also demonstrated stability, as evidenced by lower standard deviations across repeated runs. This reduction in variance indicates better generalization to unseen data, greater training robustness, and reduced sensitivity to initialization or data splits, factors that are particularly important in real-world e-commerce systems, where model stability directly impacts operational reliability.

The results provide empirical support for the decoupled approach using self-supervised pretrained UCR strategy proposed in this thesis. Not only does it outperform traditional end-to-end learning in predictive accuracy and consistency, but it also aligns well with the operational constraints and architectural modularity required for scalable and maintainable e-commerce systems.

5.6.2 Evaluation of different Touchpoint Modalities

In the context of the Breinify use case, a crucial evaluation step involved assessing the impact of different customer touchpoint modalities, namely, URL-level touchpoints and product-level touchpoints, on the quality of the learned UCR embeddings. While product identifiers offer a more abstract view of customer behavior, URL-based touchpoints are hypothesized to convey finer-grained contextual and navigational information. This evaluation aims to validate whether such granularity contributes to richer, more predictive representations of customer behavior. Table 5.5 shows the performance of the touchpoint modality evaluation. The results clearly indicate that URL-based touchpoints substantially outperform product-based representations in both predictive accuracy and stability. The pretrained UCR derived from URL touchpoints achieves a higher AUC score, compared to the product-based inputs. Likewise, the F1-score is markedly higher for URL data, while also exhibiting a significantly lower standard deviation, demonstrating improved generalizability and robustness. This substantial performance gap aligns with prior thoughts that URL-level granularity captures more semantically rich and temporally coherent behavioral cues.

Table 5.5 Results on purchase prediction of different touchpoint modalities used to build the pretrained UCR embedding

Touchpoint Modality	AUC		F1	
	Mean	Std	Mean	Std
URL	**0.942**	**0.0028**	**0.922**	**0.0019**
Product-ID	0.649	0.0067	0.617	0.0197

These results strongly emphasize the importance of touchpoint modality in the representational quality of learned UCR embeddings. Unlike product identifiers, which offer a narrow view of customer activity tied strictly to transactional engagement, URLs often contain additional contextual information about customer journeys, such as details about each page view rather than product views alone. This richer informational capacity provides the embedding model with a broader and more diverse signal space to capture subtle patterns in customer behavior. The higher diversity of URL-level touchpoints is also reflected empirically in the dataset statistics: for example, as shown in Table 5.2, the Breinify dataset contains 66,205 unique URL touchpoints in the training set compared to only 35,499 unique product-based touchpoints. This greater variety means that URL-based sequences can encode more fine-grained browsing actions, allowing the representation to distinguish nuanced differences in customer intent that product IDs alone cannot capture. As a result, the downstream LSTM model benefits from more semantically rich and varied input and is better able to learn behavioral nuances that contribute to improved predictive performance.

Taken together, these results highlight that the granularity and informativeness of the input modality are key determinants of downstream model success. They further validate the design choice to use URL-level touchpoints as the default input for the Breinify dataset, reinforcing the notion that richer, contextually grounded representations lead to more effective customer behavior modeling.

5.6.3 Evaluation of Different Learning Models Using UCR

To comprehensively assess the effect of model architecture on downstream task performance, a diverse set of learning models is employed, encompassing both traditional ML methods and neural network-based architectures. The aim is to evaluate how well different model types are able to leverage the pretrained UCR embeddings across heterogeneous datasets, including YooChoose, OpenCDP, and Breinify.

The selection of models is motivated by three key considerations:

1. Comparability with prior literature: The models chosen are commonly used in the literature for similar tasks, allowing for direct comparisons with existing results.
2. Coverage of different model classes: The evaluation includes a range of model types, from traditional classifiers to advanced neural architectures, to capture the impact of inductive biases and model capacity on performance.
3. Suitability for sequential input formats: The models are selected based on their ability to effectively process sequential data, which is crucial for capturing the temporal dynamics of customer behavior embedded in the UCR features.

The following models are included in the experiments:

- **Traditional models** such as LR, DT, RF, and GB have been widely adopted in industrial and academic settings due to their robustness, interpretability, and strong performance on structured tabular data (cf. Sect. 3.2). These models only use fixed-size vector inputs and require concatenation of the UCR embeddings to form a single feature vector. They are computationally efficient and serve as strong baselines for evaluating the added value of learned representations. LR provides a linear baseline, while DT, RF, and GB capture nonlinear relationships and decision boundaries, which are important for modeling complex customer behavior patterns.
- **Neural models** include MLP and Transformer encoders. MLPs represent a natural extension of traditional models into the nonlinear neural space and are efficient for learning higher-order interactions among the elements of the UCR. Similar to traditional models, MLPs require the UCR embeddings to be concatenated into a single vector. Transformer encoders are included due to their proven ability to model global dependencies in input sequences through self-attention mechanisms. They have emerged as the de facto state-of-the-art architecture across a wide range of domains, including NLP, vision, and increasingly in tabular and sequential behavior modeling tasks. Recent research has demonstrated their competitive or superior performance compared to both traditional and recurrent architectures, especially in scenarios where contextual relationships and nonlinear feature interactions play a crucial role in prediction. Their scalability, flexibility, and ability to learn from large volumes of data should make them par-

ticularly well-suited for e-commerce environments, where customer behavior signals can be sparse, noisy, or irregular.

- **Sequential models**, in particular LSTM networks, are selected to evaluate the utility of UCR embeddings in sequence-aware contexts. Unlike the other models, LSTMs can directly process time-ordered sequences of touchpoint embeddings without aggregation, thus preserving temporal structure. This allows for the investigation of whether retaining sequential dynamics, rather than compressing them into a fixed-size representation, leads to improved predictive accuracy.

By employing this broad model spectrum, the evaluation aims to determine which model architectures are best suited to extract predictive signals from the learned UCR across different e-commerce environments. Additionally, the analysis reveals how sensitive downstream performance is to model choice, helping to inform future design decisions for integrating UCR into real-world systems.

For the evaluation, all models received as input the proposed UCR embeddings, ensuring that observed performance differences stemmed from model capacity and inductive biases rather than representation quality. Table 5.6 presents the performance metrics of the different learning models on the purchase prediction task. Across all datasets and configurations, the LSTM consistently achieved the highest F1 and AUC scores, indicating superior effectiveness in exploiting the sequential structure of customer behavior embedded in the UCR features.

Table 5.6 Results of different learning models using UCR to predict customers' purchase intention

Dataset	Model	DT	RF	GB	LR	MLP	LSTM	Transformer		
								1-Layer	3-Layer	6-Layer
Breinify	F1	0.851	0.882	0.865	0.830	0.87	**0.922**	0.854	0.853	0.858
	AUC	0.895	0.929	0.916	0.891	0.915	**0.943**	0.91	0.909	0.912
YooChoose	F1	0.636	0.670	0.662	0.637	0.672	**0.676**	0.651	0.628	0.592
	AUC	0.670	0.667	0.655	0.672	0.673	**0.683**	0.652	0.663	0.643
OpenCDP	F1	0.757	0.765	0.763	0.755	0.841	**0.875**	0.827	0.845	0.847
	AUC	0.806	0.817	0.814	0.809	0.912	**0.922**	0.874	0.896	0.906

While traditional models such as RF and GB delivered competitive results, especially in the Breinify dataset, they are consistently outperformed by neural models.

Notably, the MLP achieved high performance on OpenCDP, yet still fell short of the LSTM on the same dataset.

The Transformer-based models underperformed relative to LSTM across all datasets in the purchase prediction task. Even as the depth of the Transformer increased, no substantial gains are observed. This is particularly evident in the YooChoose dataset, where Transformer with six layer achieved only 0.643 AUC compared to LSTM 0.683. Different from expected, such results suggest that Transformers may not optimally capture the nuances of short, session-based interaction sequences typically seen in e-commerce.

The results reveal important insights into how different learning architectures exploit the pretrained UCR embeddings across heterogeneous datasets and behavioral prediction tasks. While all models receive the same representation input, their performance varied substantially, reflecting the interaction between architectural inductive biases and the nature of customer behavior data in e-commerce. In the following, the results are examined in more detail.

The effectiveness of the LSTM architecture is further highlighted by its training and generalization behavior. As illustrated in Fig. 5.3, the LSTM model maintains stable or improving AUC scores on the test set throughout training, while avoiding overfitting on the training set. This is notable given its small model size with just 8,481 parameters, suggesting that the LSTM benefits from a favorable bias-variance trade-off and is well-matched to the sequential structure of the UCR input. This robustness is likely due to two architectural strengths: (1) the ability to model temporal order and contextual dependencies across sequences of embeddings, and (2) the use of internal gating mechanisms that allow for adaptive memory control, which is particularly useful when handling variable-length customer journeys. As already highlighted in Sect. 2.3, LSTMs are particularly effective at capturing mid-range dependencies, which aligns well with the structure of session-based customer interactions. Given that customer sessions in the examined datasets have an average length of approximately 10 events (cf. Table 4.1), the LSTM's memory span is well-suited to modeling behavior at this scale, sufficient to capture short-term intent without introducing the complexity or overfitting risk.

Transformer-based models underperformed across all tested configurations. As shown in both Table 5.6 and Fig. 5.3, deeper Transformer architectures consistently achieved lower test AUC scores compared to LSTMs while overfitting on the train data reaching a perfect score at around 30 training epochs for the three and six-layer version and in around 50 epochs for the one-layer Transformer. Notably, the six-layer Transformer performed worst on smaller datasets like YooChoose, where the AUC dropped to 0.643, substantially lower than the LSTM's 0.683. While the one-layer Transformer achieved better performance than deeper variants, its results still lag behind the LSTM, indicating that depth does not provide meaningful gains in this context.

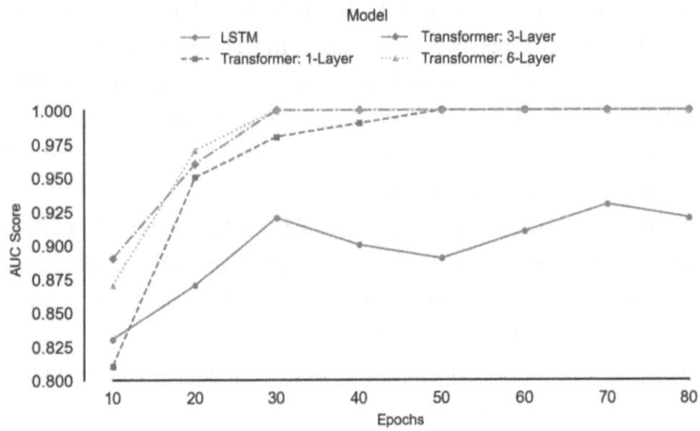

(a) Train AUC score of the LSTM and Transformer models using the UCR embedding over the training epochs.

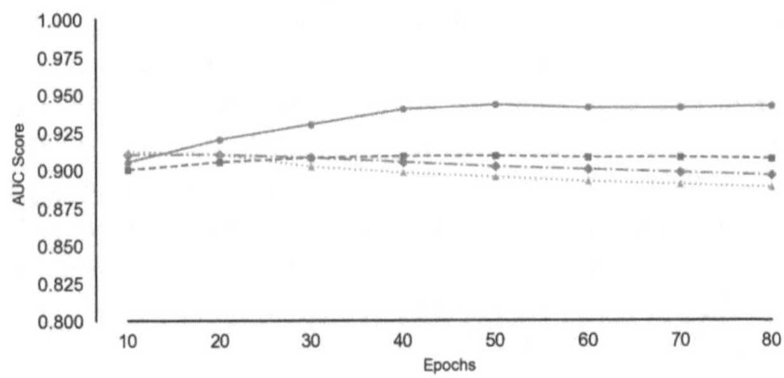

(b) Test AUC score of the LSTM and Transformer models using the UCR embedding over the training epochs.

Fig. 5.3 Train and test AUC score of the LSTM and Transformer models using the UCR embedding over the training epochs. The results are shown for the purchase prediction task on the Breinify dataset

These findings suggest that deeper Transformers may be overparameterized for the relatively small session-level training data available in e-commerce datasets. Parameter analysis reinforces this conclusion: the one-layer Transformer used approximately 25,441 parameters, while the six-layer version had 88,961. Despite their modest parameter counts relative to modern NLP-scale models, this capacity still exceeds the complexity needed for the UCR-based input, leading to overfitting and poor generalization.

Furthermore, Transformer architectures may suffer from limited robustness to sparse or fragmented interaction sequences, which are common in e-commerce logs. Unlike LSTMs, Transformers rely mainly on self-attention, which assumes meaningful token-to-token interactions. In short sessions with few interactions, this mechanism may amplify noise rather than meaningfull behavior signals, reducing predictive reliability.

Among traditional models, RF and GB performed competitively. These models are robust and interpretable but limited by their reliance on fixed-size, aggregated features. They are unable to exploit temporal dependencies or latent structure encoded in the sequential layout of UCR embeddings. The MLP model performed reasonably well, especially on the OpenCDP dataset. However, having the same fixed-input size problem as the traditional models, it failed to match the LSTM in any dataset, suggesting that while it captures higher-order feature interactions, it cannot model sequential dependencies as effectively.

The results of this evaluation highlight the transferability and robustness of the pretrained UCR embeddings and confirm the decisive role of model architecture in fully exploiting these representations. The consistently superior performance of the LSTM model across Breinify, YooChoose, and OpenCDP demonstrates that the learned UCR embeddings generalize effectively beyond a single platform or data context. Despite substantial differences in dataset scale, interaction structure, and available information, the LSTM model reliably extracted meaningful sequential patterns from the same embeddings, outperforming all other tested architectures and achieving high predictive accuracy in purchase prediction across all scenarios.

Overall, the results reinforce the importance of choosing architecture in alignment with data characteristics, and validate the effectiveness of decoupling representation learning from downstream modeling, as it enables lighter models like LSTMs to achieve high predictive performance with minimal risk of overfitting. Therefore, the LSTM is selected as the primary model for subsequent evaluations of the proposed UCR approach.

5.6.4 Comparative Evaluation Against Baseline Approaches

To validate the effectiveness and generalizability of the proposed UCR approach, an extensive evaluation is conducted against established baseline models, as described in Sect. 5.5, across all four datasets, YooChoose, RetailRocket, OpenCDP, and the

Breinify use case, as well as three prediction tasks: purchase prediction, churn prediction, and CTR prediction.

Table 5.7 summarizes the results for each approach. The proposed UCR embedding approach consistently achieved the highest or near-highest F1 and AUC values across all datasets and tasks, indicating robust performance across diverse prediction settings.

This comparative evaluation provides empirical evidence for the effectiveness and generalizability of the proposed self-supervised UCR embedding strategy. While the traditional and end-to-end baselines show partial strengths, they consistently fail to generalize across tasks and domains, highlighting a central advantage of the proposed decoupled UCR approach in this experimental setup.

The traditional baselines (purchase and churn) exhibited high performance only in the tasks and datasets for which they are explicitly engineered. This is unsurprising, as their design incorporates domain-specific inductive biases and handcrafted features tailored to narrow behavioral signals (e.g., product view sequences or inactivity periods). For instance, the churn baseline achieved an outstanding F1 score of 0.902 and an AUC of 0.928 on RetailRocket's churn prediction, which is a similar high score to the one proposed by Berger et al [22], highlighting that even with less features the proposed approach reaches similar high score as in their work. However, this performance sharply declined when evaluated on other tasks such as purchase or CTR prediction, and on structurally different datasets like OpenCDP or Breinify, even when using historical data. This pattern highlights the limited transferability of specialized heuristics and underscores a key limitation of manually engineered pipelines, they are not robust to data schema shifts, evolving behavioral patterns, or new task definitions. Moreover, traditional approaches are inherently incapable of predicting item-level click behavior, as there is no systematic mechanism to encode the identity of a seen or recommended item into the model's representation without extensive modification of the feature space. This lack of flexibility makes such baselines unsuitable for scenarios requiring fine-grained item interaction modeling, such as CTR prediction.

In contrast, end-to-end-based baselines (CTR and UCR) are able to generalize across all evaluated tasks, demonstrating functional coverage. These models directly learn task-specific representations from raw sequences and can be flexibly applied across use cases. However, as shown in Table 5.7, their performance still falls short of the proposed pretrained UCR with LSTM combination. A deeper investigation of their learning dynamics reveals the root cause: both end-to-end baselines overfit, achieving perfect AUC scores on the training set (AUC = 1.0) after just 30 epochs, while simultaneously degrading in test performance. This is visualized in Fig. 5.4, where test AUC scores steadily decline with continued training. The overfitting

Table 5.7 Performance comparison of the proposed UCR embedding approach against multiple baseline methods across four datasets and prediction tasks

Dataset	Task	Baseline Approaches								Proposed	
		Purchase		Churn		CTR		UCR		UCR Embeddings	
		F1	AUC	F1	AUC	F1	AUC	F1	AUC	F1	AUC
Breinify	purchase	0.632	0.679	0.491	0.596	0.748	0.805	0.748	0.807	**0.922**	**0.943**
	churn	0.585	0.551	0.662	0.629	0.625	0.659	0.987	0.713	**0.989**	**0.731**
	click	0.446	0.527	0.469	0.498	0.933	0.963	0.934	0.971	**0.945**	**0.981**
YooChoose	purchase	0.657	**0.690**	0.597	0.627	0.612	0.609	0.671	0.679	**0.676**	0.683
	click	✗	✗	✗	✗	0.733	0.781	0.660	0.705	**0.777**	**0.890**
RetailRocket	purchase	0.585	0.578	0.643	0.629	0.663	**0.724**	0.629	0.637	**0.674**	0.707
	churn	0.690	0.772	0.902	**0.928**	0.575	0.592	**0.980**	0.667	**0.980**	0.706
	click	✗	✗	✗	✗	**0.661**	**0.663**	0.357	0.496	0.660	0.659
OpenCDP	purchase	0.779	0.836	0.522	0.563	0.874	**0.923**	0.867	0.916	**0.875**	0.922
	churn	0.556	0.508	0.565	0.563	0.528	0.488	0.567	0.537	**0.568**	**0.567**
	click	✗	✗	✗	✗	**0.891**	**0.951**	0.021	0.499	0.612	0.549

behavior is attributed to the high parameter count of these models. The UCR baseline contains 212,710 trainable parameters, and the CTR baseline includes 747,186 parameters. These large capacities make them susceptible to memorization, particularly when training data is imbalanced, noisy, or sparse a common characteristic in e-commerce interaction data. Moreover, the tight coupling between representation learning and task optimization limits their reusability: representations tuned for one task are unlikely to generalize well to others, which reduces long-term deployment flexibility.

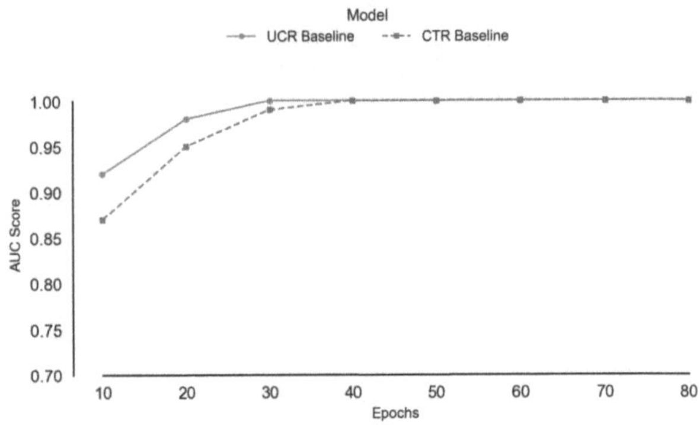

(a) Train AUC score of the two end-to-end approaches over the training epochs.

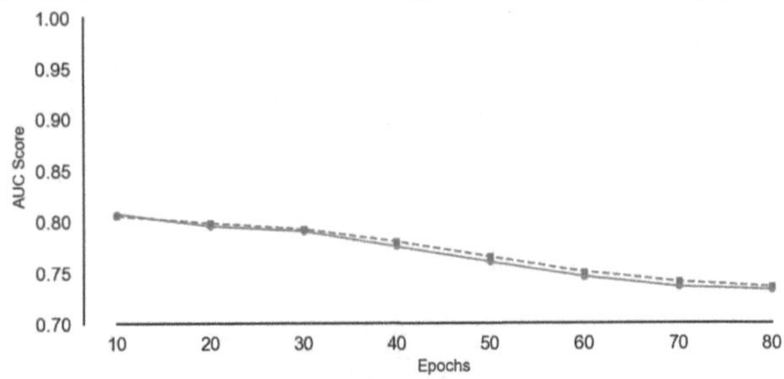

(b) Test AUC score of the two end-to-end approaches over the training epochs.

Fig. 5.4 Train and test AUC score of the two end-to-end approaches over the training epochs. The results are shown for the purchase prediction task on the Breinify dataset

The proposed UCR embedding approach directly addresses these challenges. First, the separation of representation learning and task modeling provides modularity, enabling pretraining of embeddings on rich behavioral sequences without being biased toward specific output labels. This decoupling not only reduces overfitting (as evident from the stable or improving test AUC curves shown in Fig. 5.3) but also allows reuse across tasks and datasets. Second, the pretrained UCR embeddings are compact, semantically meaningful, and task-agnostic, making them ideal input features for lightweight and robust downstream models such as the LSTM. This compositional architecture yields both performance and interpretability benefits: model capacity is distributed across components, and intermediate representations can be reused or analyzed independently.

Most importantly, the proposed approach significantly outperformed all baselines on the Breinify dataset, which represents the most realistic scenario examined in this thesis due to its industrial origin and the high granularity of its real-world clickstream interactions. Thereby, the granular URL-based interaction data provided rich semantic signals, and the UCR embeddings are able to capture these signals in a generalizable way. Across all tasks (purchase, churn, and CTR), the pretrained UCR approach achieved the best F1 and AUC scores, demonstrating that combining high-resolution behavioral data with a self-supervised embedding objective yields the most expressive and transferable customer representations.

Another critical factor influencing the effectiveness of customer behavior prediction is the information richness of the input modality. As demonstrated in the comparison between URL-based and product ID-based touchpoints (cf. Table 5.5), semantically richer inputs lead to substantially better representation quality and downstream task performance. Similarly, across datasets, those that include diverse and fine-grained interaction types such as "add-to-cart" or "checkout" (e.g., OpenCDP, RetailRocket, Breinify) consistently result in higher predictive performance than those containing only basic interactions, such as YooChoose, which includes only view events. This diversity of interaction types increases the potential information that can be captured in the behavioral sequences and provides critical intermediate signals for learning customer intent. For instance, an "add-to-cart"event is often a necessary precursor to a purchase; if the model can learn to recognize and weigh this event appropriately, it can more accurately predict purchase outcomes. In this work, a random sample analysis confirmed that the LSTM model effectively learns this relationship: when an "add-to-cart"action is present in a session, the model systematically increases the probability of predicting a purchase, demonstrating that the richer interaction data directly supports more precise behavior forecasting. These findings indicate that behavioral detail and semantic granularity embedded in the interaction sequences are crucial for effective representation learning. Consequently, the generalizability of the UCR approach is not only rooted in its architectural decoupling but also in its ability to extract latent signals from richly structured input data.

Taken together, these results demonstrate not only the strong predictive accuracy of the proposed UCR embeddings but also their practical transferability and scalability. The consistent outperformance across YooChoose, RetailRocket, OpenCDP, and Breinify shows that the learned customer representations generalize well beyond a single platform, use case, or task-specific design. Importantly, the OpenCDP results highlight that the UCR approach remains robust and computationally feasible even at industrial scale, handling hundreds of millions of interaction events while maintaining stable predictive quality. This confirms that the proposed architecture is capable of scaling to real-world production workloads and adapting to diverse behavioral data landscapes, validating its suitability for modern, dynamic e-commerce environments.

5.6.5 Real-Time Capability Evaluation

In addition to predictive performance and generalizability, real-world deployment of a customer behavior modeling system requires strict adherence to latency constraints. E-commerce platforms increasingly depend on real-time personalization, such as dynamic recommendations or triggered marketing actions, which must occur within milliseconds to retain customer attention and maximize engagement. As outlined in Sect. 4.2 and supported by prior literature [33, 162], a system is considered real-time capable if predictions are delivered within approximately 0.1 seconds.

To assess whether the evaluated approaches meet this threshold, an inference time benchmark is conducted. Specifically, the number of predictions each approach could generate within a 0.1-second window is measured under controlled conditions (single-threaded, CPU-only environment). Hardware constraints are not considered a confounding factor in the evaluation, as all approaches are executed under identical conditions on the same hardware configuration. Table 5.8 summarizes the outcomes.

Table 5.8 The number of predictions done within 0.1 seconds for each approach

Approach	Number of Predictions in 0.1 Seconds
Purchase Baseline	170
Churn Baseline	30
CTR Baseline	7,000
UCR Baseline	10,000
UCR Embedding	**12,000**

The proposed pretrained UCR embedding approach achieved the highest throughput, producing 12,000 predictions in just 0.1 seconds. In contrast, traditional feature-engineered baselines performed dramatically worse, most notably, the churn baseline managed only 30 predictions, and the purchase baseline only 170. Even the CTR baseline, which is comparatively more optimized, fell significantly short with just 7,000 predictions, a 42% reduction relative to the proposed approach.

These differences are attributable to the computational structure of each method. The proposed approach benefits from its modular architecture. Once the customer touchpoint embeddings are learned, each representation can be constructed through simple lookups. This contrasts with the handcrafted baselines, which require complex feature extraction pipelines that hinder scalability and increase latency. Similarly, end-to-end models like the CTR or UCR baselines incur a higher runtime cost due to on-the-fly sequence processing and larger model footprints.

The experimental results confirm that the proposed UCR method not only meets, but surpasses real-time performance constraints, making it a highly practical candidate for deployment in latency-sensitive applications. Its computational efficiency stems from three architectural advantages:

1. Pretrained Representations: Since customer behavior embeddings are precomputed using self-supervised learning, no deep model inference is required during prediction time enabling rapid vector lookup for customer representation. Furthermore, the representation can be built incrementally, allowing for efficient updates as new customer interactions occur.
2. Model Simplicity at Inference: The downstream learning model, here an LSTM with only around 8,000 parameters, is compact and efficient, allowing fast execution even on resource-limited hardware.
3. Task Decoupling: Unlike end-to-end models, which must recompute internal representations for each task, the pretrained UCR allows for flexible reuse across different prediction scenarios with minimal overhead.

Taken together, these findings demonstrate that the proposed method provides a compelling balance of accuracy, transferability, and computational efficiency. It satisfies the operational requirements of modern e-commerce systems, where scalability and response time are as critical as predictive accuracy.

5.7 Summary and Contribution

In this chapter, a novel approach for learning Universal Customer Representation in e-commerce environments has been proposed and empirically validated. The results demonstrate that customer behavior in e-commerce environments can be effectively represented through self-supervised embeddings learned from different, semantically rich clickstream data. The resulting representation generalizes across different predictive tasks, remains robust under real-world privacy constraints and session-based conditions, and operates within strict latency requirements, thereby directly addressing the central research question of this chapter.

To address this, a three-stage methodology is introduced, consisting of:

1. customer information collection from arbitrary touchpoints;
2. self-supervised representation learning using a Skip-Gram embedding architecture; and
3. downstream prediction using lightweight learning models.

The embedding representation learns dense vector representations from sequences of customer touchpoints, which are then aggregated to form a task-agnostic, privacy-preserving UCR.

To evaluate the effectiveness and generality of the proposed method, extensive experiments are conducted across four e-commerce datasets and three representative tasks.

The results demonstrate that the proposed pretrained UCR in combination with an LSTM consistently outperformed task-specific and end-to-end baselines in predictive accuracy and robustness. Moreover, the decoupling of representation learning from task modeling provided operational advantages, such as model reuse, interpretability, and modularity, while eliminating the need for manual feature engineering. Furthermore, the use of URL-level touchpoints led to superior representations compared to product identifiers, emphasizing the importance of input modality and data granularity. The proposed method achieved real-time capability, generating over 12,000 predictions in under 0.1 seconds significantly outperforming baseline models in latency-constrained settings.

In summary, the findings confirm that UCR can be learned directly from real-world interaction data in a self-supervised manner. These representations are generalizable, efficient, and privacy-compliant, and they enable accurate behavior prediction across diverse e-commerce tasks and deployment scenarios.

Enhancing Customer Behavior Embeddings with Additional Information 6

Building upon the findings from Research Question 1, it has been demonstrated that self-supervised embeddings derived solely from customer interaction data serve as effective UCR.

However, in the domain of product embeddings, which share methodological similarities with the customer embedding strategies discussed in this work, incorporating auxiliary features has been shown to be beneficial. For instance, Vasile et al. [236] proposed Meta-Prod2Vec, which enriches product embeddings with product category as input and output improving its recommendation performance. In previous work, SkipGramEx was proposed, which uses category information that is implicitly learned by the product embedding which improved the recommendation performance [11]. This highlights the potential of enhancing self-supervised embeddings by integrating additional contextual information.

Whether a measurable benefit can be achieved is examined in greater detail in this chapter through the second research question:

> **What impact does integrating additional customer behavior data have on self-supervised learned embeddings and how can this integration be practically implemented in e-commerce?**

Temporal features, such as the point in time at which a customer interaction occurs, have been repeatedly identified in the literature as essential for modelling customer intent. For example, Esmeli et al. [67] demonstrated that the time of activity represents a highly predictive signal for customer behavior. Therefore, this chapter investigates how temporal information can be effectively integrated into customer behavior embeddings to enhance their predictive capabilities. In addition, the underlying data model (cf. Sect. 4.2) explicitly supports the inclusion of temporal infor-

M. Alves Gomes, *Utilizing Embeddings to Learn a Universal Customer Behavior Representation in E-Commerce*, https://doi.org/10.1007/978-3-658-50781-7_6

mation as a core feature alongside touchpoint data, ensuring that temporal aspects can be systematically utilised.

To address this research question, a method for integrating time information into embedding representations is proposed. The approach extends the pretrained UCR embedding model with temporal signals through multiple encoding strategies. These strategies are then evaluated empirically across the introduced use cases, Breinify, YooChoose, and OpenCDP, which are deliberately selected to validate the generalizability of the approach under diverse real-world conditions. As highlighted in Sect. 4.2, Breinify represents an industrial, high-granularity dataset with rich URL-level interactions. YooChoose serves as a well-known public benchmark for purchase prediction with minimal metadata and no persistent customer IDs, aligning with privacy-friendly, session-based modeling, and OpenCDP tests the scalability of the proposed temporal extensions on a large-scale, multi-category platform with extensive behavioral diversity.

The remainder of this chapter is structured as follows. In Sect. 6.1, the foundations of encoding time are established. Subsequently in Sect. 6.2, the proposed methodology is detailed, including the architectural components of the embedding, as well as the strategies employed for encoding time. The experimental setup is then described in Sect. 6.4. Thereafter, in Sect. 6.5, the empirical results are presented, analyzed, and discussed in relation to the UCR embedding without time information.

6.1 Methods of Time Encoding

Time is a critical dimension in many ML tasks, particularly in e-commerce, where customer behavior, demand patterns, and product relevance evolve continuously. Traditionally, time has been incorporated into predictive models as explicit engineered features. For example, Esmeli et al. [67] and Xiahou and Harada [255] demonstrated that representing time as periodic components, such as hour of the day, day of the week, or day of the year, can reveal recurring customer activity patterns. These features are typically discretized and added to the model alongside other input variables. While such transformations introduce useful cyclical structure, they are inherently limited in their ability to represent non-linear trends and fine-grained temporal dependencies. Simple categorical encodings cannot fully capture how customer intent or item popularity shifts over continuous time horizons [125].

To address these limitations, more recent research has focused on learning temporal representations directly within the model's embedding space. Instead of treating time merely as an auxiliary categorical input, these approaches transform timestamps, time intervals, or decomposed periodic features into dense, trainable vectors. This enables the model to learn complex patterns, such as periodicity, drift, or sequential dependencies, jointly with behavioral embeddings, resulting in representations that are both temporally informed and contextually meaningful [121, 122, 125, 169, 232].

For instance, Kim et al. [125] embed both raw Unix timestamps and decomposed periodic features, including hour of day, day of week, and month of year to learn graph-based representations that model how user-item relationships evolve over time. Similarly, Nalmpantis and Vrakas [169] proposed Signal2Vec, which extends the Word2Vec paradigm to time series by embedding subsequences based on their co-occurrence in temporal context windows, without explicit manual feature engineering. Karingula et al. [121] introduced a GB approach that uses normalized time deltas as scalar inputs to learn dense representations tailored for forecasting tasks.

A foundational variant of this idea is the use of sinusoidal positional encodings, as introduced by Vaswani et al. [237] in the Transformer architecture. This method assigns each position or time step a deterministic vector consisting of sine and cosine functions at multiple frequencies. Such encodings provide unique representations for each position while preserving relative distances, enabling the model to infer sequential order [99, 274].

Building on this concept, Kazemi et al. [122] proposed Time2Vec, which generalizes sinusoidal encodings into a learnable approach. Time2Vec represents any scalar time input t as a vector of the form $[w_0 t + b_0; \sin(w_1 t + b_1); \sin(w_2 t + b_2), \ldots]$, where the weights w_i and phases b_i are trainable parameters. The linear term captures global trends, while the periodic terms model multiple seasonal cycles simultaneously.

In summary, the literature establishes two primary strategies for integrating temporal information into ML models:

1. Feature-based encoding, where time is explicitly decomposed into interpretable categorical components (e.g., hour of day, weekday) and treated as discrete inputs alongside other variables.
2. Learned time embeddings, where continuous timestamps or time deltas are transformed into dense, trainable vectors (e.g., using sinusoidal bases or neural encoders) that capture both periodic and non-linear temporal dynamics.

6.2 Time Extended Embedding

In this section, a method combining both strategies is introduced and adapted to the self-supervised UCR embedding architecture employed in this work. Specifically, the proposed Time Extended Embedding (TEE) approach extends the UCR embedding architecture introduced in Sect. 2.4. Inspired by the Meta-Prod2Vec model of Vasile et al. [236], which augments product embeddings with metadata (e.g., product categories), the TEE model introduces temporal information as an additional input during customer behavior learning. In contrast to Meta-Prod2Vec, which leverages static item attributes, TEE incorporates the time of interaction thereby modeling temporal dynamics in customer behavior sequences.

Specifically, let each touchpoint $t_j \in T$ be associated with a set of z discrete temporal features, denoted by the vector $\boldsymbol{\tau}_j = (\tau_j^1, \tau_j^2, \ldots, \tau_j^z)$, where τ_j^z is a discrete variable representing a specific time dimension (e.g., hour of the day, day of the week). For each t_j^z, a corresponding embedding matrix $e_{\tau_j^z} = \theta^{\tau_j^z} \in \mathbb{R}^{|\tau_z| \times D}$ is defined, where $|\tau_z|$ is the cardinality of the z-th temporal feature and D is the embedding dimensionality. Each interaction is thus embedded into a composite vector by concatenating the base touchpoint embedding e_{t_j} with the embeddings of each temporal feature:

$$e_{t_j}^{\text{TEE}} = e_{t_j} || e_{\tau_j^1} || e_{\tau_j^2} || \ldots || e_{\tau_j^z}, \tag{6.1}$$

where $||$ denotes vector concatenation, and $e_{\tau_j^z}$ is the embedding corresponding to the z-th temporal input. The overall architecture is illustrated in Fig. 6.1. The model consists of one-hot encoded input layers for both the interaction t_j and each temporal component τ_j^z, individual embedding layers, a concatenation step to form the joint latent representation $e_{t_j}^{\text{TEE}}$, and a fully connected output layer that predicts context interactions in the Skip-Gram setup.

The learning objective remains consistent with the formulation from Sect. 5.4, but now incorporates both the touchpoint and its temporal context. The modified training objective is defined as:

$$\mathcal{L}(\theta) = \prod_{j=0}^{n} \prod_{\alpha=-m \ \alpha \neq 0}^{m} P\left((x_{j+\alpha}, \boldsymbol{\tau}_{j+\alpha}) \mid (x_j, \boldsymbol{\tau}_j); \theta\right), \tag{6.2}$$

where θ represents the model parameters, including all embedding matrices.

This formulation encourages the embedding model to learn not only semantic similarity between the context of sequential touchpoints, but also alignment in the temporal context behavior of touchpoints. By conditioning the context on both the identity and time of interactions, the TEE model captures richer customer dynamics across daily and weekly patterns, seasonal variations, and other temporal regularities. Assigning equal weighting to both temporal and touchpoint signals ensures

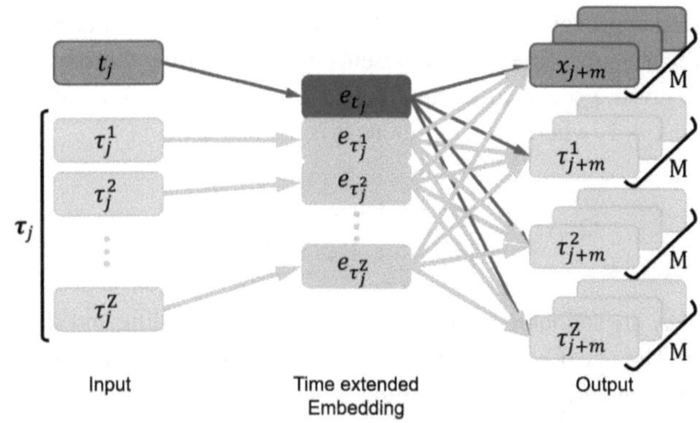

Fig. 6.1 Proposed TEE which consists of an one-hot encoding input layer for the touchpoint t_j (blue) and interaction time $\boldsymbol{\tau}_j$ (yellow), the concatenated time extended embedding layer, and a fully connected output layer

that neither semantic nor temporal information is implicitly underrepresented during training. This balanced treatment allows the model to preserve the complementary nature of content and timing. By avoiding a dominance of either signal type, the learned embeddings remain sensitive to situations in which identical touchpoints convey different meanings depending on their temporal context, such as variations in intent across time of day or seasonal cycles. Consequently, equal weighting provides a principled means to capture nuanced dependencies that would otherwise be suppressed by unequal signal as evident by other works [71, 125].

6.3 Time2Vec Incorporated Embeddings

An alternative approach used to investigate the effect of time on the UCR embeddings is the incorporation of time information through Time2Vec. This approach aims to capture periodic patterns in customer behavior, such as increased purchasing activity during weekends or holidays, by representing time as a dense, trainable vector using periodic functions. A key motivation for employing Time2Vec is that this method has been demonstrated by Kazemi et al. [122] to be model-agnostic, enabling temporal information to be incorporated seamlessly into embeddings in a manner analogous to positional encodings in Transformer models. Consequently, it can be added directly to the embedding layer without requiring architectural modifications, making it a flexible choice for enriching the UCR embeddings. Furthermore, unlike the TEE approach that relies on decomposed temporal features (e.g., day of week, month, or hour), Time2Vec represents continuous time directly.

Formally, given a scalar time input τ, the Time2Vec representation $t2v(\tau)$ is a vector of size $k + 1$, where each component is defined as:

$$t2v_i(\tau) = \begin{cases} \omega_i \cdot \tau + \varphi_i, & \text{if } i = 0 \\ \mathcal{G}(\omega_i \cdot \tau + \varphi_i), & \text{if } 1 \leq i \leq k \end{cases} \tag{6.3}$$

Here, ω_i and φ_i are trainable parameters that control the scaling and shifting of the time input τ. The periodic activation function $\mathcal{G}$, which is typically chosen as the sine function, transforms the scaled time input into a bounded, oscillatory signal that repeats over time. This design allows the representation to capture recurring patterns, such as daily or weekly cycles, by mapping continuous time onto a periodic space. The component for which $i = 0$ is defined as a purely linear term, which enables long-term trends or gradual changes in customer behavior over time to be learned directly from the data. In contrast, the components for which $i \geq 1$ apply the periodic activation function to enable the model to represent cyclic phenomena at multiple frequencies simultaneously. By combining these linear and periodic terms, Time2Vec provides a flexible mechanism for representing both non-repeating trends and repeating temporal patterns within a unified, continuous embedding.

To incorporate the Time2Vec embeddings with the UCR embeddings, both representations are combined by element-wise addition. Specifically, for a given touchpoint t_j and its associated timestamp τ_j, the final representation is computed as:

$$e_{t_j}^{\text{T2V}} = e_{t_j} + t2v(\tau_j), \tag{6.4}$$

where e_{t_j} denotes the UCR embedding of the touchpoint t_j as introduced in Sect. 5.4, and $t2v(\tau_j)$ represents the time embedding for the scalar timestamp τ_j, such as the mean session time delta. To ensure that this addition is mathematically valid and that each dimension aligns correctly, the output dimensionality of the Time2Vec representation must be identical to that of the UCR embedding. This design ensures that each temporal component is directly aligned with its corresponding semantic dimension in the touchpoint representation, allowing temporal patterns and semantic signals to be integrated seamlessly within a unified latent space.

This addition-based fusion should allow the touchpoint embedding to be modulated by time, enabling the model to learn time-sensitive behavioral patterns without altering the embedding dimensionality or requiring architectural changes in downstream components.

6.4 Experimental Setup

The experimental procedure employed in this chapter follows the same structure as established in Sect. 5.4. It consists of four main phases: (1) data preprocessing, (2) training of the embedding models (TEE, Time2Vec and UCR embedding), (3) training of the downstream learning model, and (4) evaluation of all approaches on predictive performance and real-time capability. For the learning model, a mere LSTM is used as it produces the most accurate prediction as shown in Sect. 5.6.

In analogy to the n-gram generation procedure described in Sect. 5.4.1, temporal trigrams are constructed for training the TEE. Specifically, the same context window of size $M = 2$ is used to generate trigrams from each session in the training data. For each customer interaction t_j and its associated timestamp $\boldsymbol{\tau}_j$, the resulting training instance is of form

$$((t_j, \boldsymbol{\tau}_j), (t_{j+1}, \boldsymbol{\tau}_{j+1}), (t_{j-1}, \boldsymbol{\tau}_{j-1})).$$

Similarly, for the edge case $j = 0$ or $j = n$, the special start and end tokens are used with the time set to match those of the first and last touchpoints in the session, respectively. Also as stated in Sect. 5.4.1, real-world e-commerce systems frequently encounter new touchpoints (e.g., newly introduced products). Since embeddings require a fixed input vocabulary the special "UNKNOWN" token is used. Temporal components, however, are drawn from predefined categorical sets and therefore do not require unknown handling.

All three tested approaches are trained separately on each dataset. For the TEE approach, the interaction time $\boldsymbol{\tau}_j$ is decomposed into $z = 4$ discrete temporal features, each capturing complementary aspects of customer behavior across different time scales. The following features are selected based on their empirical relevance in e-commerce and their theoretical grounding in consumer behavior literature [67, 125, 255]:

- **Day of the year** captures seasonal patterns and macro-level temporal trends. This is particularly important in e-commerce, where customer behavior is heavily influenced by calendar events such as holidays, sales cycles, and promotional campaigns (e.g., Christmas, Black Friday, back-to-school season). These events often exhibit sharp temporal spikes in interaction and conversion rates.
- **Day of the week** models weekly behavioral cycles, which are known to affect both browsing and purchasing behavior. For instance, customer engagement and transaction likelihood often peak on specific weekdays (e.g., Fridays for last-minute purchases, Mondays for planning), reflecting habitual usage patterns and marketing rhythms.

- **Hour of the day** reflects diurnal activity patterns, which are critical for understanding when customers are most active. E-commerce platforms often observe predictable peaks in traffic during lunch breaks, evenings, or late-night browsing sessions. Incorporating this feature enables models to contextualize actions based on daily temporal routines.
- **Minute of the hour** allows for fine-grained temporal resolution, capturing intra-hour variations that may reflect bursty behavior within sessions or micro-patterns in short-term customer engagement. This is particularly valuable in distinguishing between fast navigation, dwell time, or pacing of actions within active sessions.

Each of these temporal components is embedded independently and concatenated with the touchpoint embedding, as detailed in Sect. 6.2. This design allows the model to capture temporal semantics alongside interaction semantics while preserving modularity and transferability. Together, these four temporal components cover long-term, medium-term, short-term, and session-level behavioral patterns, with the goal of providing a robust and generalizable basis for enhancing the customer behavior representation.

For the Time2Vec-based approach, no n-gram construction is necessary, as the model operates on entire sessions rather than on local context windows. Time2Vec requires only a scalar temporal input, which is computed as the average time delta in seconds since the earliest recorded timestamp $\mathcal{T}_0$ in the dataset. Specifically, for a given session with start time τ_o and end time τ_n, the time input δ_τ is computed as:

$$\delta_\tau = \frac{(\tau_0 - \mathcal{T}_0) + (\tau_n - \mathcal{T}_0)}{2}. \tag{6.5}$$

The Time2Vec model is trained by predicting whether the session resulted in a purchase, effectively learning to encode time in a way that correlates with conversion likelihood. This embedding is then added to the interaction representation, as described in Sect. 6.3, and used in subsequent downstream learning.

6.5 Results and Discussion

6.5.1 Evaluation of Temporal Features on Prediction Performance

Analogous to the evaluation of the UCR embedding, both performance and real-time capability are evaluated. Table 6.1 summarizes the results of the three evaluated

Table 6.1 Comparison of three different embedding approaches, UCR embedding, TEE, and Time2Vec, on purchase prediction cross the YooChoose, OpenCDP, and Breinify datasets

Dataset	UCR Embedding		TEE		Time2Vec	
	F1	AUC	F1	AUC	F1	AUC
Breinify	0.922	0.943	**0.929**	**0.952**	0.923	0.935
YooChoose	0.676	0.683	**0.843**	**0.922**	0.708	0.757
OpenCDP	0.875	0.922	**0.930**	**0.965**	0.908	0.946

embedding approaches across the YooChoose, OpenCDP, and Breinify datasets. The proposed TEE approach consistently achieves the highest performance in both F1 score and AUC across all datasets.

These results show evidence that enriching the UCR embedding with temporal information significantly improves predictive performance across all datasets. A particularly notable finding is the substantial improvement observed on the YooChoose dataset. Here, the TEE approach yielded a dramatic increase in F1 score (+0.167) and AUC (+0.239) over the baseline UCR. This gain is especially meaningful given that YooChoose contains only coarse interaction data, specifically, product view events without any add-to-cart or purchase step granularity. As discussed in Sect. 5.6, the information content and semantic richness of input data are expected to affect representation quality. The observed performance gains of the TEE approach on this limited dataset indicate that temporal context can potentially compensate for limited input signals by providing additional information.

In contrast, datasets with inherently richer behavioral signals, such as OpenCDP and Breinify, show more moderate but still consistent gains. On OpenCDP, TEE improved F1 by +0.055 and AUC by +0.043 over the baseline. On Breinify, where input granularity is already high due to detailed URL and more event information like page visits and click events, the improvements are more modest (+0.007 F1 and +0.009 AUC). This diminishing return suggests that the marginal value of temporal signals is inversely related to the baseline informativeness of the dataset. Nonetheless, TEE consistently delivered the best results across all datasets, reinforcing its robustness and general applicability.

This result aligns with an important theoretical perspective: adding structured temporal features increases the distinctiveness of customer touchpoints by introducing additional dimensions along which they can vary. When touchpoints are combined with temporal attributes the space of possible event representations becomes significantly more fine-grained. This expanded granularity enables the model to learn behavioral distinctions that would otherwise remain hidden in coarser representations. Even when customer activity follows routine patterns, the temporal features introduce orthogonal variation that allows subtle intra-session and cross-session dynamics to be captured. This enhanced capacity to differentiate events contributes to the consistent performance improvements observed with the TEE approach, particularly in datasets such as YooChoose, where the touchpoint information alone provides only limited resolution.

The comparison with Time2Vec further supports the strength of the proposed TEE design. While Time2Vec captures temporal periodicity and offers improvements over the baseline UCR, it fails to match the performance of TEE in any setting. A potential limitation of the Time2Vec approach lies in the fact that it is trained jointly with the same objective as the task model, namely, purchase prediction. As a result, the temporal embedding may become biased toward this specific task and encode patterns that the predictive model itself also captures. This redundancy can reduce the added value of Time2Vec as a source of complementary contextual information. In contrast, the TEE embeddings are learned in a self-supervised manner by predicting surrounding context, which encourages the extraction of temporally relevant structure independently of the downstream task objective and thereby supports greater generalization.

The results also indicate that the predictive benefits of adding temporal context are transferable across very different e-commerce environments. The fact that TEE improves results not only on the proprietary Breinify dataset but also on the public benchmarks YooChoose and OpenCDP confirms that the time-augmented embeddings generalize well across use cases with varying scale, touchpoint granularity, and data structure. This cross-dataset consistency highlights that the TEE enhancement is not limited to a single narrow scenario but rather strengthens the core UCR concept as a robust and versatile representation for real-world behavioral prediction in diverse e-commerce contexts.

In summary, the findings confirm that temporal patterns encode meaningful behavioral cues not captured by sequence information alone, offering a valuable augmentation to customer behavior modelling. This effect is particularly pronounced in coarse-grained datasets, such as YooChoose, where the semantic richness of touchpoints is limited and temporal features help compensate for the lack of detailed interaction signals. Furthermore, explicit temporal embeddings, as introduced in the TEE approach, outperform general-purpose encodings such as Time2Vec. While Time2Vec is optimised jointly with the prediction task, potentially biasing the embedding toward the target objective, the TEE approach leverages a self-supervised context prediction strategy. This allows temporally relevant structure to be extracted independently of downstream task signals, supporting more generalisable and behaviorally grounded representations. Overall, the results show that the TEE approach complements and enhances the original UCR design.

6.5.2 Importance of Time Features in Time Extended Embedding

To evaluate the individual contributions of temporal features to the performance of the TEE approach, an ablation study is conducted across three datasets. As aforementioned, the TEE approach incorporates four discrete time components, day of year (dy), day of week (dw), hour of day (hd), and minute of hour (mh) each embedded independently and concatenated with the touchpoint representation. The goal of this study is to isolate the effect of each feature on prediction performance by selectively removing or retaining them. To ensure that the impact of each temporal component can be attributed unambiguously, only one feature is removed at a time. This strategy prevents interactions between multiple omitted features from confounding the interpretation of individual contributions, thereby ensuring that the performance change can be linked directly to the absence of a specific temporal signal.

Table 6.2 reports the F1 score and AUC for each ablated configuration. The results indicate that the minute of hour feature is by far the most influential. When the minute of hour is removed from the full model, performance drops significantly, most notably in the YooChoose dataset, where the F1 score declines from 0.843 to 0.782 and AUC from 0.922 to 0.887. Across all datasets, removing minute of hour causes the largest degradation in both metrics.

Table 6.2 Performance comparison of the TEE model and its ablated variants across three datasets, reported in terms of F1-score and AUC

Dataset		TEE Approach					
		full	w/o dy	w/o dw	w/o hd	w/o mh	only mh
Breinify	F1	0.929	0.927	0.926	0.924	0.923	0.928
	AUC	0.952	0.951	0.950	0.949	0.944	0.950
YooChoose	F1	0.843	0.828	0.820	0.796	0.782	0.823
	AUC	0.922	0.912	0.901	0.892	0.887	0.903
OpenCDP	F1	0.930	0.925	0.917	0.909	0.892	0.915
	AUC	0.965	0.961	0.957	0.953	0.930	0.955

Interestingly, a simplified configuration retaining only the minute of hour feature performs nearly as well as the full TEE model. For example, in the Breinify dataset, using only minute of hour yields an F1 score of 0.928 and AUC of 0.950 nearly indistinguishable from the full model's 0.929 and 0.952, respectively. This finding suggests that minute of hour captures the majority of the temporal signal used in downstream prediction.

These results highlight the importance of fine-grained temporal signals in capturing intra-session behavioral dynamics. While broader time features such as day of the year or day of the week may encode global temporal trends, e.g., holidays or weekly shopping cycles, they typically remain constant throughout individual sessions. As a result, they offer limited variation for modelling real-time or session-level behavior, especially in datasets that span only a few months (cf. Sect. 4.2), where the temporal diversity of such features is inherently restricted. In contrast, finer-grained signals such as the minute of the hour vary meaningfully within sessions and allow the model to distinguish subtle behavioral patterns, such as rapid navigation bursts versus idle browsing. This increased intra-session variability enhances the granularity of each touchpoint, enabling the model to capture distinctions that coarser features overlook. Moreover, broader temporal features may encourage the model to reconstruct predictable attributes, rather than learning genuinely contextual relationships, which can result in redundant or weakly informative signals when fine-grained behavioral prediction is required. An important limitation that is further discussed in the critical reflection in Chap. 9. These factors are an explanation, why the minute of the hour component consistently delivers the strongest performance gains and underscores the value of high-resolution temporal context in real-time behavior modelling.

In summary, the ablation study indicates that, within the scope of the test cases investigated, global temporal features contribute only marginal additional value, whereas fine-grained intra-session time signals prove to be the most impactful for real-time behavior modelling. This insight may inform future model design by guiding the selection of time features, particularly in latency-sensitive or resource-constrained deployment scenarios.

6.5.3 Real-Time Evaluation

Table 6.3 presents the results of the real-time evaluation, which measured the runtime required to generate customer representations and to perform predictions using an LSTM model. Similar to the real-time evaluation in Chap. 5, the evaluation focused on the scalability and suitability of each embedding approach for real-time

Table 6.3 The number of predictions done within 0.1 seconds for each tested approach and TEE using only one temporal feature

Approach	Number of Predictions in 0.1 Seconds
UCR Embedding	12,000
TEE	2,000
TEE only mh	6,000
Time2Vec	1,500

e-commerce applications, where low-latency inference is critical due to high request throughput.

The baseline UCR embedding approach delivered the fastest inference speed, generating 12,000 predictions within the time constraint. This efficiency stems from its compact, precomputed vector representations, which act as a lightweight lookup mechanism requiring minimal runtime computation. As such, the UCR model is highly suitable for deployment in high-throughput, latency-sensitive environments such as real-time personalization engines or triggered email systems.

By contrast, the full TEE approach, which concatenates embeddings for four discrete time features, produced only 2,000 predictions within the same time window, a 6x slowdown compared to UCR. This performance degradation is attributable to the additional memory and compute demands imposed by embedding multiple categorical time variables and performing vector concatenation for each interaction. While the TEE model provides superior predictive accuracy (cf. Sect. 6.4), this comes at the cost of significantly higher inference latency. This trade-off illustrates a central tension in real-world system design: representational richness versus real-time responsiveness.

To better balance this trade-off, a reduced variant of the TEE model using only the minute of hour feature is evaluated. This version achieved 6,000 predictions in 0.1 seconds which is three times faster than the full TEE. This highlights the potential for optimizing temporal feature sets to achieve a favorable compromise between performance and real-time applicability.

Lastly, the Time2Vec approach, despite its theoretical advantages in modeling periodicity, performed worst in terms of real-time applicability, supporting only 1,500 predictions within the time budget. This low throughput likely reflects the need to compute sinusoidal transformations dynamically, making it less compatible with stateless embedding-based inference pipelines.

In summary, these findings emphasize the critical role of architectural and feature selection decisions when designing customer representation systems for real-world deployment. While full temporal embeddings deliver superior modeling power, practical constraints often necessitate a trade-off favoring reduced feature sets and computational simplicity.

6.6 Summary and Contribution

This chapter has shown that integrating additional temporal customer behavior data into self-supervised embeddings has a positive and measurable impact on representation quality and downstream predictive accuracy, and that this integration can be practically implemented by extending the UCR embedding by including time signals jointly with interaction events. This provides a positive and comprehensive answer to the second research question.

Specifically, building on the foundational UCR approach introduced in Chap. 5, this chapter explored the incorporation of temporal context into customer behavior embeddings. Motivated by extensive evidence in customer modeling research highlighting the significance of temporal dynamics, a novel TEE architecture is proposed. TEE augments the Skip-Gram-based self-supervised embedding approach by jointly embedding discrete time components, such as minute of hour, hour of day, day of week, and day of year alongside interaction events. A comparative approach based on Time2Vec, a general-purpose continuous time representation, is also evaluated.

To assess effectiveness, the proposed approaches are benchmarked across three real-world datasets, under a consistent experimental protocol. Results demonstrated that TEE consistently outperforms both the original UCR and the Time2Vec-based method across all datasets in terms of predictive performance. The most significant improvements are observed in the YooChoose dataset, which features coarse-grained interactions with limited semantic depth, thereby underscoring the value of temporal augmentation in sparse behavioral settings.

Real-time capability is also assessed as a critical deployment factor. Although the full TEE model introduces greater complexity due to the joint embedding of multiple time features, the resulting increase in inference latency remains within acceptable bounds for production use. Importantly, a simplified variant of TEE that incorporates only the minute of hour feature demonstrated a favorable trade-off: it preserved the majority of the performance gains while substantially reducing runtime overhead. The accompanying ablation study confirmed that this feature alone captures the most behaviorally informative temporal signal, whereas additional components (e.g., day of week, day of year) contributed marginally but increased computational cost.

In conclusion, this chapter contributes an effective and practical method for enhancing self-supervised customer embeddings through temporal feature integration. It shows that temporal context, when explicitly encoded during training, improves predictive accuracy without.

7 Lifelong Learning Embeddings for Adaptive Customer Behavior Modeling

Building upon the previous chapter, which demonstrated how enriching the UCR approach with temporal information enhances its expressiveness and predictive power, this chapter extends the discussion to another critical challenge, which is relevant for academia and industry alike: the need for continuous adaptability in dynamic e-commerce environments. While TEE addresses the question of how to encode additional session-based behavioral signals, they do not fully resolve the problem of how to maintain and evolve customer representations over time as new products, interactions, and behavioral patterns emerge. Accordingly, this chapter tackles the challenge of adaptability by addressing the third research question of this thesis:

> **How can self-supervised customer behavior embeddings be improved to adapt to the dynamics of real-world e-commerce applications?**

The domain of e-commerce is characterized as one of the most rapidly evolving and highly competitive environments in modern digital ecosystems. The rapid and continuous introduction of new products, services, and customer interaction patterns challenges the underlying infrastructure of ML systems deployed in such environments. As illustrated in Fig. 7.1, use cases such as YooChoose, RetailRocket, and Breinify demonstrate a substantial weekly influx of new touchpoints such as products or visited URLs. This phenomenon exemplifies the real-world dynamism that any robust e-commerce system must accommodate.

A foundational component of the proposed UCR are embeddings, which encode discrete inputs in continuous vector representations as already highlighted in Chap. 2. However, conventional embedding strategies as the proposed UCR embedding are inherently static: once trained, these representations remain fixed in dimensionality and content, requiring full retraining to integrate new tokens or data distri-

M. Alves Gomes, *Utilizing Embeddings to Learn a Universal Customer Behavior Representation in E-Commerce*, https://doi.org/10.1007/978-3-658-50781-7_7

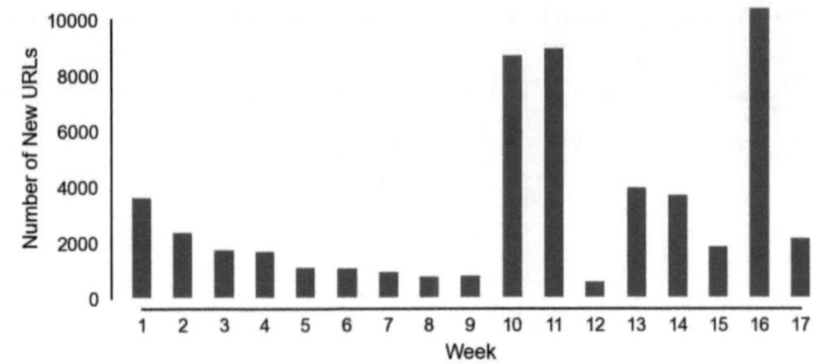

(a) Number of new URLs introduced weekly in the Breinify dataset.

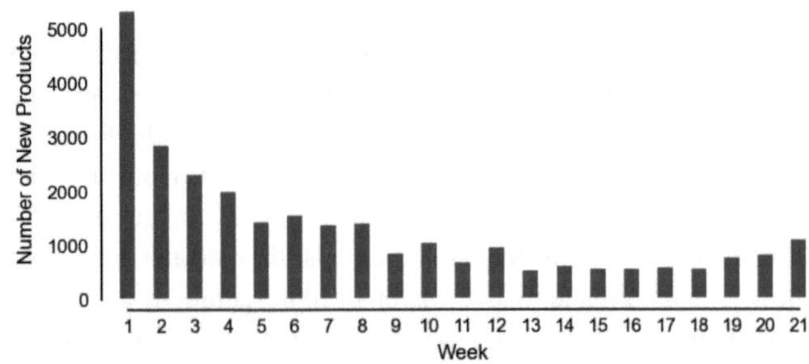

(b) Number of new products introduced weekly in the YooChoose dataset.

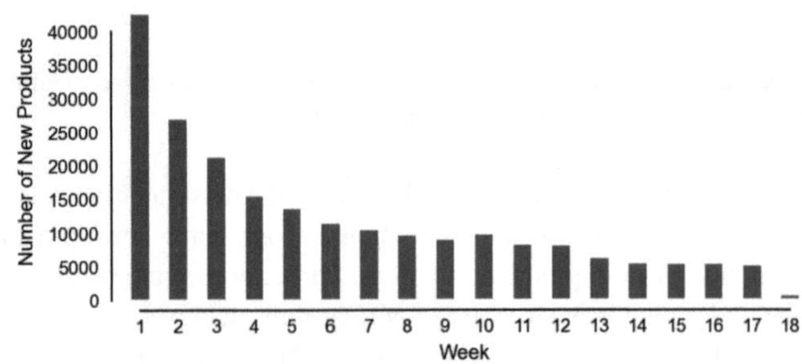

(c) Number of new products introduced weekly in the RetailRocket dataset.

Fig. 7.1 Number of new touchpoints introduced weekly in the YooChoose, RetailRocket, and Breinify datasets

butions. This inflexibility results in substantial inefficiencies and scalability issues, especially in contexts where change is the norm rather than the exception. Moreover, due to regulatory requirements such as the GDPR (cf. Sect. 4.2), which mandate the minimization and timely deletion of personal or behavioral data, historical interaction records cannot always be retained indefinitely. Consequently, any practical embedding mechanism must remain effective even when long-term historical data is unavailable, thereby necessitating strategies that preserve essential knowledge without relying on persistent access to raw historical data.

This dynamic setting places three critical demands on the UCR embedding and any other embedding mechanism used in e-commerce:

- **Extendability**: The embedding model must support the seamless integration of new items, such as products, customers, or interaction types, without necessitating retraining from scratch, which is computationally expensive at industrial scale.
- **Knowledge Retention**: Previously acquired representations must be retained and reused, thereby mitigating the risk of catastrophic forgetting commonly observed in sequential training scenarios, while complying with data minimization requirements that may prohibit the reuse of historical raw data.
- **Compactness**: The embedding space must accommodate growth or reduction in vocabulary size and dimensionality, maintaining a balance between representational capacity and computational efficiency.

Conventional static embedding approaches are fundamentally limited in this context. When retrained or updated, they are prone to knowledge degradation and lack mechanisms for generalization across continuously evolving item catalogs and customer behavior patterns. To overcome these limitations, a novel incremental embedding approach, referred to as LLE is proposed in this chapter. The LLE approach is designed to meet the aforementioned criteria by integrating incremental algorithms and Continual Learning (CL) principles into the core of representation learning for e-commerce applications.

The remainder of this chapter is structured as follows: First in Sect. 7.1, foundational concepts and methodologies from the field of CL are introduced. Subsequently, in Sect. 7.2 a literature review on dynamic embedding approaches is conducted and their limitations are discussed. Sect. 7.3 presents the technical details of the proposed LLE approach. Then in Sect. 7.4, the experimental setup is described, followed by Sect. 7.5, which details the experimental results and their implications.

7.1 Foundations of Continual Learning

In order to build self-supervised customer embeddings that remain useful and reliable over time, it is essential to first understand the fundamental principles of how ML models can adapt to continuous streams of new data without losing previously acquired knowledge. This section therefore introduces the core ideas, mechanisms, and practical design considerations of CL as a necessary conceptual basis for developing an adaptive UCR that can withstand the dynamics of real-world e-commerce environments.

CL, also referred to as lifelong learning, has emerged as a critical paradigm in ML, aiming to enable models to accumulate knowledge over time without succumbing to catastrophic forgetting. This phenomenon, whereby previously acquired knowledge is lost when new information is learned represents one of the principal challenges in learning from time-evolving information. It arises due to the parameter updating nature of learning models, which, when trained on unseen data and not constrained, tends to overwrite earlier learned representations during the assimilation of new tasks or data distributions [92].

In e-commerce scenarios, particularly those involving customer behavior modeling, this issue is magnified by the rapidly changing data landscape, wherein new products, services, and customer preferences are introduced continuously as previously highlighted. Prapas et al. [186] state, that static models, which require retraining from scratch upon data shifts, have been shown to be inefficient and inflexible in such dynamic environments. Thus, CL offers a pathway to model adaptation by retaining stability in prior knowledge.

A central challenge in CL lies in managing the trade-off between plasticity and stability [159]. Plasticity refers to a model's capacity to integrate and adapt to new information, allowing it to generalize to novel tasks or data distributions. In contrast, stability denotes the ability to preserve knowledge acquired from previous tasks, safeguarding it from being overwritten by subsequent learning episodes. An effective CL system must achieve an optimal balance between these two opposing forces: excessive plasticity can lead to catastrophic forgetting, while excessive stability can hinder the learning of new information.

The interplay between plasticity and stability has been recognized as a fundamental aspect of CL methods. Therefore, multiple CL approaches have been developed to address the challenge of catastrophic forgetting and maintaining new information. De Lange et al. [55] provide a comprehensive overview of CL techniques, categorizing them into three main types: regularization-based methods, replay methods, and parameter isolation methods. Regularization-based methods constrain the learning process to preserve important parameters from previous tasks, while replay methods store and replay past data to maintain performance on earlier tasks. Parameter isolation methods modify the model structure to accommodate new tasks without interfering with previously learned representations by introducing new parameters or modules and freezing existing ones to mitigate forgetting.

In the context of this work, regularization-based CL methods have been favored over replay-based methods and parameter isolation methods due to both practical and architectural considerations specific to real-world e-commerce systems. Replay methods rely on storing and accessing past data samples or regenerating them during training. While effective in preserving prior knowledge, such strategies raise significant scalability and privacy concerns, particularly in industrial settings where data storage is restricted by regulatory or infrastructural constraints as it is part of the use case in this thesis. Moreover, the growing volume of e-commerce interactions exacerbates the memory footprint, making long-term deployment infeasible without extensive resource allocation. Parameter isolation methods do not align well with the goals of the proposed UCR, which require generalizable, shared feature spaces across tasks. In dynamic e-commerce environments, where data distributions evolve continuously and unpredictably, such approaches are impractical. The rigid separation of knowledge can hinder the adaptability and relevance of learned representations, making it challenging to respond effectively to rapidly shifting customer behavior and market trends.

In contrast, regularization-based methods, such as Elastic Weight Consolidation (EWC) [128], Memory Aware Synapses (MAS) [4], and Learning without Forgetting (LwF) [143], operate without retaining raw data, instead constraining parameter updates based on their estimated importance. These methods introduce minimal architectural overhead and offer compatibility with embeddings, where the goal is to maintain representational integrity. Given these advantages, regularization-based approaches are identified as a more suitable choice for dynamic, privacy-sensitive, and resource-constrained customer modeling environments, where continual adaptation must be achieved without sacrificing scalability or compliance.

Kirkpatrick et al. [128] proposed EWC to address catastrophic forgetting by estimating the importance of neural network parameters for prior tasks using the Fisher Information Matrix. The Fisher Information Matrix quantifies the sensitivity of the model's output to changes in its parameters, providing a measure of how critical each parameter is for maintaining performance on previously learned tasks. By penalizing deviations from previously learned parameter values, EWC effectively anchors important parameters while allowing less critical ones to adapt to new tasks. The underlying assumption is that parameters with high Fisher information are more critical for maintaining performance on previously learned tasks. The Fisher Information Matrix is calculated at the conclusion of each task, approximating the curvature of the log-likelihood loss landscape and thus identifying parameters that significantly affect the model's output. Formally, for each trainable parameter θ_i of a learning model, its importance F_i is computed as the diagonal of the Fisher Information Matrix:

$$F_i = \mathbb{E}_{(x,y)\sim\mathcal{D}}\left[\left(\frac{\partial \log p(y|x;\boldsymbol{\theta})}{\partial\theta_i}\right)^2\right], \tag{7.1}$$

where $\mathbb{E}_{(x,y)\sim\mathcal{D}}$ is the expectation over the joint distribution of inputs x and labels y in dataset $\mathcal{D}$. The EWC objective function incorporates this parameter importance by penalizing deviations from the previously learned parameter values θ_i^*, resulting in the following regularized loss function:

$$\mathcal{L}_{\text{total}} = \mathcal{L}_{\text{new}} + \frac{\lambda}{2}\sum_i F_i(\theta_i - \theta_i^*)^2. \tag{7.2}$$

Here, $\mathcal{L}_{\text{new}}$ represents the loss associated with the current task, and λ is a hyperparameter controlling the impact of the regularization. By anchoring important parameters and allowing unimportant ones to adapt, EWC strikes a balance between plasticity and stability, effectively preventing catastrophic forgetting while enabling CL.

A similar approach called MAS was proposed by Aljundi et al. [4]. MAS is a regularization-based CL method that estimates parameter importance based on the sensitivity of a model's outputs to changes in its weights. Unlike approaches that require labeled data or task boundaries, MAS operates in an unsupervised manner by leveraging the distribution of inputs during training. The importance of each model parameter θ_i is quantified through a sensitivity measure, computed as the expected squared gradient of the model's output function $f(x;\theta)$ with respect to that parameter over the input distribution $\mathcal{D}$:

$$\Omega_i = \mathbb{E}_{x\sim\mathcal{D}}\left[\left\|\frac{\partial f(x;\boldsymbol{\theta})}{\partial\theta_i}\right\|^2\right], \tag{7.3}$$

where, $\mathbb{E}_{x\sim\mathcal{D}}$ is the expecation over the input data distribution $\mathcal{D}$, representing all inputs x encountered during training. After completing a task, the sensitivity scores Ω_i are used to construct a regularization term that penalizes changes to important parameters while training on new data. The total loss function used during subsequent training is defined as:

$$\mathcal{L}_{\text{total}} = \mathcal{L}_{\text{new}} + \frac{\lambda}{2} \sum_i \Omega_i (\theta_i - \theta_i^*)^2, \tag{7.4}$$

where θ_i^* are the parameters optimized on the previous task and λ is a hyperparameter controlling the trade-off between preserving old knowledge and learning new information. By discouraging large updates to critical weights, MAS enables the model to retain previously learned behavior while incorporating new knowledge, thus mitigating catastrophic forgetting in a scalable and data-efficient manner.

While MAS and EWC rely on parameter importance estimates to constrain updates, LwF proposed by Li and Hoiem [143], takes a different approach by leveraging knowledge distillation from previously learned tasks using the trained model as a teacher. Specifically, before learning a new task, the model's predictions for the old tasks are recorded as soft targets. During the training phase on the new task, the model is regularized to reproduce these stored predictions, thus maintaining prior functionality. Let p_c^{old} denote the soft target probability for class c from the previous model and p_c^{new} the current prediction. The distillation loss is then computed using a cross-entropy function:

$$\mathcal{L}_{\text{distill}} = -\sum_c p_c^{\text{old}} \log(p_c^{\text{new}}) \tag{7.5}$$

The final objective function combines this distillation term with the standard classification loss $\mathcal{L}_{\text{new}}$ on the new task, resulting in:

$$\mathcal{L}_{\text{total}} = \mathcal{L}_{\text{new}} + \lambda \mathcal{L}_{\text{distill}}, \tag{7.6}$$

where λ is a hyperparameter that controls the contribution of the distillation loss. By enforcing consistency between the old and new predictions, LwF effectively preserves previously learned knowledge while allowing for adaptation to new tasks. This property makes LwF particularly suitable for deployment in scenarios with privacy constraints, where data reuse is restricted, yet output-level consistency must be maintained.

7.2 Related Work on Incremental Learning Embeddings and its Limitations for E-Commerce

As already highlighted, embeddings cannot encode new tokens into the embedding space, which leads to the problem known as the Out-of-Vocabulary problem, which requires the retraining of the embedding representation. In NLP the Out-of-Vocabulary problem is addressed via fallback mechanisms such as the use of an unknown token [9, 222] or subword-based approaches [149, 189, 204], including byte-pair encoding [237], which have further enhanced the flexibility of embeddings by decomposing rare or novel words into smaller compositional units.

Despite their effectiveness in NLP, these methods exhibit critical limitations when transferred to the e-commerce domain. Unlike natural language, which evolves gradually over extended periods, e-commerce environments are characterized by rapid and continual change. New products are introduced at high frequencies, as already illustrated in Fig. 7.1, leading to an overwhelming prevalence of Out-of-Vocabulary tokens. In such a setting, relying on a static unknown token is ineffective, as it homogenizes representations of inherently diverse entities and thus fails to preserve meaningful distinctions between new products. Similarly, subword decomposition is inapplicable in e-commerce, as touchpoints such as product identifiers are not semantically compositional. New products cannot be inferred or reconstructed from constituent elements of existing products. Consequently, these conventional NLP-inspired fallback mechanisms fail to address the continuous and unbounded expansion of the categorical space in dynamic e-commerce systems.

Beyond these standard fallback methods, more advanced research in NLP has explored dynamic embedding learning to capture gradual semantic changes in language over time. For example, temporal word embeddings proposed by Bamler and Mandt [19] have been designed to model word meanings as time-evolving trajectories using a probabilistic state-space approach. In their approach, semantic drift is captured through a Brownian motion prior and learned via scalable variational inference, allowing smooth transitions in word representations over time. Similarly, Yao et al. [263] introduced a joint optimization strategy that learns time-specific word vectors alongside alignment mappings between time periods, enabling effective tracking of semantic shifts. Rudolph and Blei [200] proposed a dynamic embedding model based on exponential family distributions, where continuity across time slices is enforced to capture gradual linguistic change. Multilingual continual embedding models, such as the one developed by Kozal et al. [129], have also been designed to preserve semantic consistency across tasks in multilingual contexts. Despite these advances in modeling semantic drift in language, such techniques do not directly address the fundamental challenge faced in e-commerce applications, where the primary issue is not gradual semantic shift but the continual introduction of entirely new items and interaction types that cannot be derived from existing semantic structures.

Beyond the NLP domain, dynamic embedding strategies have been increasingly explored through graph-based methodologies. For instance, Daruna et al. [52] investigated several CL approaches for knowledge graph embeddings, addressing the challenges of incorporating new semantic classes and mitigating catastrophic forgetting in an industrial context. Their study introduced methods such as parameter isolation, regularization-based strategies, and generative replay. These approaches incrementally expand the embedding space by adding new parameters for unseen entities and relations while preserving existing ones. In parallel, Zhu et al. [284] applied continual graph embeddings to industrial fault diagnosis, where the embedding space is dynamically partitioned to protect semantically critical subspaces. This allows the system to integrate new fault types incrementally while preserving the consistency and accuracy of existing diagnostic representations. Bielak et al. [26] presented an incremental embedding approach, where each new graph gets its static snapshot embedding. Each embedding snapshot is subsequently aligned with previously learned embeddings. New nodes are integrated through this alignment process and then combined via convex interpolation with past embeddings. Wu et al. [250] developed a dynamic graph, where embeddings are updated by propagating changes through attentive graph convolution layers. New entities and relations are embedded based on their neighborhood context, and catastrophic forgetting is controlled via a gating mechanism that limits abrupt deviations in core representations.

In summary, while dynamic embeddings in NLP have been designed primarily to model semantic drift over time, such approaches are less suitable for the e-commerce domain, where the continual introduction of new products and interactions renders subword-based compositionality and temporal smoothing ineffective, since the abrupt appearance of entirely new items does not follow gradual or predictable temporal trajectories that can be interpolated smoothly from past representations. In contrast, graph-based methods have been identified as a more promising foundation for the development of dynamic embeddings in e-commerce systems. Notably, the concept of parameter isolation, as investigated by Daruna et al. [52], has been shown to support continual expansion of the embedding space without incurring catastrophic forgetting, by allocating dedicated parameters for new entities while preserving previously acquired representations. Additionally, catastrophic forgetting has been effectively mitigated through regularization strategies that stabilize important parameters during incremental updates. However, a critical limitation remains: the compactness of the embedding space has not been adequately addressed by these approaches. Furthermore, based on the research, none of the existing methods have been tested in the context of e-commerce before. Therefore, the proposed LLE approach aims to address these two gaps by introducing an incremental, knowledge-preserving, and compact embedding.

7.3 Lifelong Learning Embeddings Approach

Building on the findings presented in the literature review on dynamic embeddings, the proposed LLE approach translates these insights into a concrete strategy tailored to the operational and regulatory constraints of real-world e-commerce environments. Unlike conventional static embedding approaches, the LLE explicitly addresses the continual influx of new products and touchpoints, the risk of catastrophic forgetting when training solely on newly arriving data, and the requirement to comply with data protection regulations, which prohibit the indefinite storage of historical interaction data.

To operationalize these demands, the concept is formalized through a modular and extensible algorithm (cf. Algorithm 7.1) that structures the learning process into four coordinated components. Each of these components addresses one of the core challenges identified and collectively ensures that the resulting embedding remains adaptable, knowledge-preserving, and computationally sustainable over time.

Algorithm 7.1 LLE approach for incremental customer behavior representation

for each new data iteration **do**
    Incremental embedding update
    Check embedding size
    while embedding is overfitting **do**
        Reduce embedding dimension
    end while
    while loss decreases and no overfitting **do**
        Increase embedding dimension
    end while
    Train embedding with continual learning regularization
    Prune outdated touchpoints
    if outdated touchpoints are found **then**
        Remove outdated touchpoints
    end if
end for

The four components are outlined as follows:

1. **Incremental Embedding Update**: To accommodate the continuous introduction of previously unseen touchpoints, this component enables the embedding matrix to expand dynamically by adding new tokens for novel touchpoints such as products, URLs, or interaction types. This eliminates the need for complete retraining, which would be computationally prohibitive at industrial scale, and ensures that the embedding stays current with the evolving input vocabulary.
2. **Adaptive Embedding Dimensionality**: As the complexity and diversity of touchpoints fluctuate over time, this mechanism adjusts the dimensionality of the embedding space in response to empirical signals such as validation performance and overfitting trends. This ensures that the embedding remains expressive enough to capture new behavioral patterns without introducing redundant capacity that would inflate memory costs unnecessarily.
3. **Continual Learning Algorithms**: Because the deletion of historical raw data prevents the reuse of prior training samples, this component integrates regularization-based CL strategies to preserve the semantic structure of previously learned representations. By constraining parameter updates, the approach mitigates catastrophic forgetting, thereby maintaining consistency and stability in the embedding across sequential training cycles.
4. **Pruning of Outdated Touchpoints**: As the embedding grows over time, obsolete or inactive touchpoints, such as discontinued products or retired URLs, may accumulate. This component identifies and removes semantically irrelevant or unused touchpoints to maintain a compact and relevant embedding space. This pruning step complements the other mechanisms by ensuring long-term scalability and resource efficiency.

In the following, each of these four core components is described in detail, outlining their individual roles and the specific mechanisms by which they address the requirements of dynamic, continual embedding learning in real-world e-commerce contexts.

7.3.1 Incremental Embedding Update

To enable incremental updates in the embedding layer, the underlying architecture must be capable of integrating new instances, e.g., customer touchpoints, without requiring complete retraining. The proposed embedding mechanism within the LLE approach is therefore designed to support structural expandability while maintaining compatibility with downstream models and training workflows.

A conceptual foundation for this design is inspired by parameter isolation methods from the CL domain, as already highlighted previously in Sect. 7.1. However, strict parameter isolation would contradict one of the core functionalities of the proposed UCR embedding: the ability to continuously update and adapt to changes in customer behavior over time. Freezing parameters, as done in isolation-based methods, would hinder the representational plasticity required to reflect evolving customer preferences.

As such, the LLE approach adopts the ability to dynamically grow the parameter space for new instances as usually done by parameter isolation, but deliberately omits the freezing step in this initial stage. The primary objective at this point is not yet to address forgetting, but rather to structurally enable expansion. Strategies for preserving knowledge are introduced in subsequent stages through CL algorithms.

In the proposed UCR embeddings and in conventional DL models, embedding layers are typically implemented as single-layer neural networks that receive one-hot encoded inputs. As already described in Sect. 5.4, embeddings are represented by an embedding function $E(t) \to \mathbb{R}^D$, which maps each discrete touchpoint, here touchpoints $t \in T$ from the set of customer touchpoints to a D-dimensional latent space. The learned parameter matrix $\mathcal{E} \in \mathbb{R}^{|T| \times d}$ encodes these vector representations e_t, with each row j corresponding to a specific touchpoint t_j.

To support incremental updates, the embedding matrix $\mathcal{E}$ must be dynamically extendable. Specifically, given a set of customer touchpoints T_{old} at time τ and its associated embedding matrix $\mathcal{E}_{\text{old}} \in \mathbb{R}^{|T_{\text{old}}| \times D}$, a new matrix $E_{\text{new}} \in \mathbb{R}^{|T_{\text{new}}| \times D}$ is constructed at time $\tau + 1$ such that:

$$\mathcal{E}_{\text{new}}[i] = \begin{cases} \mathcal{E}_{\text{old}}[\pi(i)] & \text{if } t_i \in T_{\text{old}} \\ g(\mathcal{E}_{\text{old}}, t_i) & \text{if } t_i \notin T_{\text{old}} \end{cases} \tag{7.7}$$

where $\pi(i)$ denotes the index mapping from the new to the old touchpoint position, and g is a weight initialization function for newly introduced touchpoints. The initialization function addresses the cold start problem, where newly introduced touchpoints, lacking pretrained representations, would otherwise be initialized randomly, leading to suboptimal performance and poor generalization [144]. The initialization function g mitigates this by generating informed embeddings based on the existing matrix E_{old}, thereby preserving semantic coherence and with the goal of improving downstream task performance.

7.3.2 Adaptive Embedding Dimensionality

As the distribution of customer touchpoints evolves over time, due to factors such as the introduction of new marketing channels, seasonal product changes, or shifts in customer behavior, the representational demands on the embedding space may change accordingly. A fixed embedding dimensionality is often chosen empirically at initialization based on static datasets. However, in dynamic real-world settings, such a static configuration can become suboptimal. This misalignment arises because the expressive capacity of the embedding space must match the underlying semantic complexity of the customer touchpoints it encodes.

When the dimensionality is too low relative to the diversity and granularity of customer interactions, the embedding layer is constrained in its ability to distinguish between semantically dissimilar touchpoints. This results in information bottlenecks, where distinct touchpoints are projected into overlapping regions of the latent space, leading to underfitting and an insufficient customer representation which results in reduced downstream performance. Conversely, when the dimensionality is too high, particularly in the presence of a sparse or contracting set of interaction touchpoints, the embedding is prone to overparameterization. This scenario increases the risk of overfitting to the interaction patterns in the training set. Excess capacity may allow the model to memorize spurious correlations rather than learning robust, generalizable representations. Moreover, from a systems perspective, maintaining an excessively large embedding space becomes memory-inefficient, especially in production environments where latency and scalability are critical.

Therefore, a mechanism that dynamically adjusts the embedding dimensionality is required to balance the trade-off between expressiveness and generalization. By aligning the representational capacity of the embedding with the temporal complexity of the touchpoint distribution, the system can adaptively optimize model performance while preserving computational efficiency. This is particularly relevant in long-running systems where customer behavior and product catalogs are subject to non-stationary shifts.

Similar to the incremental update of the embedding, the methodological foundation of extending embedding dimensionality is also partly inspired by parameter isolation techniques in CL. In the context of the proposed LLE, this principle is adapted to manage representational growth: when additional capacity is required, new dimensions are added to the embedding space. However, in contrast to classical parameter isolation, existing parameters are not frozen, allowing the embedding to remain plastic and capable of continuous refinement. This ensures that the system not only accommodates growth but also preserves adaptability to evolving customer behaviors over time.

Specifically, to adjust the dimensionality D of the embedding matrix $\mathcal{E} \in \mathbb{R}^{|T| \times D}$, overfitting needs to be detected. Therefore, temporal cross-validation is conducted using a held-out validation set. Let $\mathcal{L}_{\text{train}}^{(e)}$ and $\mathcal{L}_{\text{val}}^{(e)}$ denote the training and validation losses, respectively, at epoch e. The divergence between these two quantities signals that the model may be failing to generalize beyond the training data. This is formally expressed using a ratio-based criterion:

$$\frac{\mathcal{L}_{\text{val}}^{(e)}}{\mathcal{L}_{\text{train}}^{(e)}} > \gamma \quad \text{and} \quad \mathcal{L}_{\text{val}}^{(e)} > \mathcal{L}_{\text{val}}^{(e-1)} \tag{7.8}$$

where $\gamma > 1$ is a predefined threshold that reflects acceptable divergence. If this condition holds consistently across multiple epochs, it is interpreted as a signal of overfitting. In response, the embedding dimensionality D is iteratively reduced by a fixed step size Δd, until overfitting is mitigated and the validation loss improves. Formally, for step size Δd, the dimensionality adjustment is defined as:

$$d' = d - \Delta d, \quad \text{until } \mathcal{L}_{\text{val}}^{(e)} \text{ improves and overfitting no longer occurs.} \tag{7.9}$$

Conversely, if there is no sign of overfitting and if the validation loss continues to decrease monotonically and remains tightly coupled to the training loss, it is inferred that the embedding space may be underparameterized. In this case, embedding dimensionality is expanded to improve the model's expressive capacity:

$$d' = d + \Delta d, \quad \text{until } \mathcal{L}_{\text{val}}^{(e)} \text{ no longer improves.} \tag{7.10}$$

This adaptive resizing mechanism aims to minimize model complexity while preserving representational power, thereby upholding the principle of parsimony in model design. When the embedding matrix is extended, previously learned dimensions are preserved to retain past information, and the new dimensions are initialized in a manner that maintains semantic continuity:

$$\mathbf{E}_{\text{extended}}[i][: d] = \mathbf{E}_{\text{old}}[i], \quad \forall i \in \{1, \ldots, |V\}. \tag{7.11}$$

Through this process, the embedding space is continuously re-aligned with the demands of the data distribution. Similar to parameter isolation techniques in CL, which allocate new parameter blocks to accommodate concept drift, this method introduces additional representational capacity only as needed, but without freezing existing parameters. This preserves model plasticity, enabling continued adaptation and fine-tuning in subsequent learning cycles.

However, while this adaptive resizing mechanism enables the embedding space to remain aligned with the evolving complexity of customer interactions, it also introduces specific challenges for knowledge preservation. When the dimensionality is increased, new capacity is added to the embedding matrix, but without careful constraints, this expansion may disrupt the existing latent structure and introduce instability during training. More critically, when the dimensionality is reduced, all information previously encoded in the embedding is irreversibly lost, which can degrade the semantic coherence of the entire embedding. To mitigate these risks, the proposed LLE approach integrates explicit CL strategies that regularize the training process and help preserve essential knowledge even as the embedding structure adapts dynamically.

7.3.3 Embedding Training with Continual Learning

After the embedding input space has been extended to incorporate new customer touchpoints and the embedding dimensionality has been adaptively adjusted to reflect the complexity of the current data distribution, the next step involves training the embedding matrix on the newly observed interaction data. While the previous steps enable structural flexibility, by dynamically adding new rows for unseen touchpoints and modifying the embedding dimension they deliberately avoid freezing previously learned parameters. This design choice preserves representational plasticity, allowing the embedding to continuously adapt to changes in customer behavior. However, this same flexibility introduces the risk of catastrophic forgetting, whereby previously encoded knowledge may be overwritten during training on new data. This issue is particularly critical when the embedding dimensionality has been reduced. In such cases, the embedding matrix $\mathcal{E}_{\text{new}}$ must be reinitialized, and the prior semantic structure embedded in $\mathcal{E}_{\text{old}}$ is no longer implicitly available in the parameterization of the current embedding.

To address this vulnerability of forgetting, the LLE approach integrates explicit CL mechanisms that aim to retain semantic knowledge across time. The idea is that these methods compensate for the absence of parameter freezing by injecting external regularization signals into the training process, thereby aligning the updated embedding with prior knowledge while still enabling the representation to evolve. In this way, the third step in the LLE approach serves a critical stabilizing role which ensures that the embedding retains its accumulated representational semantics, even as it adapts to new data and evolving structural configurations.

Let $E_{\text{old}}(t)$ denote the previously trained embedding function for a touchpoint $t \in T$, and $E_{\text{new}}(t)$ the embedding function under the current trained embedding. To encourage the new embedding to approximate the structure of its predecessor, an alignment loss is introduced:

$$\mathcal{L}_{\text{CL}} = \sum_{x \in \mathcal{D}_t} \ell_{\text{align}}(E_{\text{old}}(t), E_{\text{new}}(t)), \tag{7.12}$$

where ℓ_{align} denotes a vector similarity function, such as the Euclidean distance or cosine similarity, and $\mathcal{D}_t$ represents the distribution of touchpoints observed during training. This approach can be interpreted as a form of representation-level knowledge distillation [101], where the previous model serves as a teacher guiding the reconstruction of previously learned patterns.

Crucially, this strategy is agnostic to the specific CL technique used, allowing flexible integration of additional CL techniques as long as they provide a regularization signal over the embedding representations. The total loss function for embedding training is then defined as:

$$\mathcal{L}_{\text{total}} = \mathcal{L}_{\text{task}} + \lambda_{\text{CL}} \mathcal{L}_{\text{CL}}, \tag{7.13}$$

where $\mathcal{L}_{\text{task}}$ refers to the task loss, which in the case of representation learning is the self-supervised task introduced in Sect. 5.4, and λ_{CL} is a scalar hyperparameter controlling the influence of the CL term.

By preserving previously learned representations during training, this regularization has the goal to ensure that the embedding remains semantically consistent across new data distributions while preserving plasticity to incorporate new information. This balance between stability and adaptability is central to effective lifelong learning, especially in environments where customer behavior evolves gradually but persistently.

7.3.4 Pruning of Outdated Touchpoints

Following the extension of the embedding to accommodate new touchpoints, the adaptation of embedding dimensionality to align with data complexity, and the application of CL techniques to retain past knowledge, a final step is required to maintain long-term efficiency: pruning outdated or inactive instances from the embedding space.

This step is motivated by the inevitable accumulation of obsolete touchpoints, such as discontinued products, deprecated interaction types, or inactive customer events, during the continual integration of new data. While earlier steps in the LLE approach ensure that new touchpoints are incorporated and existing knowledge preserved, they do not impose constraints on the retention of inactive or semantically irrelevant entries. Without targeted pruning, the embedding matrix may grow indefinitely, degrading memory efficiency and increasing the risk of representing semantically meaningless or outdated elements. Moreover, inactive touchpoints may introduce noise into downstream models, particularly if left unregularized across multiple update cycles.

Importantly, this pruning step must follow the CL phase to ensure that any potentially useful historical information has been consolidated. Premature removal of touchpoints before CL-based knowledge alignment would risk losing useful representations that are merely underrepresented in the current training batch. Only after the semantic alignment process has stabilized the embedding, it becomes feasible to identify and remove genuinely obsolete touchpoints.

Formally, let $t \in T$ denote a touchpoint and let $e_t \in \mathbb{R}^D$ be its corresponding embedding vector. Given a representative sample set $\mathcal{S} \subset T$ that contains the known touchpoints, the pruning criterion is defined based on the frequency of occurrence and the semantic relevance of each touchpoint which can be defined by its mean activation across the embedding space:

$$\bar{a} = \frac{1}{|\mathcal{S}|} \sum_{t \in \mathcal{S}} \text{softmax}(e_t), \tag{7.14}$$

where the softmax is applied along the output dimensions. Each entry $\bar{a}_t$ of the resulting vector reflects the average activation strength of the t-th dimension across all input touchpoints. A touchpoint t is considered outdated if its mean activation falls below a predefined threshold κ:

$$\mathcal{I} = t | \bar{a}_t < \kappa, \tag{7.15}$$

with $\mathcal{I}$ denoting the set of indices corresponding to unused or obsolete components of the embedding space. Subsequently, the embedding matrix $\mathcal{E}$ is updated by removing all rows associated with the inactive elements $\mathcal{I}$.

The activation-based pruning mechanism is grounded in the observation that embeddings representing frequently occurring touchpoints tend to produce consistently high activation signals due to the self-supervised learning paradigm. Conversely, touchpoints that are no longer relevant, contribute negligibly to the overall activation distribution across the embedding space over time. By monitoring the average activation strength of each touchpoint, it becomes possible to estimate its practical utility within the current data distribution. This provides a data-driven criterion for systematically identifying and removing inactive touchpoints, thereby maintaining the embedding's semantic relevance and ensuring that model capacity is not wasted on obsolete elements.

This selective pruning strategy ensures that the embedding space remains compact, semantically relevant, and computationally efficient over time. It prevents the unbounded growth of the embedding, reduces memory usage, and avoids representational drift due to stale or irrelevant inputs. As such, this final consolidation phase complements the LLE approach by reinforcing long-term sustainability after adaptability and knowledge preservation have been achieved.

7.4 Experimental Setup

To rigorously evaluate the effectiveness of LLE under realistic incremental learning conditions and therefore answer the third research question, a series of experiments is conducted. The evaluation focuses on both the overall performance of LLE and the individual contributions of its four core components. In particular, these experiments are designed to answer whether and to what extent preserving prior embeddings enhances stability and performance in dynamic settings. Therefore, the datasets introduced in Sect. 4.2 are used to simulate the continual introduction of new products and customer touchpoints, reflecting the real-world challenges faced in e-commerce environments.

For this purpose, the training sets for the Breinify, YooChoose, and RetailRocket use cases are utilized. The same preprocessing steps described in Sect. 5.4.1 are applied to generate customer sessions, touchpoints, purchase labels, and n-grams for embedding training. Notably, the OpenCDP dataset is not included in this experimental stage because the current LLE implementation, which relies on repeated retraining and dynamic adjustment of embedding dimensionality, is not yet feasible for touchpoint vocabularies of this magnitude. The extremely large number of unique touchpoints in OpenCDP would result in excessive training time and memory requirements for each incremental update cycle. This practical limitation, along with potential strategies for extending LLE to very large-scale touchpoint spaces, is discussed in detail in Chap. 9.

To compensate for this exclusion and to validate the LLE approach across varying data dynamics, the RetailRocket dataset is included, as its distinct temporal properties and high variability in newly observed touchpoints provide a valuable test scenario for evaluating adaptability under different distributional shifts. Although RetailRocket is typically used in the literature as a benchmark for churn prediction rather than purchase prediction, it is purposefully included here to examine the transferability of the proposed LLE approach under challenging conditions. Specifically, RetailRocket exhibits substantially lower interaction volume per time window and a significantly higher proportion of newly observed touchpoints compared to YooChoose and Breinify (cf. Fig. 7.2). These properties create more challenging cold-start and representation drift scenarios, providing valuable insight into how well LLE can maintain stable embeddings when confronted with sparse data and frequent vocabulary expansion.

All datasets are temporally partitioned by a fixed timeframe, specifically, weekly increments, to simulate real-world incremental learning scenarios in which models are updated as new data arrives. Weekly slicing strikes a practical balance between granularity and stability by ensuring that each data batch contains sufficient interaction volume for meaningful representation updates, while avoiding the excessive computational overhead associated with overly frequent retraining cycles. Shorter intervals, such as daily updates, may be too sparse or noisy to support robust embedding learning, whereas longer periods can fail to capture timely trends and rapid shifts in dynamic e-commerce environments. In addition, consumer shopping patterns often follow recognizable weekly rhythms, such as weekend activity peaks or payday-driven purchasing behavior, which makes a weekly interval representative of common behavioral fluctuations, as supported by Lo et al. [151].

Due to the temporal partitioning of the datasets into weekly increments, it is essential not only to consider the introduction of new, previously unseen touchpoints as highlighted in Fig. 7.1, but also to examine the overall distribution of interaction volume across time. This context is critical for understanding the learning dynamics of incremental embedding updates. To this end, the proportion of newly observed, previously unseen touchpoints (unknown touchpoints) is measured on a weekly basis for each dataset. Fig. 7.2 illustrates the total number of weekly interactions and the percentage share of unknown touchpoints.

In the Breinify dataset, a steady increase in total touchpoint volume is observed over time, which likely reflects growing customer activity or product assortment. Despite this increase, the proportion of unknown touchpoints remains relatively low, ranging between 1.4% and 4.8%, indicating a stable product catalog and high overlap between weeks. In the YooChoose dataset, the number of weekly touchpoints remains consistently high, while the share of unknown entries fluctuates between approximately 2% and 4%. This suggests moderate system dynamism with high interaction density.

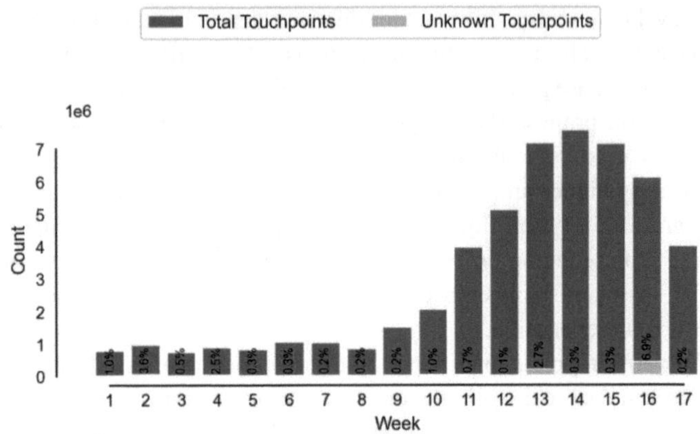

(a) Number of total and unknown touchpoints at each week in Breinify dataset.

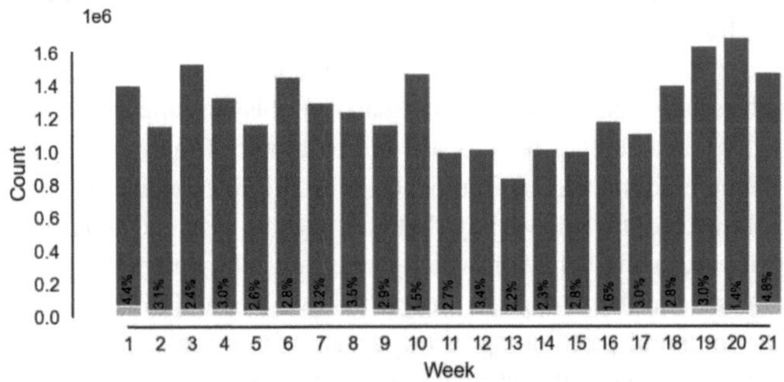

(b) Number of total and unknown touchpoints at each week in YooChoose dataset.

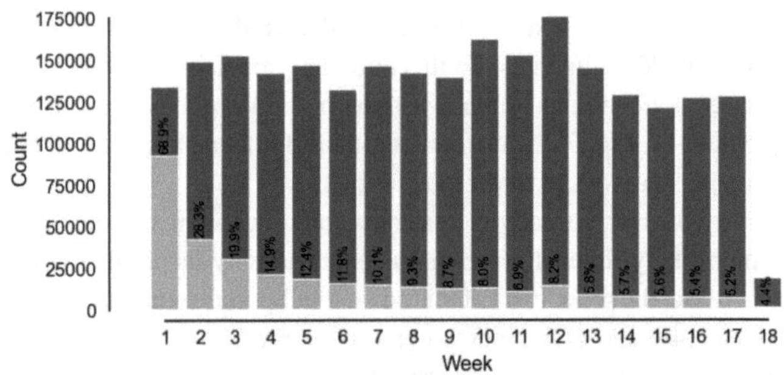

(c) Number of total and unknown touchpoints at each week in RetailRocket dataset.

Fig. 7.2 Number of total and unknown touchpoints per week in the three datasets, YooChoose, RetailRocket, and Breinify

In contrast, the RetailRocket dataset exhibits significantly fewer touchpoints per week but a markedly higher proportion of unknown touchpoints. The initial weeks include up to 69% new touchpoints, and even later stages maintain shares between 5% and 28%, suggesting more volatile item turnover or frequent catalog expansion. These dataset-specific characteristics are considered essential for contextualizing the experimental findings presented later in this chapter. They reflect different levels of temporal volatility and representation drift, and thus impose distinct challenges for embedding models operating under CL constraints.

After data preprocessing, the training process starts. The initial UCR embedding is trained using the first week's data, employing a self-supervised context prediction task based on surrounding touchpoints as described in Chap. 5. Then the embedding is incrementally updated with data from subsequent weeks using the LLE approach. Thereby, the following variables are systematically varied to assess the impact of each component:

- **Initialization Strategy:** None (retraining from scratch), random initialization, unknown-touchpoint reuse, or average-based initialization.
- **Embedding Adaptation:** Dynamic adjustment of embedding dimensionality (enabled vs. disabled).
- **Pruning Strategy:** Pruning of outdated touchpoints (enabled vs. disabled).
- **Continual Learning Regularization:** Presence or absence of regularization-based CL methods. Specifically, the following strategies are evaluated:
  - **None:** This baseline scenario omits any CL mechanism. It reflects a naïve approach where the embedding is updated solely based on the current batch of data. As such, it is expected to suffer from catastrophic forgetting, particularly in scenarios where older touchpoints remain relevant but are not explicitly reinforced during retraining. This baseline provides a reference point for evaluating the benefits of the more sophisticated CL techniques.
  - **EWC** penalizes changes to parameters that are deemed important for previously learned tasks, based on the Fisher information matrix. In the context of embeddings, this means discouraging updates to dimensions that have high context relevance based on earlier data. Kirkpatrick et al. [128] state that, EWC is particularly well-suited when task boundaries are explicit and discrete, e.g., here new touchpoints of new behavior distribution, making it applicable in dynamic environments where new data streams continuously without erasing the past.
  - **MAS** estimates the importance of each parameter based on the sensitivity of the embedding's output, measured without labels. Unlike EWC, which is

task-dependent, MAS offers a label-free alternative, making it suitable for models trained where class labels are sparse or unavailable, which is often the case in session-based customer modeling due to the high variability of customer interactions.

- **LwF** distills knowledge from the previous embedding by enforcing similarity between current and past outputs. This output-level regularization does not require access to prior data but instead compares activations across models, making it ideal for embedding representations. It directly aligns with the semantic stability objective in LLE by maintaining consistent latent representations for touchpoints across time.
- **Combinations:** To explore potential synergies between different CL mechanisms, combinations of the aforementioned CL techniques are evaluated. Specifically, (EWC, MAS), (EWC, LwF), (MAS, LwF), and (EWC, MAS, LwF). Combining CL techniques can potentially provide complementary protection against forgetting, balancing both structural and functional alignment across learning steps. This is particularly relevant in setups, where the embedding matrix undergoes both dimensional and distributional shifts across time, and no single method may be sufficient to ensure knowledge retention in isolation.

Each experimental configuration is evaluated over weekly data increments. Therefore, at each new data arrival, the following update cycle is executed (cf. Algorithm 7.1):

1. **Touchpoint Integration:** The embedding is extended to incorporate newly observed touchpoints. Several initialization strategies are evaluated, including random initialization, average embedding initialization, unknown-touchpoint reuse, and full reinitialization of the embedding. The choice of these strategies reflects the heterogeneity of customer behavior data. For instance, product IDs often carry categorical information, which would also allow category-based initialization strategies like category average. However, other types of touchpoints, such as URLs are more unique, rendering such strategies less effective. Therefore, to balance generality and simplicity in the experiments, the focus lies on these three most basic and broadly applicable strategies.
2. **Dimensionality Adjustment:** The embedding dimensionality is adaptively resized to avoid underfitting or overfitting, based on the validation loss divergence condition. This ensures that the embedding remains compact and expressive as the touchpoint distribution evolves.

3. **Continual Learning Integration:** The embedding is trained for five epochs on the current week's data using one or more CL techniques. Limiting the number of epochs per update cycle follows best practice in CL, where short, efficient retraining is preferred to maintain scalability and low latency, as stated by De Lange et al. [55]. The focus is placed on regularization-based methods, excluding memory- or rehearsal-based strategies. As aforementioned, this decision is motivated by practical concerns: memory-based approaches such as generative replay [208] require explicit storage of previous data, which is often, as already highlighted, infeasible in commercial environments due to privacy regulations and storage constraints [31, 69].
4. **Task Model Training:** As a final step, an LSTM model is trained using the updated embedding to perform downstream prediction tasks and is then evaluated on interaction data from the subsequent week. This forward-looking evaluation ensures that model performance is measured on previously unseen, temporally disjoint data, thereby preventing feature leakage between training and testing phases. By systematically using the following week's data as the test set, each update iteration replicates realistic deployment conditions in which the learned embeddings must generalize to new customer interactions that were not available at the time of training. This temporal hold-out strategy is essential to guarantee that the predictive performance reflects the true adaptability and robustness of the LLE approach under incremental, real-world data streams.

By analyzing the purchase prediction performance at each stage while testing different combinations, the experiments provide insight into the trade-offs between stability and plasticity in the LLE approach. As aforementioned (cf. Sect. 5.6), purchase prediction is chosen as the primary downstream task because it relies on explicit, observable labels derived directly from transaction events. Performance metrics, including training and validation AUC scores, are logged to assess stability, adaptability, and generalization of the embeddings over time. To isolate the effect of the embedding representation from downstream model complexity, the task model is retrained from scratch at each timestep to avoid residual knowledge transfer. This constraint ensures that changes in performance reflect modifications to the embedding alone. Although CL for the task model would be necessary in practical applications, it is deliberately omitted here to maintain strict experimental control.

7.5 Experimental Results and Discussion

Building on the experimental setup described previously, this section presents and discusses the empirical findings that demonstrate how the proposed LLE approach performs under realistic, incremental learning conditions. By evaluating the LLE across the datasets, the results highlight how well the method handles evolving customer behavior streams and tests its ability to preserve learned representations over time.

7.5.1 Performance Evaluation of Lifelong Learning Embeddings Under Incremental Learning Conditions

Table 7.1 summarizes the top three performing configurations for each dataset. Each row shows a specific combination of three key factors: the initialization strategy used to integrate new touchpoints into the embedding (Strat column), the CL method(s) applied (CL column), and whether dynamic embedding dimensionality adaptation was enabled (Dynamic column). The resulting performance is quantified by the mean AUC score and its standard deviation (std) across all time steps. The final column, Δ Baseline, indicates the average improvement in AUC over the baseline approach that retrains embeddings from scratch without leveraging prior knowledge. This provides a concise comparison of how well different configurations balance stability and adaptability under continual data streams.

The results demonstrate that across all three datasets, all selected LLE configurations outperform the baseline by substantial margins, ranging from 0.073 in YooChoose to 0.092 in RetailRocket, demonstrating that reusing previously learned embeddings meaningfully enhances predictive performance. Notably, while the specific CL techniques and initialization strategies differ across top configurations, the performance margins between them remain minimal. For instance, in the RetailRocket dataset, the difference in mean AUC between the best (0.6767) and third-best (0.6764) configuration is only 0.0003, which is well within the standard deviation range $\tilde{0}.017$. Similar patterns are observed in the other datasets. This indicates that no single strategy universally dominates across settings, and instead, various combinations of CL methods and initialization strategies can achieve comparably strong results when integrated into the LLE approach. Furthermore, configurations that included dynamic embedding dimensionality, used in five out of the nine top entries, appear to offer minor yet consistent improvements in expressiveness, particularly in datasets with larger or evolving touchpoint vocabularies.

Table 7.1 Top three LLE configurations for the conducted experiments for each dataset with their average AUC and standard deviation over all time steps, as well as the average improvement over the baseline approach that retrains embeddings from scratch

Dataset	Component			AUC		
	Strat	CL	Dynamic	Mean	Std	Δ Baseline
Breinify	avg	ewc	True	0.8173	0.0509	0.0863
	avg	mas+lwf	False	0.8164	0.0479	0.0854
	avg	ewc+mas	False	0.8156	0.0525	0.0846
YooChoose	unknown	mas+lwf	True	0.6607	0.0173	0.0730
	random	mas+lwf	True	0.6605	0.0161	0.0728
	random	ewc	True	0.6601	0.0166	0.0723
RetailRocket	avg	ewc+lwf	True	0.6767	0.0168	0.0920
	None	ewc+lwf	False	0.6765	0.0166	0.0918
	random	ewc+mas+lwf	False	0.6764	0.0171	0.0917

Nevertheless, the results indicate that the choice of a particular initialization strategy or CL method exerts limited influence on overall performance. While all LLE variants consistently outperform the non-incremental baseline, no single configuration demonstrates clear superiority across datasets or time steps. This suggests that general performance gains stem less from the specific mechanisms employed and more from the reuse of prior knowledge in dynamic settings. To investigate this further, a weekly analysis of AUC progression is conducted to assess whether different configurations provide systematic advantages under varying data conditions.

Fig. 7.3 illustrates the weekly AUC difference between various LLE approaches and a baseline embedding model retrained from scratch at every time step. Results are shown separately for the YooChoose, RetailRocket, and Breinify datasets. The plot distinguishes three categories of LLE configurations: (1) those combining both incremental initialization and CL techniques (orange), (2) those using only initialization strategies (blue), and (3) those using only CL (green). Shaded bands around each curve represent the variability across runs, reflecting stability over time.

In the YooChoose dataset, where only a modest proportion of touchpoints per week are unknown (typically under 4%) and interaction volume remains consistently high, all LLE variants achieve sustained improvements over the baseline. The combination of CL and incremental initialization yields the most stable results, as evidenced by narrower confidence intervals. This stability likely stems from the

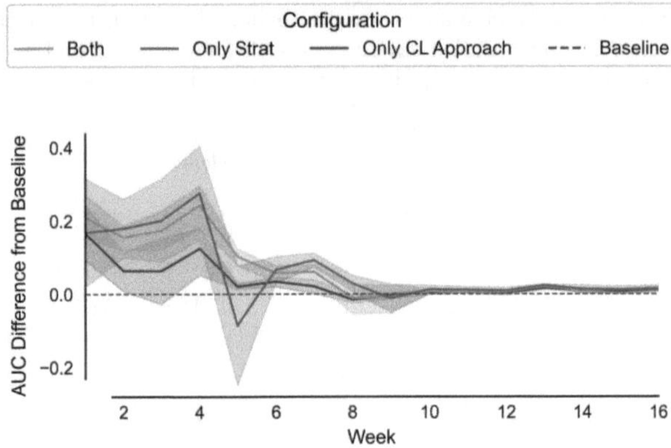

(a) AUC performance differences of different LLE configurations compared to the baseline configuration on the Breinify dataset over 16 weeks.

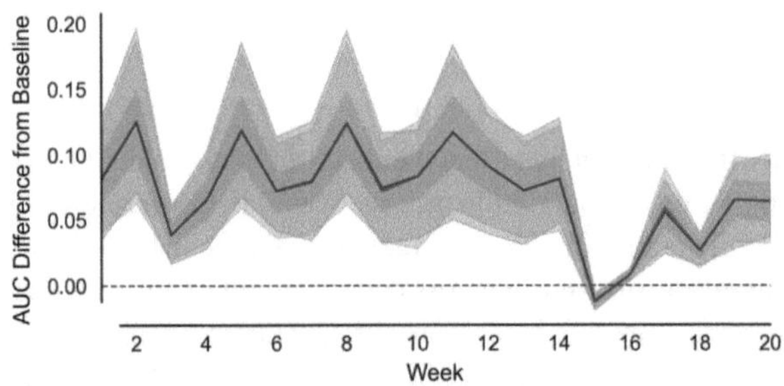

(b) AUC performance differences of different LLE configurations compared to the baseline configuration on the YooChoose dataset over 20 weeks.

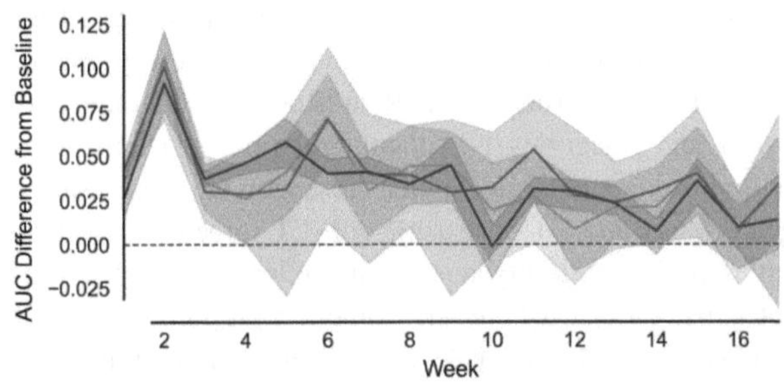

(c) AUC performance differences of different LLE configurations compared to the baseline configuration on the Retailrocket dataset over 17 weeks.

Fig. 7.3 AUC gap differences between the LLE configurations and the baseline embedding retrained from scratch for the three datasets, YooChoose, RetailRocket, and Breinify

balanced effect of incremental strategies, providing quick adaptation to new touchpoints, and CL methods preserving previously acquired semantic structures.

Similar is observed from the results on the Breinify dataset, where the combination of incremental strategies and CL techniques yields the most stable performance. Additionally, although it also contains a moderate number of unknown touchpoints per week (1% on average), the volume of total interactions increases substantially over time, especially starting with week ten (cf. Fig. 7.2a). Notably, from week eight onward, all strategies converge in performance. This convergence aligns with a data-rich regime, where the need for prior knowledge decreases, and the embedding model can rely on the most recent training signals alone. The diminishing gap between approaches indicates that when sufficiently high-quality interaction data is available, CL and initialization strategies provide diminishing returns.

In contrast, the RetailRocket dataset exhibits a somewhat different behavior. While all LLE variants maintain a performance advantage over the baseline, the CL-only configurations (green line) achieve comparably lower AUC scores, but also have the least performance fluctuation across time steps. This stability is particularly notable given the characteristics of the dataset: RetailRocket consistently introduces a high proportion of unknown touchpoints, on average around 13% per week, while also exhibiting significantly lower overall interaction volume compared to Breinify and YooChoose. These conditions appear to favor CL methods, which rely on previously acquired semantic structures to stabilize learning when new data is sparse.

The hypothesis is that the higher share of unknown touchpoints, coupled with fewer touchpoints per week, enables CL techniques such as EWC, MAS, or LwF to effectively preserve and extend existing embedding knowledge. By constraining drastic shifts in embedding space, CL methods help maintain consistency and allow newly observed touchpoints to be integrated more robustly using historical context. This mechanism reduces variance and improves reliability in performance, particularly important in low-resource settings where initialization alone may lack sufficient data support. Consequently, the use of CL alone appears especially well-suited to the dynamics of RetailRocket, offering a stable and generalizable solution in environments characterized by high touchpoint turnover and limited weekly context.

7.5.2 Evaluation of Dynamic Embedding Dimensionality

Besides the incremental strategies and CL methods, the impact of dynamic embedding dimensionality is also evaluated. Performance-wise, there is no indication that the dynamic adjustment of embedding dimensionality significantly improves the overall performance of the LLE approach. However, it helps to maintain a compact and efficient embedding space, which is particularly important in production environments where memory and computational resources are limited. Fig. 7.4 illustrates the weekly evolution of the average embedding size produced by the LLE approach for the three datasets. Each line represents the mean embedding dimensionality across configurations with dynamic resizing enabled, while shaded areas indicate variance across runs. The figure visualizes how the embedding capacity is automatically adjusted in response to changing data characteristics during continual training.

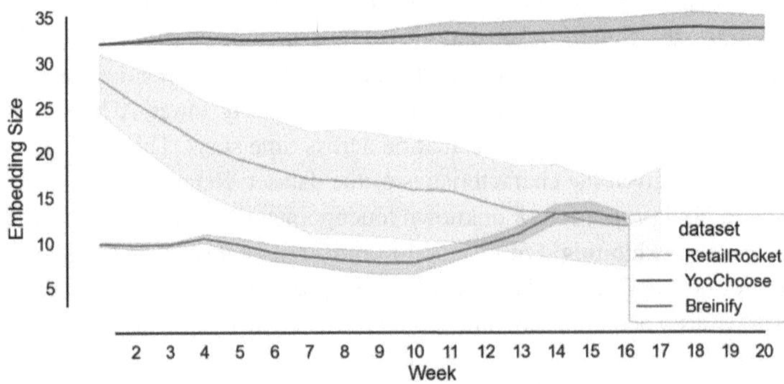

Fig. 7.4 Change in embedding size over time due to dynamic dimensionality adaptation in the LLE approach, as it adapts to evolving data distributions. Average embedding size across all trained configurations are shown for the RetailRocket, YooChoose, and Breinify datasets

In the YooChoose dataset, the embedding size remains consistently high and stable, fluctuating only slightly between 32 and 34 dimensions. This behavior reflects the relatively uniform and high interaction volume per week observed in this dataset, along with a low percentage of new or unknown touchpoints (typically below 4%). The consistently high embedding size indicates that a broad representational space is needed to maintain fine-grained distinctions in a diverse but stable touchpoint vocabulary. The steady growth across weeks corresponds to a continuous influx of new touchpoints in small quantities, with the dimensionality adapting gradually. This stability in the embedding size correlates with the observed stable performance when both CL and incremental strategies are applied, as discussed previously.

In contrast, RetailRocket exhibits a markedly different pattern. The average embedding size begins at approximately 28 in the first week and steadily decreases to about 13 by week 17. This trend reflects an initial overprovisioning of capacity, caused by the high initial touchpoint vocabulary and the elevated proportion of unknown touchpoints during early stages (up to 19%). As the embedding model gains a better understanding of touchpoint relevance and distribution over time, dimensionality is compressed, converging toward a more efficient representation. The limited number of weekly interactions compared to YooChoose reduces the diversity of touchpoint co-occurrences, resulting in a lower effective dimensionality need. The downward trend also aligns with the dataset's limited input variability over time, once key patterns are learned, fewer dimensions suffice to encode meaningful distinctions. This stable compression likely supports the stronger performance of CL-only configurations on RetailRocket, as regularization becomes more effective when the representational space is fixed and less prone to fluctuation.

The Breinify dataset exhibits the most dynamic behavior. Initially, embeddings are compact at around nine dimensions, then decrease further until week ten before undergoing a sharp expansion, reaching a peak of 15 dimensions by week 15. This inflection point closely mirrors the increase in total touchpoints and the surge in unknown touchpoints seen previously in Fig. 7.2. The adaptive dimensional growth ensures that the model can accommodate the surge in data complexity as new touchpoints and customer interactions are introduced in large quantities. This flexibility is critical for maintaining representation quality in high-velocity settings where touchpoint variety and customer behavior patterns shift rapidly. The ability of LLE to expand the embedding space when needed, rather than adhering to a static structure, is particularly beneficial in industrial contexts where data evolution can be abrupt, such as during seasonal campaigns, promotional bursts, or sudden product line expansions. This behavior demonstrates that the dimensionality adaptation mechanism is sensitive to both touchpoint influx and the semantic diversity embedded in new interactions, dynamically scaling model capacity to align with the increased representational demand. Moreover, the fact that the embedding dimensionality begins to stabilize again after week 16 suggests that the model is able to find a new representational equilibrium once enough training signals from the new touchpoint distribution have been absorbed. This indicates that the dimensionality control mechanism does not simply grow without bound but responds to empirical signals such as overfitting or underfitting risks in a data-driven manner. In practice, this self-regulating capacity is vital for balancing expressiveness and efficiency. It ensures that the embedding space remains sufficiently large to encode new semantic nuances without introducing unnecessary parameters that could lead to overfitting or waste memory resources. Together, these dynamics validate the effectiveness of the LLE's dimensionality adaptation principle as a key pillar for robust, incremental representation learning in real-world, rapidly evolving e-commerce systems.

Based on these results, it can be assumed that embedding representations with adaptive dimensionality is more capable of maintaining high semantic resolution under volatile or expanding touchpoint distributions, as seen in the Breinify scenario. In contrast, static or overprovisioned embedding spaces, as observed in RetailRocket, tend to shrink when data sparsity or stable touchpoint sets make excess capacity redundant, highlighting the risk of overfitting when dimensionality is not matched to actual input complexity. This supports the general assumption that dynamic dimension control improves representational compactness without sacrificing the model's ability to distinguish semantically diverse touchpoints over time.

In summary, the figure highlights one of the core strengths of the LLE approach: dynamic embedding adaptation. When interaction volume and touchpoint diversity remain steady (as in YooChoose), dimensionality can be kept stable. In more constrained or lower-volume settings like RetailRocket, dimensional compression is beneficial and reflects the efficiency of representational learning. In contrast, for datasets characterized by bursts of new interactions and structural change (like Breinify), the ability to expand embedding size allows the model to absorb complexity without sacrificing expressiveness. This adaptability enables LLE to balance efficiency with capacity, offering a robust mechanism to support evolving touchpoint landscapes in real-world e-commerce environments.

7.5.3 Evaluation of Pruning of Outdated Touchpoints

Another component of the LLE approach is the optional pruning of outdated touchpoints, which is executed after the CL phase and is intended to remove semantically inactive or obsolete elements from the embedding space. In practice, however, this mechanism was not activated during any of the experimental runs. As outlined earlier, pruning decisions are based on touchpoint activation statistics: a touchpoint is considered for removal only if its usage frequency falls below a defined threshold. This threshold is systematically tuned during initial experiments, yet it consistently produces one of two extremes. In some configurations, the threshold is set too aggressively, leading to the removal of nearly all touchpoints, risking the loss of valid information, while in other settings, no touchpoints are removed at all. To avoid inadvertently discarding potentially useful knowledge, the final configuration ensures that any touchpoint activated at least once is preserved. Under this conservative setting, no touchpoints are pruned during the entire experimental period.

Despite the fact that the pruning mechanism did not remove any touchpoints during this limited experimental period, it remains an integral component of the LLE approach because it addresses a practical scenario that inevitably arises in real-world production systems operating over longer time horizons. For example, in e-commerce, entire product lines may be discontinued, promotional URLs may expire, or seasonal interaction types may no longer appear in customer sessions. In such cases, the associated touchpoints become permanently inactive and unnecessarily occupy rows in the embedding matrix, increasing the memory footprint without contributing semantic value. The pruning mechanism provides a structured way to remove these obsolete rows, complementing the adaptive dimensionality control that adjusts the number of columns. Together, these two mechanisms ensure that the embedding space remains both dimensionally compact and semantically relevant. This design choice is critically examined in Chap. 9, where the limitations of the current threshold setting and strategies for more robust touchpoint lifecycle management are discussed in detail.

This also underscores that while the pruning component is critical for managing touchpoint lifecycle in extended real-world deployments, its absence in the experimental results is primarily explained by two interrelated factors. First, the temporal scope of the experimental design spanned only several weeks. Within such a relatively short window, most touchpoints introduced in early iterations continued to appear in subsequent data slices, confirming their behavioral relevance. Second, the touchpoint vocabularies in all evaluated datasets, whether representing product views, page visits, or interaction categories, were inherently semantically dense and stable. Many touchpoints, such as high-traffic URLs, persistent products, or category pages, retain functional relevance for extended periods in production contexts. As a result, the pruning criterion did not find sufficient evidence to classify any touchpoints as obsolete in the short term. Furthermore, although this outcome means that the influence of pruning on predictive performance cannot be validated directly within this study, this is not unexpected given the limited timeframe and the continued relevance of nearly all touchpoints under these conditions.

To further investigate the practical feasibility of the pruning mechanism under conditions that approximate longer operational horizons, an additional controlled simulation is performed. Specifically, one commonly occurring touchpoint was deliberately removed from the incoming touchpoint stream to emulate a real-world scenario in which a product, URL, or category becomes obsolete. The system was then allowed to continue incremental training and after approximately 150 embedding training epochs, the activation-based relevance score would decay below the pruning threshold. This test demonstrated that it is indeed technically possible for the pruning strategy to identify and remove truly inactive touchpoints.

Therefore, although pruning showed limited operational relevance within the bounded experimental timeframe, its role remains highly significant for sustainable, large-scale, long-term usage.

In summary, the experimental results validate that LLE remains stable and robust even without pruning over short increments, but they also imply that without a more nuanced, adaptive pruning mechanism, the long-term scalability and maintenance efficiency of the embedding space could be constrained. Consequently, this opens a clear path for future research into smarter touchpoint lifecycle management strategies that preserve semantic integrity while ensuring that the representation space remains compact and computationally efficient over extended deployments.

7.6 Summary and Contribution

This chapter demonstrates that self-supervised customer behavior embeddings can be improved to adapt to the dynamics of real-world e-commerce applications by extending the proposed UCR embedding approach with lifelong learning capabilities through the introduction of LLE. This enhancement enables static representations to be incrementally updated over time to accommodate the continuous arrival of new products, services, and behavioral signals typically encountered in dynamic, production-scale environments. Based on these findings, the third research question can be positively answered.

LLE is a modular and extensible learning approach based on four core components:

1. incremental touchpoint integration for new touchpoints
2. adaptive resizing of embedding dimensionality
3. regularization-based CL to preserve prior knowledge
4. and optional pruning of outdated touchpoints

This extension builds directly upon the foundations of the previously proposed UCR, which demonstrated that semantically rich customer behavior can be effectively represented through self-supervised embeddings trained on arbitrary touchpoints. While the original UCR approach provides task-agnostic, privacy-preserving, and low-latency representations, it remains limited to static data snapshots. The LLE approach addresses this limitation by enabling the continuous integration of new touchpoints and evolving behavior patterns, without retraining from scratch, thus making the UCR architecture applicable under the dynamic constraints of real-world e-commerce systems.

To validate the proposed method, comprehensive experiments are conducted across three datasets, each simulating weekly data arrivals. A range of LLE configurations is evaluated, varying initialization strategies, CL methods, and dimensional adaptation mechanisms. Performance is assessed using a downstream purchase prediction task and measured by AUC scores relative to non-incremental baselines.

The results demonstrate that all LLE variants consistently outperform the static retraining baseline, highlighting the value of preserving and extending previously learned representations. While no single combination of CL strategy and initialization method emerged as universally superior, the reuse of prior embedding knowledge is identified as the primary contributor to performance gains. Additionally, it is shown that adaptive control over embedding dimensionality enables compact yet expressive representations, with behavior differing across datasets based on interaction volume and touchpoint novelty.

Further, the LLE approach is shown to support robust performance across varying data regimes: in high-volume, low-volatility environments such as YooChoose and Breinify, embedding updates stabilized over time; in contrast, in the low-interaction, high-turnover RetailRocket dataset, CL techniques yielded greater performance stability. Although the pruning module is not activated during the evaluation period due to the ongoing relevance of all touchpoints, its inclusion ensures long-term scalability under extended deployment scenarios.

Taken together, these findings demonstrate that the proposed LLE approach equips the original UCR representation with the core properties required for CL in production-grade e-commerce systems: adaptability to evolving touchpoint spaces, retention of past knowledge, and dynamic complexity control, all while ensuring semantic stability and operational scalability.

8 Beyond E-Commerce: Generalizing Self-Supervised Behavior Embedding Representation

The empirical findings presented in the preceding chapters demonstrated that customer behavior in e-commerce can be effectively captured using a self-supervised learning approach that constructs a UCR from interaction data alone. The proposed UCR embeddings have been shown to be effective across diverse prediction tasks, including purchase prediction, churn estimation, and CTR forecasting, when tested on different datasets. Furthermore, the approach satisfied critical operational requirements, such as low inference latency, adaptability to heterogeneous data sources, and robustness under dynamic conditions. These outcomes establish a strong empirical basis for investigating whether such embeddings may also be transferred to domains beyond e-commerce.

This chapter explores the open research question

> **Can the proposed three-stage approach using self-supervised learning embedding representation be used on other application domains outside of e-commerce?**

Specifically, it investigates whether self-supervised embeddings, as developed for e-commerce applications, can be extended and applied to other domains characterized by sequential event-based behavioral data. Many real-world systems, such as those found in healthcare, education, finance, mobility, cybersecurity, wildlife, and digital communication, generate rich behavioral data streams that exhibit structural similarities to the interaction logs seen in e-commerce. These include time-ordered sequences of user actions, visits, events, or observations that reflect underlying behavioral processes.

To establish whether and how the approach can be generalized, three core sub-questions are formulated and addressed sequentially:

M. Alves Gomes, *Utilizing Embeddings to Learn a Universal Customer Behavior Representation in E-Commerce*, https://doi.org/10.1007/978-3-658-50781-7_8

1. **Abstracting the E-Commerce Use Case for General Behavior Prediction:** Which core properties of the e-commerce scenario enable effective behavior prediction, and can these properties be generalized to define requirements for behavior prediction in other domains? This subquestion is necessary because any transfer of the proposed approach must begin with a clear understanding of the domain characteristics that make behavior learnable from raw interaction data. Without an abstracted model of the original use case, aligned with the formalized data model, it cannot be ensured that the fundamental assumptions, such as the availability of sequential symbolic events, contextual dependencies, and repeatable behavioral patterns, are satisfied elsewhere. By formally describing these conditions, transferable design requirements can be derived that guide the selection of suitable target domains.
2. **General Properties of the Three-Stage Approach and UCR Embeddings:** Which structural elements of the proposed three-stage approach and the resulting UCR embeddings can be transferred beyond e-commerce, and under which methodological constraints are these elements valid? This subquestion is essential because transferability depends not only on the nature of the data but also on the methodological generality of the representation learning pipeline itself. The three-stage architecture, which decouples behavior observation, representation learning, and downstream prediction, must be examined to identify which components are intrinsically independent of e-commerce specifics but also identify method-specific assumptions to avoid overgeneralization. By formalizing the approach as a modular, reusable design, its core mechanisms, such as the distributional learning assumption, context windowing, and embedding aggregation, can be tested for compatibility with new behavioral domains.
3. **Transfer Realization:** Under what conditions can a transfer be practically realized, and what constraints or adaptations must be considered when applying the approach to other non-e-commerce use cases? This subquestion addresses the operational feasibility of the transfer. Even if a target domain shares the required structural properties and the approach is theoretically domain-agnostic, practical constraints may arise. These may include domain-specific challenges such as data sparsity, rare event distributions, temporal irregularities, or regulatory constraints not accounted for in the original assumptions, all of which may influence the design and operationalization of the approach. By identifying such constraints and possible adaptations in advance, informed guidelines for implementing and validating the approach in other domains can be derived. This step ensures that the transfer is not only theoretically grounded but also technically achievable in practice.

To answer these subquestions systematically, this chapter is structured as follows. In Sect. 8.1, the essential properties of the original e-commerce use case are formalized, and an abstract model for general behavior prediction is derived. In Sect. 8.2, the general structural elements of the three-stage approach and the properties of the resulting UCR embeddings are analysed. Based on this analysis, generalisable requirements and constraints are formulated. In Sect. 8.3, these insights are synthesized into a conceptual framework for cross-domain transfer, including the necessary boundary conditions. Sect. 8.4 identifies and discusses related application domains in which a transfer of the proposed approach may be feasible, drawing on published studies and empirical precedents.

8.1 Abstracting the E-Commerce Use Case for General Behavior Prediction

A fundamental aspect of the e-commerce use case in this thesis is the sequential structure of the customer interaction data, where each touchpoint preserves its relative order and contextual dependency within the customer journey. This sequential structure has been shown to be essential for uncovering latent intent and behavioral patterns, as evidenced by empirical results in this thesis (cf. Sect. 5.6) and other related work (cf. Chap. 3).

Another defining feature is the symbolic discreteness of interaction events. Each customer action, such as a page view, product click, or search query, has been mapped to a finite, domain-specific vocabulary of symbolic identifiers. This abstraction mirrors the tokenization step in NLP, where the Skip-Gram objective relies on co-occurrence patterns among discrete symbols to learn semantically meaningful embeddings [161]. The repeatability and contextual reuse of these symbols make the distributional hypothesis applicable in this context.

Also, the privacy-preserving minimalism of the employed data model is a possible transferable property. Explicit personal identifiers and static demographic attributes have been deliberately omitted to ensure full compliance with stringent data protection requirements. By relying exclusively on the sequence of observed behavioral interactions, it has been demonstrated that latent intentions, such as purchase likelihood, churn risk, or click engagement probability, can be accurately inferred without access to sensitive personal information. This capability indicates that behavioral signals are sufficient to encode the decision-making patterns of individuals when captured with adequate temporal and contextual detail. This highlights the potential of predicting future behavior and intention using past behavior.

The operational time scale in e-commerce is generally short, with interactions often occurring within minutes. However, this temporal granularity can vary significantly in other domains. For example, patient journeys in healthcare or student learning trajectories in education may span days, months, or even years. This variation does not necessarily invalidate the sequential embedding approach, as long as the temporal ordering of events remains behaviorally meaningful and the learned representations capture stable context-dependent co-occurrence patterns.

An additional essential aspect is the coherence of the behavioral unit. In the e-commerce setting, each sequence captures the actions of a single customer acting independently within a bounded environment of available options, such as products, categories, or navigation elements. In other domains where multiple entities may act together, for example, flocks of animals, coordinated teams, or user collectives, the unit of representation must still preserve behavioral coherence. This means that the sequential signal must reflect the actions of either a single behavioral entity or a clearly defined group whose members share a unified behavioral intention. Without this coherence, the learned representation cannot reliably encode latent intent or enable meaningful prediction based on the symbolic sequence.

Bringing these observations together, the general characteristics that must be satisfied by a domain to support the transfer of self-supervised behavior embeddings can be formulated as follows:

1. **Event-Based Interaction Stream**: A continuous stream of discrete, observable actions must be produced that reflect behavior. Thereby, each event must be mappable to a finite set of symbolic identifiers that abstract domain-specific actions.
2. **Temporal Attribution**: Each event must carry a timestamp or equivalent temporal marker that enables ordering of the actions within the behavioral sequence.
3. **Sequence Delineation**: Events must be groupable into bounded, coherent sequences that represent logically or temporally connected behavioral episodes.

When these conditions are met, the construction of behavior-only embeddings becomes possible. Therefore, to support the transfer of self-supervised behavior representation learning across domains, a generalized data model is defined that captures the essential structural properties of temporally ordered interaction data. This model abstracts the core components necessary for sequence-based embedding methods, while remaining agnostic to different domains.

Formally, let $\mathcal{D}$ denote a dataset of behavioral interactions observed in a given domain. The dataset $\mathcal{D}$ is composed of N discrete events:

$$\mathcal{D} = \{e_i \mid i = 1, 2, \ldots, N\}$$

Each event e_i is defined as a tuple:

$$e_i = (\text{action}_i, \text{order}_i, \text{sequenceId}_i)$$

where `action` represents the symbolic action drawn from a finite vocabulary $\mathcal{T}$, `order` encodes when the action occurs, e.g., a timestamp, and `sequenceId` denotes a unique identifier assigned to each bounded behavioral episode, ensuring that discrete events are correctly grouped into coherent sequences.

The successful transfer of the proposed self-supervised representation learning approach thus hinges on verifying that these minimal structural properties hold in the target domain. If so, the conditions required for the distributional hypothesis, context-driven co-occurrence modeling, and task-agnostic embedding reuse are satisfied. This abstraction provides the necessary theoretical basis for the methodological generalization explored in the sections that follow.

8.2 General Properties of the Three-Stage Approach and UCR Embeddings

To facilitate a rigorous investigation of transferability, the three-stage approach developed in this thesis is not revisited here as a domain-specific solution for e-commerce alone, but rather is abstracted as a generalizable architectural principle for learning task-agnostic behavioral representations. Accordingly, this section delineates the fundamental properties that render each stage transferable across domains and articulates the theoretical conditions that constrain or enable its applicability beyond the original e-commerce use case.

A central premise of the proposed design is its strict separation of unsupervised learning of latent patterns into embeddings and task-agnostic reuse for diverse predictive goals. This modularization aligns with foundational principles of representation learning which posit that decoupling the representation stage from the downstream task enables the learned features to generalize beyond the training domain [21].

In the first stage, the requirement is that the behavior of an entity can be recorded as a temporally ordered stream of symbolic actions as described in Sect. 8.1.

The second stage's transferability hinges on whether the distributional hypothesis can be assumed in the new domain. The central assumption is that events share contexts that convey latent semantic similarity. Literature shows that it holds for NLP with words in a sentence and in e-commerce for product views in a session. Thus, the Skip-Gram objective (cf. Equation 2.17) is not tied to any NLP or e-commerce setting. It is an instance of a broader contextual co-occurrence maximization principle. The transferability of the Skip-Gram approach depends only on whether the context windows can be constructed meaningfully, and co-occurrences are frequent enough to provide a learning signal. If these hold, the specific neural architecture Skip-Gram may be adapted but the learning principle remains valid.

Finally, the third stage operationalizes the representation as a general-purpose feature space. Its key transfer property is that once learned, the embedding does not encode a task-specific output. Instead, any downstream learning model is left open. For transfer, the only requirement is that the target behavior is predictable from the encoded latent signal.

However, these abstractions highlight that transferability is not guaranteed solely by the existence of the three-stage architecture. It is bounded by several structural and operational conditions that must be satisfied in any target domain. Sufficient symbol set richness must be present to ensure that the domain's symbolic vocabulary is neither too sparse nor dominated by unique or unrepeated events, otherwise, meaningful co-occurrence patterns necessary for distributional learning cannot be established. Furthermore, context reliability must be maintained such that a meaningful contextual window can be defined to capture dependencies among events. In addition, signal stability must be ensured so that the underlying behavioral patterns are sufficiently repeatable and not dominated by random noise, which would otherwise hinder the generalizability of learned embeddings. Only when these boundary conditions are met can the proposed representation learning approach be expected to yield transferable and robust behavior embeddings beyond the original e-commerce scenario.

By clarifying these conditions, the three-stage pipeline can be positioned not as a universal template but as a constrained yet reusable approach for self-supervised behavior representation. This theoretical scaffold ensures that transferability is analyzed systematically and not assumed by superficial analogy.

8.3 Transfer Realization

To realize a transfer several points need to be considered. A first practical consideration is the sufficiency of behavioral signals. Data sparsity and rare event distributions, which are frequently encountered in domains where behavior signals are limited or highly uneven are a concern. For instance, in healthcare or fraud detection scenarios, specific symbolic events (e.g., rare diagnoses, infrequent malicious actions) may appear too infrequently to produce robust co-occurrence patterns. In such cases, the risk arises that the learned embedding space becomes unstable or undertrained for low-frequency tokens. Moreover, overly fine-grained tokenization may lead to vocabularies that are too large to train effectively, while excessive generalization may obscure critical behavioral distinctions. Empirical calibration of symbolic representations, potentially involving domain experts, may therefore be necessary to ensure that the constructed vocabulary is both meaningful and tractable.

A second important consideration is the temporal structure of the interaction data. While e-commerce sessions typically produce dense, short-lived sequences, many alternative domains, such as patient monitoring, wildlife tracking, or educational progress, generate events at irregular or extended intervals. Such temporal heterogeneity can dilute contextual co-occurrence or render fixed-size context windows inadequate. In these settings, adaptive context windowing, temporal decay functions, or explicit time-aware embedding extensions as the proposed TEE (cf. Chap. 6) may be required to capture relevant sequential dependencies without introducing noise.

The practical feasibility of transfer also depends on the availability of reliable sequence delineation mechanisms. While session identifiers are well defined in e-commerce through browsing sessions, such boundaries may be less obvious in domains such as mobility or open-ended user interaction. In these cases, robust heuristics or segmentation algorithms must be devised to partition continuous event streams into analytically useful sequences that reflect coherent behavioral episodes.

Furthermore, operationalization must account for compliance with domain-specific regulatory or ethical requirements, particularly in contexts where behavioral signals may intersect with sensitive attributes. Although the proposed approach is designed to minimize reliance on explicit personal identifiers, additional safeguards may be needed to align with sector-specific standards for data anonymization and usage consent.

By systematically identifying such operational constraints and feasible adaptations, the conditions under which a theoretical transfer becomes technically achievable are clarified. In this way, informed guidelines for extending the proposed approach to novel domains can be established.

In summary, the practical realization of transfer requires that the following conditions are satisfied in any target domain:

- Adequate symbolic event frequency to provide robust co-occurrence signals for representation learning.
- Reliable temporal structure that allows meaningful sequential dependencies to be captured.

- Well-defined symbolic vocabulary granularity that balances semantic expressiveness with statistical tractability.
- Clear sequence delineation to ensure that behavioral episodes are coherent and properly bounded.
- Compliance with regulatory and ethical constraints to safeguard privacy and data integrity.

8.4 Related Behavior-Based Use Cases for Transferability

The feasibility of transferring the proposed self-supervised behavior embedding approach beyond the e-commerce domain is supported by empirical evidence from several fields in which temporally structured interaction data are routinely generated and behavior prediction tasks are of critical operational relevance. In these domains, the structural and methodological requirements outlined in Sects. 8.1 and 8.2 are theoretically examined and discussed.

8.4.1 Healthcare

In the healthcare sector, patient interaction trajectories derived from electronic health records have been utilized to predict outcomes such as medication adherence, disease progression, or unplanned readmissions. Large-scale studies have demonstrated that event logs consisting of diagnostic codes, treatment procedures, and prescription sequences can be mined using unsupervised and ensemble learning models to capture latent disease patterns and patient state transitions [84, 96]. A compelling example is provided by Asare et al. [17], who demonstrated that passive smartphone behavioral data can be leveraged to predict clinical depression levels without relying on traditional surveys or direct self-reporting. By modeling 22 features derived from everyday phone interactions, such as screen time regularity, phone usage entropy, and connectivity patterns, for 629 participants, the authors trained supervised ML models to estimate individual depression scores. This work illustrates that latent mental states can be inferred from unobtrusive, sequential behavioral signals alone, underscoring the practical value of transferring self-supervised embedding strategies to mental health monitoring where explicit personal profiling is impractical or undesired.

However, this example also presents challenges that must be addressed in any practical transfer. For example, the relatively limited participant pool in Asare et al.'s study may restrict the diversity of behavioral patterns captured, raising questions about the generalizability of learned representations across populations. Moreover, event sparsity, temporal irregularity in patient visits, and heterogeneous coding standards can complicate the symbolic standardization needed for robust embedding training. Nonetheless, the structural fit between medical interaction data and the key requirements of symbolic discreteness, sequential context, and privacy preservation makes the healthcare sector a promising candidate for transferring self-supervised behavior embedding approachs. Successfully adapting the approach in this domain will require careful design of context windows, data integration across disparate systems, and evaluation of fairness and bias mitigation to ensure predictive reliability and ethical compliance.

Looking ahead, large-scale public datasets such as the eICU Collaborative Research Database [91, 183, 184] and MIMIC-IV [91, 118, 119] offer a valuable opportunity to empirically validate the theoretical transferability assumptions outlined in this work. Both datasets contain timestamped symbolic interactions, including diagnoses, medications, laboratory events, and procedures, that can be used for sequential modeling and representation learning. While these data may not originate from self-initiated behavior in the strictest sense, they can still reflect meaningful temporal dynamics in care delivery or patient response patterns. Future investigations should systematically assess whether embeddings learned from such structured clinical sequences capture transferable behavioral signals to create a robust patient representation that supports robust downstream prediction, thereby testing the limits and potential of applying behavior-based representation learning in complex medical environments.

8.4.2 Education

In the field of education, sequential student activity data, such as assignment submissions, learning management system interactions, or participation in digital forums, are increasingly used to forecast outcomes like retention risk, dropout probability, or academic performance [57, 157]. These tasks bear structural similarity to customer behavior prediction in e-commerce, just as repeated product views or cart interactions may signal purchase intent, patterns of learning activity can serve as proxies for engagement, persistence, or academic success. A representative example is provided by Zhu et al. [285], who developed an approach to predict final course grades in twelve Massive Open Online Courses. In their work, a diverse set of behavioral features was engineered to capture individual patterns of engagement, including metrics such as the number of submissions, forum interactions, and time spent on course components. To complement these static counts, an entropy-based metric was introduced to quantify fluctuations in learner behavior over time, providing a dynamic signal of engagement consistency. When tested with four different supervised ML models, the inclusion of these behavioral signals significantly improved the prediction of final grades and enabled early identification of at-risk students with greater accuracy than previous benchmarks on the same platform.

This use case is suited for the transfer of the proposed three-stage self-supervised embedding approach because learning activities form temporally ordered, symbolically discrete sequences is possible. Each interaction, such as completing a quiz, posting a comment, or submitting an assignment, represents a clear symbolic event that can be embedded in a latent space. The structure of courses and modules provides an inherent context window, ensuring that sequential co-occurrence of actions can be exploited to model latent learning behaviors. This also allows for the representation learning to capture the distributional patterns of student engagement, based on the assumption that students engaging in similar educational trajectories tend to exhibit similar behavioral sequences. This student learning behavior representation can then be reused for diverse downstream tasks, such as predicting course completion likelihood, identifying at-risk students, or tailoring personalized learning interventions.

Nevertheless, practical challenges must be considered when transferring the approach to real-world educational settings. One limitation is that overly coarse or sparse symbolic representations, for example, encoding only high-level events such as "course completion" without more granular sub-events, may fail to provide sufficient contextual richness for effective self-supervised embedding learning. It is therefore essential to design an adequately detailed activity space, distinguishing between specific learning milestones (e.g., "completed task 1", "viewed lecture 3", "attempted quiz 2") to generate a symbolic vocabulary with meaningful co-occurrence patterns. Another challenge lies in the variability of learning pathways and educational platforms: students often follow non-linear, self-paced trajectories, and interaction data may differ significantly in structure, frequency, or completeness depending on platform design and course format. Moreover, education unfolds over much longer time horizons than typical e-commerce sessions, ranging from weeks to months or even years, which introduces additional complexity in maintaining meaningful temporal dependencies across extended periods. This temporal span must be considered when defining context windows, modeling long-range dependencies, and validating the stability of learned behavior embeddings. Careful attention must therefore be paid to sequence delineation, symbolic standardization, and time-aware modeling to ensure that the resulting representations capture relevant pedagogical dynamics while remaining robust across diverse educational environments.

While the task-agnostic design of the embedding approach enables broad reusability across educational prediction tasks, it may also fail to capture task-specific nuances that are more easily learned in end-to-end supervised pipelines. In such cases, hybrid architectures that fine-tune the embedding layer for domain-specific targets may improve performance without sacrificing generalizability. Furthermore, relying solely on behavioral signals, though aligned with privacy-preserving design principles, may exclude critical contextual factors such as prior educational background or socioeconomic conditions that shape observed behavior and learning outcomes. This omission can pose challenges for fairness, bias detection, and causal interpretability. Future implementations should therefore explore fairness-aware constraints or integrate auxiliary signals in a post-processing step to address potential disparities while maintaining privacy compliance.

Despite these challenges, the structural fit between online learning interaction logs and the sequential, symbolic assumptions of the three-stage approach indicates that education remains a promising application domain for transferring self-supervised behavior embeddings. Enriching the activity design, validating the semantic consistency of symbolic events, and ensuring fair modeling of student diversity are essential adaptations to unlock the full potential of transferable representation learning in this context.

8.4.3 Wildlife

The domain of wildlife monitoring presents a structurally compatible, yet operationally complex, candidate for transferring self-supervised behavior embedding approaches. In this context, sequential behavioral data are typically derived from GPS tracking devices or sensor-based telemetry systems, producing time-stamped movement traces or activity logs for individual animals or animal groups. These data can be discretized into symbolic states, such as habitat zones, movement phases, or behavioral markers (e.g., resting, foraging, traveling), which makes the first stage of the three-stage approach, symbolic behavior observation, in principle feasible.

A representative example is provided by Browning et al. [30], who proposed a method to predict seabird foraging behavior using only GPS-based features. The task was framed as a binary classification problem (diving for food vs. not diving), with inputs such as altitude changes, positional deltas, and "coverage ratio" of GPS fixes, indirect proxies for stationary behavior. Although they achieved promising performance (around 80% accuracy), the approach relied on a secondary sensor (time-depth recorders) to provide training labels. When assessing the transferability of the proposed self-supervised embedding approach, this case illustrates that when continuous sensor signals can be discretized into repeatable symbolic states, for example by segmenting GPS trajectories into location clusters or behavioral phases, then temporally ordered sequences suitable for distributional learning can be constructed. The three-stage approach could, in such settings, leverage symbolic co-occurrence to encode behavioral patterns and enable downstream prediction of latent activity phases.

In contrast, Ahmed et al. [2] examined a different use case: predicting the spread of chronic wasting disease in deer populations. Their model used aggregate spatio-temporal features, such as land cover, past infections, and harvest density, to estimate future outbreaks at the county level. This task highlights a structural misalignment with the proposed three-stage approach. While temporal progression is present, the data do not originate from behavior sequences, but rather from population-level summaries. In such cases, discrete behavioral episodes are not explicitly observed, and the events do not form symbolic trajectories. As a result, the direct application of Skip-Gram-style embedding may be impractical without additional processing steps that reconstruct movement paths or infer interaction networks from raw telemetry or contact data. Thus, while the disease task appears to be a promising application for transfer, it requires careful consideration of how to construct meaningful symbolic sequences from aggregated or population-level data.

Moreover, wildlife movement prediction itself presents a particularly challenging transfer scenario. Unlike customer journeys, animal behavior is heavily influenced by environmental stochasticity (e.g., predation risk, food availability, and human activity), which can alter movement patterns independently of prior behavior. These exogenous factors introduce substantial noise and reduce the effectiveness of sequence-only modeling approaches. Even when symbolic sequences can be constructed, their predictive utility may be undermined if the behavior is more reactive to external triggers than shaped by internal state. Furthermore, the symbolic abstraction process, i.e., discretizing raw movement trajectories or location data into meaningful event tokens, requires substantial domain expertise. Poorly chosen abstractions may obscure meaningful variation or lead to unstable embeddings due to vocabulary sparsity or semantic inconsistency.

Still, the wildlife domain is not without promise. In cases where behavior is structured and repeatable, e.g., nesting, foraging bouts, migration corridors, symbolic co-occurrence can encode context, and therefore, behavior modeling is possible. Furthermore, tasks such as identifying movement anomalies, habitat preference shifts, or social synchronization patterns may benefit from task-agnostic embeddings learned from sequences of discrete actions. Yet successful transfer of the decoupled approach will depend on domain-specific adaptations, including discretization of continuous inputs, appropriate context windows, and careful interpretation of learned embeddings in light of ecological variance. In summary, while the wildlife domain satisfies many formal preconditions for transferring the quality and granularity of available data, combined with high external variability, posing significant challenges. Tasks like fine-grained movement prediction may struggle due to ecological confounders, whereas more structured or population-level behaviors, when well-defined, offer viable opportunities for applying and adapting the UCR methodology.

8.4.4 Other Domains

Besides Healthcare, Education, and Wildlife there are other domains that deal with behavior and predictions based on it. Similar to the e-commerce domain, the financial sector is characterized by interaction logs and transactional sequences, which have been modeled to predict fraudulent activity, assess credit risk, and anticipate default events. Advanced ML methods, including graph-based representations and recurrent architectures, have consistently demonstrated the predictive value of capturing transaction co-occurrence patterns and behavioral anomalies within time-constrained account activity streams [38, 239]. In this context, transaction types or account actions naturally form a finite symbolic vocabulary that repeats across diverse customer populations, satisfying the requirements for the first stage of the three-stage approach. Furthermore, the sequential and contextual nature of financial actions, such as payment sequences or spending routines, creates an opportunity to apply the distributional hypothesis for behavioral embeddings in the second stage, with co-occurrence of actions serving as a latent signal.

In the mobility and transportation domain, spatial-temporal trajectory data derived from GPS logs have been widely applied to model individual movement behavior, forecast traffic flows, and identify anomalous routes [77, 253]. Here, the symbolic tokens correspond to discretized locations, transit modes, or movement phases, all of which naturally form repeatable event streams with clear temporal ordering. This alignment directly supports the first stage of the proposed approach. The embeddings of the second stage can exploit the sequential co-occurrence of location visits and transit transitions, mirroring customer navigation paths in e-commerce. However, the inherently continuous nature of spatial data requires robust symbolic discretization, such as clustering locations into states, to ensure the event space remains tractable yet informative. Moreover, the granularity of symbolic states must balance capturing meaningful movement patterns against the risk of data sparsity if too many unique tokens are defined. If resolved, the learned mobility embeddings can serve as general-purpose inputs for diverse downstream tasks such as congestion forecasting, route optimization, or abnormal route detection in the third stage.

In the field of cybersecurity, system logs, user access traces, and command execution histories represent classic examples of symbolic, time-ordered event sequences [27, 78]. These log streams align closely with the structural assumptions of the three-stage design: symbolic discreteness is inherent in command or log types, sequential ordering is explicit in event timestamps, and context windows can be defined by user sessions or system processes. This makes the first and second stages highly feasible. Embedding models can learn distributional representations of typical versus anomalous command patterns, thereby enabling effective reuse for diverse prediction tasks such as intrusion detection or insider-threat monitoring in the third stage. However, practical constraints include the extreme imbalance between frequent normal activity and rare malicious actions, which may lead to embedding spaces dominated by benign patterns. Consequently, careful adaptation may be required to ensure that subtle anomalies remain distinguishable.

8.5 Summary

This chapter addresses the open research question about the transferability of the proposed three-stage approach and whether UCR embeddings can be transferred as behavior embeddings in other domains. For this investigation, the structural and operational properties of the original e-commerce scenario are first abstracted, showing that the approach depends critically on the existence of symbolic, temporally ordered, and repeatable interaction sequences. It hypothesizes that when such behavioral signals are available, the distributional hypothesis, originally validated in NLP and adapted here for customer journey modeling, can be generalized to encode latent intent across diverse domains.

Through formalizing the data model and three-stage approach the conceptual characteristics for cross-domain transferability are made explicit. This modular separation is feasible only when domains provide a sufficiently rich symbolic vocabulary, stable co-occurrence contexts, and coherent sequences. Furthermore, practical constraints such as data sparsity, class imbalance, event rarity, symbolic granularity, and temporal irregularity must be actively managed to ensure operational feasibility in real-world applications.

A review of literature across healthcare, education, finance, mobility, cybersecurity, and wildlife monitoring confirmed that these structural conditions can be satisfied in practice. In many of these domains, behavior-based prediction tasks still rely heavily on manual feature engineering, despite the availability of rich interaction traces. This highlights a clear opportunity, by adopting the proposed self-supervised embedding approach, such pipelines can shift toward task-agnostic, reusable representations.

Also key limitations are identified, including the challenge of capturing evolving intent over long time spans, the design of context windows for irregular behavior, and the operational demands of symbolic abstraction in highly heterogeneous domains. Addressing these limitations points to concrete directions for future research, such as adaptive temporal modeling, hybrid embedding objectives, and systematic benchmarking against feature-engineered baselines.

In conclusion, the general conditions, empirical evidence, and conceptual refinements presented in this chapter collectively show that the three-stage behavior embedding approach, originally designed for e-commerce targeting, can be transferred to a wide range of domains that share the foundational properties of symbolic, sequential behavior data. By satisfying these structural requirements and addressing domain-specific constraints, self-supervised universal behavior representations can serve as a viable and more general alternative to traditional, manually engineered features in modern behavior prediction pipelines.

9 Critical Reflection and Outlook

Building upon the preceding chapters, in which the design, implementation, and evaluation of the UCR, TEE, and LLE approaches were presented in detail, this chapter provides a critical reflection of their limitations and unresolved challenges, including constraints arising from the experimental design, methodological choices, and aspects of the implementation that could have been strengthened. While the proposed approaches demonstrate that the integration of privacy-awareness into customer representation learning is feasible, it must be acknowledged that alternative architectures and methods offer complementary capabilities in terms of efficiency, robustness, or adaptability. Furthermore, by discussing theoretical, architectural, and experimental shortcomings a more balanced perspective on the generalizability, scalability, and practical feasibility of the contributions is provided.

This chapter is structured to systematically examine the principal components of this thesis by identifying methodological, architectural, and experimental limitations for each. Sect. 9.1 addresses the core assumptions and constraints of the UCR design, with particular emphasis on experimental design, synthetic labeling, and data granularity. Sect. 9.2 critically analyzes the TEE approach, highlighting the trade-offs between temporal expressiveness and computational feasibility. Sect. 9.3 then discusses the LLE approach, focusing on its modularity, dimensionality adaptation, and pruning strategy. The chapter concludes with an outlook that synthesizes these limitations and outlines potential avenues for addressing them in future work.

9.1 Reflection on Universal Customer Representation with Embeddings

The proposed approach demonstrates the ability to produce compact and computationally efficient customer behavior representations within the specific boundaries

M. Alves Gomes, *Utilizing Embeddings to Learn a Universal Customer Behavior Representation in E-Commerce*, https://doi.org/10.1007/978-3-658-50781-7_9

of the conducted experiments. These boundaries are primarily defined by the use of session-level interaction data, a constrained range of data distributions across the selected e-commerce datasets, and a focus on binary classification tasks. While the datasets differ in scale and domain, they do not comprehensively reflect the diversity of real-world customer behavior, particularly with respect to temporal dynamics, cross-platform activity, and long-tail phenomena. Moreover, the evaluation is limited to binary classification tasks, which, represent only a subset of the broader set of customer-centric tasks outlined in Sect. 2.1. Consequently, although the pretrained UCR embeddings modestly exceed strong baselines in these controlled settings, the current evaluation does not fully capture the generalizability or applicability of the approach in more heterogeneous and dynamic environments.

9.1.1 Limitations of the Three-Stage Approach

While the proposed three-stage approach was designed to address well-known shortcomings of traditional feature engineering and tightly coupled end-to-end approaches, several conceptual and practical limitations remain.

A primary limitation arises from the exclusive reliance on session-level behavioral data for customer representation learning. As detailed in Sect. 5.2, the approach deliberately omits persistent identifiers, demographic information, and longitudinal customer histories to align with privacy-preserving principles under the GDPR [69]. However, as acknowledged in Sect. 4.2, the GDPR does not categorically prohibit the use of personal or persistent data, but instead, it requires lawful grounds such as explicit consent, contractual necessity, or sufficient anonymization or pseudonymization. This conservative design decision therefore sacrifices richer behavioral signals, such as cross-session continuity, or evolving customer preferences that could substantially enhance the semantic depth and predictive power of the learned representations. For instance, Asad et al. [16] provide an extensive overview of practical privacy-preserving mechanisms that could enable the secure incorporation of such data while maintaining regulatory compliance. Specifically, techniques such as differential privacy and local differential privacy allow for controlled noise injection either server-side or client-side to protect individual-level information. Secure multi-party computation can enable multiple data holders to collaboratively compute shared customer models without exposing raw behavioral records. Homomorphic encryption allows computations to be performed directly on encrypted persistent profiles, safeguarding sensitive attributes during processing. Additionally, methods like tokenization, anonymization, and pseudonymization offer practical pathways for masking or generalizing identity-linked data, thereby balancing semantic richness with legal safeguards. By integrating such advanced privacy-enhancing technologies, richer behavioral histories could be exploited to produce more robust and generalizable UCR without breaching the strict data minimization principles of the GDPR. For instance, by associating repeated sessions with an anonymized but persistent customer identifier, it becomes feasible to model long-term behavioral patterns, such as repeated interests, evolving preferences, or customer lifecycle stages, which are typically unobservable in isolated session data. This enables the construction of more semantically enriched representations while ensuring that personally identifiable information remains protected.

The assumption of touchpoint homogeneity and static semantics imposes another structural constraint. The UCR approach treats each touchpoint equally within its context window, relying on the Skip-Gram model's distributional assumption that co-occurrence implies similarity. However, touchpoints may vary significantly in semantic weight, e.g., a "checkout success" carries far more behavioral signal than a casual page view. The current design does not incorporate explicit weighting or contextual enrichment for different touchpoint types. Nonetheless, some degree of importance weighting can be captured at the task-specific model level, i.e., in the third stage of the approach. Here, learning models are capable of assigning higher predictive relevance to semantically richer touchpoints, thereby inducing an implicit weighting during downstream optimization. This effect has been partly examined by analyzing the increase in purchase prediction probabilities conditioned on the presence of "add to cart" events (cf. Sect. 5.6). However, this exploration remains preliminary and lacks the depth of a controlled, foundational ablation study that systematically varies or excludes specific touchpoint types to assess their marginal contribution. Such an ablation would offer stronger evidence for the implicit weighting capabilities of the downstream model. Importantly, by localizing this weighting to the task-specific layer rather than the universal embedding itself, the semantic neutrality of the UCR representation is preserved. This aligns with the objective of universality: if a particular weighting were hard-coded into the embeddings, it would compromise their transferability to tasks where different touchpoints carry different levels of importance. However, incorporating such structured attributes, through feature-aware embeddings or other architectures combining sequence, could yield alternative approaches on the representation level. For example, Wu et al. [249] explicitly model multiple customer behaviors such as clicks and views separately within each session and combine them through a list-wise DNN, showing that treating different behavior types with learned combination weights yields more informative session embeddings. Similarly, Celik and Omurca [35] demonstrate that supplementing Skip-Gram embeddings with a Transformer layer enables the model to learn the varying importance of items in a session sequence through self-attention, effectively capturing both short-term and long-range behavioral dependencies. These results suggest that extending the proposed UCR approach with touchpoint-type-specific embeddings, learned importance weights, or attention-based mechanisms could improve the representational quality at the representation level, thereby enhancing the model's ability to capture the semantic richness of customer behavior. Such extensions need to be investigated in future work to determine whether they can be integrated into the existing three-stage approach without compromising the universality of the learned representations.

Another limitation of the proposed three-stage approach, concerns the third stage. A key empirical finding, as reported in Sect. 5.6, highlights that the performance of downstream predictive tasks is substantially influenced by the choice of learning architecture, even when all models receive identical UCR input representations. This dependency underscores a structural limitation of the three-stage pipeline: the quality and utility of a UCR are not determined in isolation but are instead jointly conditioned on the compatibility between the embedding space and the inductive biases of the downstream model and available data. Although Transformer-based architectures have demonstrated superior performance across multiple domains, such as NLP and computer vision, they were consistently outperformed by LSTM-based models in the present experimental evaluation. Notably, even deeper Transformer configurations (e.g., 3-layer and 6-layer variants) failed to generalize effectively. These models rapidly achieved near-perfect AUC scores on training data within 30 to 50 epochs but exhibited strong overfitting behavior, particularly on smaller datasets such as YooChoose.

This underperformance of Transformer models represents a critical limitation of the third stage. It reveals that increased model complexity and capacity do not automatically translate into improved generalization, particularly in the context of session-based customer behavior modeling where sequences are short and semantically sparse. The evidence suggests that the inductive bias of attention-based architectures may not align well with the structure and scale of customer interaction data as captured by UCR embeddings. Furthermore, the lack of improved generalization in deeper Transformer models indicates that the embedding space, while rich, may not provide sufficient long-range dependencies or structural cues for self-attention mechanisms to exploit effectively. It is plausible that the data scarcity and short context lengths limit the advantage that Transformers are designed to leverage. In retrospect, this limitation could have been partly mitigated through more rigorous model capacity control and regularization. In addition, the exploration of architectural modifications (e.g., bottleneck attention, reduced number of heads, or session-aware inductive biases) may have yielded configurations better aligned with the short-sequence nature of the tasks.

A central open question emerging from these findings is the identification of the threshold at which Transformer architectures become advantageous over recurrent models in customer behavior modeling. This inflection point is likely conditioned by multiple latent factors, including sequence length, event diversity, and the availability of temporally extended supervision (e.g., customer lifetime value or cross-session patterns). Controlled evaluations that systematically vary these parameters could yield insight into this regime shift and inform best practices for architecture selection. Given the observed overfitting tendencies, it is further hypothesized that Transformer models require substantially larger and more heterogeneous datasets to generalize effectively. Therefore, future research should explore evaluations on longer-term and cross-platform datasets, spanning months or years of behavioral traces, to assess whether Transformers benefit disproportionately from richer temporal dynamics and structural complexity.

9.1.2 Limitations of the Experimental Design

Despite the systematic structure of the experimental pipeline and the rigorous methodological controls applied, several limitations inherent in the conducted experiments must be acknowledged to properly contextualize the reported findings. This should help clarify the boundaries within which the reported results should be interpreted.

The scope of empirical validation in this work was confined to a limited set of four e-commerce datasets, each subjected to highly controlled and standardized preprocessing procedures. Such methodological rigor is essential in a research context, as it ensures consistency, comparability, and reproducibility of results across experiments. However, this level of control also introduces a structural limitation: the curated nature of these datasets does not fully reflect the variability and complexity encountered in real-world customer interaction logs. In production environments, event data often exhibit significant heterogeneity, including noise, missing values, inconsistent schema definitions, and sparsely populated behavioral traces. These conditions can compromise the reliability of preprocessing pipelines and downstream inference mechanisms. As such, the robustness and adaptability of the proposed UCR approach in less curated, more operationally realistic data settings remain insufficiently evaluated. Addressing this gap through experiments on noisier or semi-structured datasets would be crucial to assess the practical viability of transferring the approach beyond research-grade environments.

The downstream prediction tasks were deliberately framed to exclude any task-specific adaptation or fine-tuning of the pretrained embeddings. This isolation clarifies the representational capacity of the learned UCR but precludes insight into how partial or full joint optimization with downstream objectives might affect performance. In practice, modern representation learning pipelines often blend self-supervised pretraining with targeted fine-tuning or domain adaptation to address domain shift, drift, or evolving task requirements, aspects that remain unexplored in the current design and which are used in some related work (cf. Chap. 3).

In addition to the core tasks of purchase, churn, and click-through prediction, the conducted experiments do not address other downstream tasks that are highly relevant in modern e-commerce practice but were left unexplored in this thesis. For example, predicting demographic attributes, customer segmentation, explicit product ratings, or personalized item ranking and recommendation are common operational tasks (cf. Sect. 2.1) that place additional demands on the generalizability of a UCR. The absence of empirical tests on these tasks, e.g. customer demography prediction, limits the extent to which the learned embeddings can be claimed to capture all aspects of latent customer intent or cross-domain behavior. Incorporating such additional tasks in future experiments would help to verify whether the proposed representations maintain universal predictive power when applied to tasks that depend on softer, non-transactional signals or external profile enrichment, and whether the current touchpoint-only strategy remains sufficient in such scenarios. In particular, tasks such as demographic attribute inference present an interesting research direction. It remains an open question whether demographic characteristics, such as age group, gender, or income bracket, can be reliably inferred from behavioral patterns alone. If so, this would suggest that explicit demographic information is not strictly required and is, at least partially, encoded implicitly in customer interaction behavior. Investigating such hypotheses would offer a deeper understanding of the representational capacity of the proposed UCR and its applicability to profile enrichment, personalization, and compliance-sensitive inference tasks. Future work should therefore incorporate a broader range of downstream tasks, particularly those involving soft or inferred attributes, to more rigorously assess the universality and task-transfer potential of the learned representations.

An important limitation of the current evaluation concerns the absence of live A/B testing. While extensive offline benchmarking provides valuable insights into representational quality and computational feasibility, practical targeting approaches ultimately rely on real-world customer interaction feedback to validate their utility and acceptance. An A/B test with production traffic, systematically comparing the proposed UCR-based models against established baselines in a live environment, would enable measurement of business-relevant outcomes such as conversion uplift, engagement retention, or revenue per session. Such online experimentation would also expose the approach to the aforementioned unpredictable noise, drift, and behavioral dynamics that only emerge in authentic customer journeys, thereby revealing practical trade-offs not captured in purely offline evaluation. Incorporating robust A/B testing pipelines should therefore be considered a critical next step to strengthen the evidence for the real-world viability of the approach.

9.1.3 Limitations Regarding the Baseline Approaches

While strong end-to-end baseline architectures were selected to compare with the effectiveness of the proposed UCR method, important limitations arise from the need to adapt these models to the specific experimental and data constraints of this thesis. As a result, several original input features required by the baseline models were excluded, thereby limiting their operational capacity within the experimental setting.

The selected CTR prediction baseline, DIN, is designed to leverage four primary groups of features: customer profile attributes, historical behavior signals, Ad metadata, and contextual session features. However, only customer behavior features could be retained in the implementation used in this thesis. Customer profile features, such as age, gender, and location, and detailed contextual features (e.g., device type, geographic region) were omitted due to data privacy constraints. Consequently, DIN was limited to using only clickstream-derived signals, including event types and product metadata extracted from the session logs.

Similarly, the UCR baseline DUPN was originally proposed as a multi-task learning approach integrating both short- and long-term behavioral data, enriched with persistent customer identifiers and historical customer profiles. In the experiments conducted for this thesis, however, the use of long-term customer trajectories and profile information was not feasible. Only short-term session-based behavior data were available for model input. As a result, the DUPN architecture was adapted to operate without its full set of originally designed input signals.

These feature reductions represent a critical limitation in the evaluation of the baselines. The exclusion of profile and contextual features from the baseline architectures has critical implications for both model behavior and the validity of comparative performance evaluation. First, it introduces a representational bottleneck that reduces the expressive capacity of models like DIN and DUPN, which are architecturally designed to integrate heterogeneous signals. By removing entire input channels the model's inductive bias is altered, potentially destabilizing optimization and degrading the alignment between feature space and output targets. Second, the absence of personalized information removes the capacity to adapt predictions to customer-specific patterns, thereby disproportionately affecting models that explicitly encode personalization, such as attention-weighted customer profiles in DIN. This loss of personalization likely leads to underutilization of key architectural mechanisms and a deviation from the conditions under which these models are typically benchmarked. Third, the fairness of the evaluation is complicated by this reduction: although feature parity ensures methodological comparability, the full potential of the baselines cannot be demonstrated, and any performance deficits must be interpreted within this constrained feature regime. In practical terms, this underscores the necessity of context-aware benchmarking, in which models are assessed under realistic deployment constraints rather than idealized or maximal-capacity configurations. In their complete configurations, both DIN and DUPN could be capable of achieving significantly higher predictive performance, especially when trained on rich datasets containing personalized, cross-session, and cross-contextual information. In real-world deployments where such data is legally accessible and ethically justifiable, these models could outperform the approach proposed in this thesis. Therefore, the intention of this evaluation is not to position the proposed method as universally superior, but rather to demonstrate its robustness under realistic operational constraints imposed by privacy-preserving environments.

These findings are conceptually aligned with the limitations observed in the third stage of the proposed approach, where Transformer models, despite their theoretical capacity, failed to generalize effectively due to a mismatch between model complexity and the structure of the available session-based data. In both cases, model performance is not only a function of architecture but is fundamentally constrained by the availability and quality of input signals. As with Transformers, the reduced baselines operate under suboptimal data conditions that limit their ability to exploit their full inductive strengths. This convergence reinforces the broader insight that evaluation in privacy-preserving, resource-constrained environments must carefully consider the alignment between model assumptions and feasible data regimes.

This constraint is particularly salient in European e-commerce contexts, where strict data protection regulations prohibit the use of personally identifiable data, without consent, for most forms of behavioral modeling. Under such legal frameworks, end-to-end architectures that depend on persistent customer identifiers or fine-grained contextual profiles become increasingly difficult to operationalize. The practical consequence is a growing need for models that function effectively under anonymized, session-based data regimes.

In conclusion, while the adapted baseline models serve as strong and meaningful benchmarks within the experimental constraints, their performance must be interpreted with respect to their reduced representational capacity. The imposed feature limitations are not indicative of architectural inferiority but are the result of essential trade-offs necessary to ensure legal and ethical compliance. The proposed UCR approach is therefore not positioned as a universal replacement for full-capacity end-to-end systems, but rather as a viable, privacy-compatible alternative suited for deployment in real-world scenarios where data protection is a binding constraint.

9.1.4 Synthetic Labeling for Churn and CTR Tasks

A key methodological choice in this thesis was the inclusion of three distinct prediction tasks, purchase prediction, churn prediction, and CTR prediction, to evaluate the generalizability and task transferability of the proposed UCR approach. While this multi-task setup offers important insight into the representational flexibility of the learned embeddings, it simultaneously introduces a significant methodological constraint, which is the reliance on heuristic or synthetic labels for the churn and CTR tasks.

For purchase prediction, the labeling procedure benefits from direct behavioral signals. The occurrence of a checkout event constitutes a clear, verifiable, and semantically robust indicator of purchase intent. As such, the ground truth labels for this task are unambiguous and closely aligned with actual customer outcomes, providing a sound basis for benchmarking model performance with minimal noise or interpretive bias.

By contrast, churn and CTR prediction require the construction of proxy labels based on incomplete or indirect behavioral observations. In the case of churn, customers are classified as having churned if no activity is recorded within a predefined temporal window following their last observed session. This heuristic, though aligned with conventions in prior customer lifecycle modeling studies [22, 83], embeds rigid assumptions regarding customer engagement frequency and behavioral regularity. Specifically, it assumes that all customers interact with the platform at similar intervals and that a fixed duration of inactivity can be reliably interpreted as permanent disengagement. In practice, however, platform usage is influenced by diverse behavioral patterns, including seasonality, personal schedules, and external campaign stimuli. As a result, loyal but infrequent customers may be incorrectly labeled as churned, while sporadic or low-engagement customers may be labeled as retained solely due to incidental activity near the cutoff window.

A related challenge arises in the CTR prediction task, where only positive click events are recorded in the underlying logs. The absence of negative feedback necessitates the use of negative sampling to simulate non-clicks. This common technique [141, 172, 280] involves randomly selecting items not associated with click events and treating them as negative instances. However, this approach conflates unseen items with "seen-but-ignored" ones and assumes that random samples are representative of true non-interest. In reality, many sampled items may never have been shown to the customer or may have been ignored for reasons unrelated to customer preference, such as display fatigue, ranking position, or contextual irrelevance. Consequently, the synthetic negative class is noisy, and the semantic boundary between positive and negative labels is blurred.

These issues result in a shared set of limitations for both churn and CTR prediction tasks. First, the reliance on heuristic or synthetic labels introduces label noise, which can distort both model training and evaluation. This noise may cause models to overfit spurious patterns or dataset-specific artifacts, thereby compromising generalization. Second, the reduction of complex behavioral states into binary labels (e.g., churned vs. retained, clicked vs. not-clicked) limits the capacity to capture more nuanced engagement phenomena, such as gradual disengagement, dormant reactivation, or partial interest. A further limitation is introduced by the temporal truncation of the datasets. All labels are constructed based on customer behavior within a bounded observation window. As a result, instances of churn or non-clicking may reflect only temporarily unobserved behavior rather than permanent disengagement or disinterest. This constitutes a classic case of right-censoring, in which the absence of future data is incorrectly treated as the final outcome. For churn, customers labeled as disengaged may simply reappear outside the dataset's time range. For CTR, unclicked items may be selected in future sessions that remain unobserved.

Taken together, these limitations indicate that the results obtained for churn and CTR prediction should be interpreted with appropriate caution. While these tasks provide informative auxiliary signals regarding the representational generality of the UCR, they do not offer definitive evidence of predictive accuracy in operational settings where customer intent is only partially observable. High evaluation metrics on these tasks may reflect the model's capacity to learn correlated behavioral regularities, rather than a true ability to infer latent intent. Importantly, the distortion introduced by heuristic label generation is uniformly applied across all evaluated approaches. As such, while the presence of label noise weakens the absolute reliability of the task formulation, it does not necessarily invalidate comparative performance differences, since all models are trained and evaluated under the same conditions. Nevertheless, this uniform distortion highlights the need for careful interpretation when extrapolating findings to production environments with more complex or uncertain customer behavior dynamics.

To mitigate these concerns, purchase prediction was designated as the primary evaluation task in this thesis, owing to its unambiguous and behaviorally grounded outcome variable. Notably, only in the case of the Breinify dataset were the CTR labels derived directly from logged customer interactions, enabling a more accurate definition of click behavior based on explicit exposure and engagement events. In all other datasets, CTR outcomes were inferred indirectly, introducing further uncertainty regarding label quality and therefore, only used to examine the generalization capacity of the approach. Furthermore, the inclusion of churn and CTR prediction remains valuable, as it reflects real-world deployment scenarios characterized by partial feedback, missing counterfactuals, and noisy supervision. These tasks expose the model to less controlled but operationally relevant conditions, testing the generalization capacity of the UCR beyond deterministic or fully observed outcomes. Future research should explore more refined labeling strategies, such as time-to-event models for churn and exposure-aware models for CTR, to reduce heuristic biases and improve alignment between experimental conditions and actual customer behavior.

9.1.5 Alternative Approaches for Universal Customer Representation

While this thesis centers on self-supervised, sequence-based embedding methods for customer representation, several alternative paradigms offer promising and complementary avenues for modeling complex customer behavior in e-commerce. These alternative approaches, particularly graph neural networks and pretrained foundation models, have gained increasing relevance in recent years due to advances in representation learning and the growing availability of multi-modal data. While they were not incorporated into this thesis due to scope and focus constraints, their potential merits are acknowledged and should be explored in future work.

A notable direction involves the use of graph-based representations, particularly graph neural networks. These models are inherently capable of capturing higher-order relational patterns such as customer-to-product and product-to-product co-engagement, as well as structural dependencies between items, sessions, and customers. GNNs have been successfully applied in tasks such as personalized recommendations, customer segmentation, fraud detection, and session-based predictions [252]. For instance, session graphs can represent intra-session navigation patterns, while heterogeneous graphs can incorporate multi-modal data, including product attributes, customer demographics, and contextual metadata. Future extensions of this work may explore hybrid approaches in which UCR embeddings are enriched with graph-based node representations, thereby improving relational expressiveness without fully abandoning sequential modeling.

Another compelling alternative lies in large-scale pretrained language models, particularly those developed under the foundation model paradigm. As highlighted in Sect. 3.1, most of the studies on UCR utilize text data to model customer behavior, where customer intent is modeled through the semantic information contained in item or product descriptions rather than solely through explicit interaction sequences. These approaches leverage the world knowledge embedded in LLMs to derive customer representations based on the semantic attributes of viewed or purchased products. This enables meaningful generalization even for unseen or infrequent items, as semantic similarity in product names or descriptions allows the model to capture latent intent patterns. Moreover, textual product metadata is typically well-structured and readily available in modern e-commerce systems, making it an accessible and privacy-friendly input source. Given the increasing capability of LLMs to encode external knowledge and contextualize product semantics, this paradigm represents an intriguing direction for future investigation into universal, text-based customer representations. However, text-based representations also exhibit important limitations, particularly in the context of modeling customer behavior. Most critically, the semantic similarity inferred from textual metadata does not necessarily align with behavioral similarity. For instance, two products such as "heavy metal vinyl" and "classical music CD" may be close in the language model's embedding space because they share genre and media-related keywords, yet they appeal to fundamentally different customer groups. Similarly, within broad product categories like wine, LLMs may embed an entry-level supermarket wine and a high-end vintage bottle as similar due to shared descriptors, despite their distinct appeal to casual consumers versus domain experts. Despite these challenges, the integration of LLM-derived product semantics remains a valuable research direction. When combined with behavior-driven representations, such as those proposed in this thesis, textual embeddings could enrich models with external knowledge, especially in cold-start or low-interaction scenarios.

An alternative direction for building UCR draws inspiration from sentence embedding research in NLP, where entire sequences are encoded as single dense vectors rather than embedding each token individually. In this paradigm, a whole customer session can be treated analogously to a sentence, capturing the aggregated behavioral intent in one compact representation. In the literature, several methods have been proposed to build sentence embeddings in a self-supervised manner by predicting surrounding context, a principle that aligns well with the structure of customer journey modeling [49, 86, 152, 175]. Such sequence-level embeddings could be integrated into the three-stage approach proposed in this thesis as an alternative to the current Skip-Gram-based touchpoint embeddings. By embedding each session directly, downstream models could operate on fixed-size, holistic representations without needing to process each interaction step by step. However, one inherent limitation of this approach is that sequence-level embeddings may overlook the relative importance of specific, high-signal events, such as add-to-cart, because they emphasize overall sequence similarity rather than preserving fine-grained distinctions between different types of customer actions. The main advantage of sequence embeddings lies in their simplicity and computational compactness, which eases deployment in forecasting pipelines and supports fast clustering or similarity search. Yet, for tasks where detailed event semantics and precise action weighting are critical for accurate predictions, the finer control offered by interaction-level embeddings may remain preferable.

9.2 Reflection on Time Extended Embeddings

9.2.1 Limitations of Temporal Representation Design

The TEE approach integrates four decomposed temporal features, minute of the hour, hour of the day, day of the week, and day of the year. While this decomposition adds expressive capacity to model customer behavior across multiple time scales, it introduces several limitations and operational challenges that merit closer examination.

The static bucketing of time into coarse features like day of the year or day of the week also struggles to capture domain-specific, irregular, or event-driven patterns that do not align with standard seasonal cycles. For instance, sharp anomalies such as promotional sales spikes, sudden demand surges, or sports events often cut across fixed calendar segments in unpredictable ways, e.g., occurring on irregular dates, varying in duration, or being influenced by external factors like competitor actions or media coverage. When discrete time bins cannot adapt to these irregularities, the model risks misattributing genuine event-driven variation to noise, undermining forecast accuracy. Kalifa et al. [120] addressed this gap by introducing GAN-Event, an architecture that explicitly augments time-series models with embeddings of external world events scraped from news or search trends, enabling the model to correct or adjust forecasts during sharp anomalies. Translating this insight to TEE, event embeddings, derived from domain calendars, marketing campaigns, or real-time signals, could be integrated as an additional input channel. This would allow the model to link temporal context not only to periodic cycles but also to high-impact, irregular drivers. Combining discrete or continuous time encodings with such dynamic event representations could help the TEE approach generalize more robustly to domain-specific spikes without relying solely on manual feature engineering.

By embedding time as categorical tokens, the model implicitly assumes that each temporal unit is equally meaningful. In reality, certain time bands, such as lunchtime shopping peaks or late-night browsing windows, may carry far more predictive weight than others. Without explicit weighting or a hierarchical encoding mechanism, the model risks underutilizing these asymmetries by treating all time slots uniformly. This shortcoming mirrors the limitation discussed previously for behavioral signals, where specific touchpoints like add-to-cart events carry more significance than generic page views. Similar solutions could be applied here: for example, learned attention weights or frequency-based priors could be introduced to modulate the relative influence of different time units based on their actual behavioral impact. Additionally, the current design does not adapt its temporal granularity to the available data density, leading to sparse time bins in low-activity regimes, which can increase the risk of overfitting to noise rather than capturing stable, generalizable cycles. A more adaptive time encoding, guided by data-driven weighting or dynamic bin merging, could help the TEE approach exploit the true predictive asymmetries present in real-world customer behavior. Even though these temporal asymmetries are not modeled at the representation level, the downstream learning model may still learn their relative importance implicitly, as supported by the results of the ablation study (cf. Sect. 6.5). Whereby the minute of the hour alone brings the biggest performance gain.

While this thesis benchmarked the discrete TEE design against Time2Vec as a baseline for continuous encodings, the Time2Vec approach did not deliver superior performance in the tested e-commerce scenarios (cf. Sect. 6.5). However, more recent continuous-time embedding methods may offer stronger alternatives. For example, Kim and Lee [123] propose the Continuous-Time Linear Positional Embedding, which learns a simple linear function to encode irregular time intervals directly, satisfying ideal properties such as monotonicity and translation invariance. Unlike fixed or static categorical time bins, their approach can flexibly handle non-uniform time gaps, making it well-suited for irregular or sparse customer behavior streams. While their approach was developed for irregular sensor and environmental forecasting, its principle could inspire future extensions of TEE by replacing discrete time buckets with a learnable linear function, potentially improving generalization in dynamic or sparse e-commerce settings without adding complex overhead.

Another central outcome of Chap. 6 is the empirical confirmation of the trade-off between temporal expressiveness and real-time inference efficiency in the context of self-supervised customer embeddings. While the full TEE model demonstrably improves predictive accuracy by incorporating multiple temporal cues, this gain is accompanied by a substantial increase in model complexity and computational latency that cannot be ignored in practical deployment scenarios.

Concretely, the conducted real-time benchmark (cf. Table 6.3) revealed that the full TEE configuration is approximately six times slower at inference than the UCR embedding. This sharp increase in latency arises from several cumulative factors: each additional time feature demands its own embedding matrix, the final vector dimensionality expands linearly with every concatenated time component, and the downstream learning model must process this larger representation space at prediction time. In high-throughput e-commerce systems, this overhead risks pushing latency beyond acceptable thresholds, directly undermining customer experience and system reliability.

9.3 Reflection on Lifelong Learning Embeddings

9.3.1 Limitations in Approach Design

A core limitation of the proposed LLE approach stems from its strictly modular, stepwise architecture, which separates the incremental update, dimensional adaptation, CL, and pruning processes into distinct and temporally sequential phases. While this separation improves transparency and maintainability, it introduces an artificial rigidity that fails to capture the interdependencies between these components.

For instance, the adaptation of embedding dimensionality is executed independently of the CL phase, despite the fact that both processes affect the model's ability to retain and integrate knowledge. When dimensionality is reduced based on overfitting criteria, previously learned embeddings may become truncated, altering the semantic space and impairing the similarity structure that CL mechanisms such as LwF or MAS rely upon. In this context, applying dimensionality reduction before representation alignment may compromise the effectiveness of the CLregularization terms, ultimately undermining knowledge retention. Ideally, these operations would be jointly optimized, so that dimensionality decisions are made in a CL-aware manner. Recent research has begun to explore such joint optimization strategies. Yan et al. [259] introduced Dynamically Expandable Representation in the context of class-incremental learning. Their approach freezes existing representation dimensions while dynamically adding new ones when encountering novel data complexity, guided by a pruning-informed mask and auxiliary diversity-inducing loss, to balance stability and adaptability. Another related possible approach was proposed by Douillard et al. [63], which performs dynamic token expansion in a Transformer architecture. It allocates task-specific tokens during training, while keeping a shared backbone constant. This modular expansion enables joint learning of new tasks without overwriting existing ones. This integrated approach ensures that new capacity is only added where needed, preserving previous semantic features and avoiding sudden drift.

Similarly, the pruning of outdated touchpoints is postponed until the end of each cycle, assuming that touchpoint relevance can be reliably assessed only after CL has stabilized the embedding. However, in practice, pruning decisions could benefit from earlier signals such as changes in interaction frequency or representation variance detected during incremental update or dimensionality adaptation. Moreover, pruning decisions made after dimensionality changes may suffer from interpretability issues, since the activation patterns used for relevance estimation are dependent on the latent space configuration, which may have just changed.

Furthermore, the deliberate choice to omit parameter freezing, common in parameter-isolation CL techniques, was made to preserve model plasticity and allow the embedding matrix to remain fully trainable. While this aligns with the goal of continual adaptation, it introduces a critical vulnerability. The embedding is left entirely exposed to drift, and the full responsibility of stability is shifted to regularization-based CL methods. These methods, rely heavily on accurate parameter importance estimates and carefully tuned regularization weights to maintain prior knowledge. In scenarios where these hyperparameters are suboptimally set, due to data scarcity, noise, or abrupt distributional shifts, the CL mechanisms may fail to prevent forgetting. This reliance also complicates deployment in practice, where robust hyperparameter tuning may not be feasible due to limited validation resources or privacy constraints.

9.3.2 Limitations in Adaptive Embedding Dimensionality

The current strategy for dynamically adjusting the embedding dimensionality in LLE is based on a heuristic criterion that effectively detects overfitting by comparing training and validation losses. Specifically, dimensionality is increased or decreased depending on whether the ratio of validation to training loss exceeds a predefined threshold. While this rule is straightforward to implement and computationally efficient, it suffers from sensitivity to noise and volatility in the validation signal, especially in data-scarce or high-variance settings such as RetailRocket.

In such environments, loss fluctuations may reflect stochastic variability rather than genuine overfitting, leading the system to misinterpret these signals and perform unwarranted resizing actions. As a result, dimensionality adjustments may be triggered too early, reducing capacity unnecessarily, or too late, allowing underfitting or overfitting to persist longer than needed. This can induce instability in representation quality and reduce the interpretability of learned embeddings over time.

Moreover, dimensionality changes are applied in fixed, manually defined step sizes, regardless of the severity of the detected overfitting or underfitting. This coarse-grained control lacks adaptivity. In cases of minor misalignment between model capacity and data complexity, even a single dimensionality step might be too disruptive, whereas in highly dynamic settings, small incremental changes may be insufficient to compensate for a surge in input diversity. The fixed-step mechanism also does not account for the local curvature of the loss landscape, which could provide a more robust signal for scaling adjustments. For example, a sharp gradient in loss divergence would ideally trigger larger dimensional shifts than a plateau, which the current design does not accommodate.

A further practical limitation lies in the computational cost of the heuristic approach. Each potential dimensionality change, whether an increase or a reduction, requires full embedding retraining and re-evaluation, typically over several epochs with updated model parameters. This iterative process imposes significant training overhead, particularly in industrial-scale settings with large token vocabularies and tight retraining windows. Although this repeated retraining is necessary to validate the appropriateness of each dimensional shift, it makes the method resource-intensive and less scalable, especially in time-constrained or budget-sensitive applications. In fact, this computational burden was the primary reason why the dimensionality adaptation could not be applied to the OpenCDP dataset within this thesis; the sheer vocabulary size and the iterative capacity tuning would have exceeded practical training time constraints and hardware resources.

To address these challenges, recent work by Tousside et al. proposes a promising alternative with the enhanced Sparsification and Expansion for CL method [229]. This approach introduces a structured heuristic for dynamic capacity expansion, in which network units are sparsely utilized and selectively expanded based on monitored unit importance across layers. Unlike the manual resizing employed in LLE, eSECL estimates the exact amount of capacity needed per layer using learned statistics from prior tasks, offering a more scalable and computationally efficient solution. This principled approach to capacity management could serve as a valuable extension for LLE's dimensional adaptation mechanism, particularly under data regimes characterized by rapid growth or non-stationarity.

9.3.3 Alternative Approaches to Touchpoint Pruning

While the core limitations of the proposed pruning mechanism have already been addressed in Sect. 7.5, this section focuses on alternative strategies that offer more adaptive and robust pruning behaviors for long-term deployments.

A promising direction is explored by Liu et al. [150], who propose dynamic vocabulary compression based on token usage frequency and relevance. Instead of removing tokens abruptly through a static threshold, their method gradually reduces the embedding capacity of infrequent or dormant tokens by shrinking their dimensionality. Applied to the LLE setting, this would allow rarely used touchpoints to retain compressed, low-resolution representations, preserving partial semantic information without occupying full embedding space. Such gradual shrinkage mitigates the risk of representational gaps and provides a smoother adaptation to behavioral drift over time.

Another complementary approach is proposed by Dorkin et al. [62], who demonstrate that corpus-driven pruning strategies can effectively identify truly obsolete tokens in multilingual models by tracking usage patterns over extended time windows. Translating this to LLE, touchpoint activity could be monitored using sliding-window statistics to distinguish permanent obsolescence from temporary dormancy caused by seasonality, campaign cycles, or irregular demand. Incorporating this temporal signal into the contrastive learning phase would ensure that pruning decisions align with the long-term representational needs of the embedding space.

Taken together, these strategies highlight the potential of combining adaptive dimension shrinking with time-aware touchpoint lifecycle modeling to build a more resilient and scalable pruning system. Future work should explore hybrid strategies that unify these principles to support efficient embedding maintenance in evolving real-world systems without compromising on semantic coverage or representational continuity.

At the same time, it should be emphasized that the pruning strategy proposed in this thesis is itself data-driven, relying on learned activation patterns during training to determine touchpoint relevance. While its simplicity and computational efficiency make it practical for real-time embedding systems, its reliance on a static threshold could be further improved. Future refinements could incorporate additional heuristics, such as the time since a touchpoint was last seen, its normalized usage frequency, or a decaying activation memory, to better distinguish between dormant and obsolete touchpoints. These enhancements would preserve the lightweight nature of the current approach while increasing its adaptability to long-term production environments.

9.4 Future Directions

Building upon the methodological and architectural limitations, several promising directions for future research are apparent suitable for dynamic and privacy-sensitive e-commerce environments.

One possible direction is the investigation of privacy-preserving extensions to incorporate persistent customer histories without violating data protection principles. Techniques such as differential privacy, secure multi-party computation, and homomorphic encryption, as discussed by Asad et al. [16], could enable richer behavioral signals while maintaining GDPR compliance. Furthermore, the current assumption of equal semantic weight for all touchpoints may be addressed by integrating touchpoint-specific weighting or attention mechanisms. Studies by Wu et al.[249] and Celik and Omurca[35] have demonstrated that modeling behavioral heterogeneity and importance through advanced architectures can yield more expressive customer embeddings.

While the proposed TEE model demonstrated that decomposed temporal features can enrich short-term behavioral signals, its design did not model long-term customer evolution or multi-scale temporal dependencies. Future work could extend this by developing unified architectures that integrate session-level, periodic, and historical-level patterns through hierarchical or multi-timescale encoders. Incorporating explicit memory components or attention across multiple temporal resolutions could help retain both short-term context and stable habitual patterns. The potential of TEE for temporal augmentation in attention-based models, such as Transformer variants, should also be explored. As discussed, the integration of semantically meaningful time embeddings can inform self-attention about the relative relevance of events, allowing the model to differentiate similar behaviors that occur at distinct times. Such temporal cues may guide the attention mechanism to prioritize recent high-signal actions, such as last-minute cart additions, while discounting stale or repetitive interactions, thereby enhancing interpretability and predictive power.

Furthermore, extending TEE with event-driven signals could address its current limitation in capturing domain-specific irregularities that do not align with static time bins. As previously highlighted, external signals such as promotional campaigns or seasonal sales spikes could be incorporated through additional event embeddings to correct forecasts when sharp anomalies occur. This combination of periodic and event-based temporal encodings could strengthen the robustness of time-extended representations under fluctuating business conditions.

The limitations identified in the LLE approach underscore the need for more adaptive and integrated mechanisms for managing embedding capacity. The current heuristic for dimensionality adaptation, based solely on static loss thresholds, could be replaced by more data-driven strategies that adjust embedding size in response to signals such as learned importance weights or representation sparsity. As discussed, research has shown that dynamic expansion and pruning, when jointly optimized with CL phases, can balance plasticity and stability more effectively than sequential, isolated operations. This integration would avoid semantic drift or misalignment when resizing embeddings during continual updates.

The pruning mechanism in the current LLE design relies on a static activation threshold and does not yet distinguish between truly obsolete touchpoints that are merely dormant due to seasonal or cyclical behavior. Future work should explore more adaptive, domain-specific, and time-aware pruning strategies that incorporate long-term usage statistics, such as frequency decay or time since last occurrence, to more accurately reflect touchpoint lifecycle dynamics. Additionally, metrics like embedding drift, representation variance, or changes in touchpoint co-occurrence structure could serve as complementary relevance signals to guide pruning decisions. Rather than abruptly removing low-activation touchpoints, soft-pruning strategies, such as gradual dimension shrinking for infrequent or dormant touchpoints, could be employed to preserve residual semantic signal without incurring unnecessary memory overhead.

The present UCR and TEE pipelines rely exclusively on touchpoint sequences and timestamps. Future extensions should incorporate structured products and contextual metadata, such as category taxonomies, price tiers, or promotional tags, to enrich the semantic content of the learned representations. As shown by related methods such as Meta-Prod2Vec and SkipGramEX, embedding side information alongside behavioral data strengthens the ability to infer latent relationships and improves robustness under sparse interaction scenarios. This is particularly relevant for enhancing cold-start performance when new or infrequent products appear in the catalog but lack sufficient behavioral co-occurrence signals.

In addition, the CL mechanisms applied in LLE should be more tightly coupled with downstream tasks such as personalization or ranking. Integrating downstream objectives into the continual training loop would enable task-aware regularization and performance monitoring, ensuring that learned representations remain aligned with operational goals. Moreover, live A/B testing pipelines should be incorporated to systematically evaluate representational drift and business impact under real production traffic, an aspect that has been identified as a critical gap in the present experimental design.

Another important direction for future research lies in the development of a standardized benchmark for evaluating privacy-preserving customer representation learning. Current evaluations benchmark always assume a rich set of information about customers, such as their demographics, preferences, and behavioral patterns, which should not be assumed in real-world scenarios due to privacy concerns. The proposed data model in this thesis, which structures customer interactions in a touchpoint-based, session-aware format, offers a suitable foundation for such a benchmark. By defining standardized tasks (e.g., purchase prediction, churn inference) alongside privacy-relevant adversarial objectives (e.g., re-identification risk, sensitive attribute inference), the benchmark could facilitate the quantitative assessment of privacy-utility trade-offs under consistent conditions. Furthermore, privacy-enhancing techniques such as differential privacy, anonymization, or embedding obfuscation could be systematically evaluated in this approach. Establishing such a benchmark would contribute significantly to the field by enabling more reproducible and comparable research on privacy-aware customer modeling in realistic e-commerce settings.

A promising future direction for addressing privacy concerns in customer representation learning involves the integration of data spaces, in which the UCR is stored and controlled directly by the customer. Under this paradigm, the representation would be securely maintained within a user-governed data environment rather than on centralized company servers, ensuring that only the customer retains full access rights. Critically, this design grants individuals explicit control over when and to whom their behavioral representations are disclosed, as well as which specific aspects are shared. By decoupling storage from service providers, the Data Space model makes it feasible to construct a general-purpose UCR that extends far beyond the task-specific and platform-constrained implementations examined in this thesis. Such a decentralized UCR could be flexibly reused across multiple e-commerce platforms, personalization services, or downstream applications without requiring redundant data collection or intrusive tracking. Only the final embedding, abstracting raw behavioral traces into a compact representation, would be shared with companies, and solely under informed consent. This approach preserves the semantic richness and cross-domain applicability of the UCR while fundamentally shifting control back to the customer. By empowering individuals to act as sovereign data custodians within interoperable Data Spaces, this direction aligns technological innovation with strict data privacy principles, fulfilling both regulatory requirements and rising societal demands for transparent, user-centric data governance. However, a central open question for future research is whether such general-purpose UCR embeddings can achieve true interoperability across heterogeneous platforms and services, or whether fundamentally new representation paradigms will be required to enable privacy-preserving, user-controlled data portability at scale.

Summary 10

This thesis contributes to the development and realization of a Universal Customer Representation (UCR) capable of accurately modeling and predicting customer behavior in e-commerce contexts. The e-commerce sector is highly dynamic and competitive, where customer satisfaction is a key driver of commercial success. To achieve this, effective personalization strategies are essential, as they enable tailored experiences that respond to individual customer needs. Given the diversity of customer behavior, personalization requires multiple marketing strategies and thus a detailed understanding of customer preferences. This, in turn, necessitates robust customer representations. A UCR is required to avoid repeated engineering of task-specific models for each new campaign, thereby ensuring scalability and modularity. Moreover, such representations must meet real-world constraints, including strict compliance with data privacy regulations and support for real-time inference, which are critical for enabling responsive personalization. To systematically address this objective, four research questions are formulated, targeting customer behavior representation from interaction data alone, integration of temporal information, continuous adaptation through lifelong learning, and applicability of the approach to other domains.

A comprehensive literature review on customer representation approaches revealed a fundamental trade-off in existing methodologies. Traditional manual feature engineering techniques offer interpretability and computational efficiency but are limited in adaptability and scalability. In contrast, automated DL methods improve generalization and reduce manual effort, albeit at the cost of increased computational requirements, data volume, and the need for personal data. The proposed UCR approach offers a balanced resolution by combining the adaptability and performance benefits of learning-based approaches with the modularity, efficiency, and strict compliance with data privacy regulations.

M. Alves Gomes, *Utilizing Embeddings to Learn a Universal Customer Behavior Representation in E-Commerce*, https://doi.org/10.1007/978-3-658-50781-7_10

To address the first research question, a decoupled three-stage methodology is introduced. This involves (1) representing customer behavior solely through timestamped symbolic interaction sequences without incorporating additional customer-specific features, (2) learning UCR embeddings in a self-supervised manner via a Skip-Gram model that captures behavioral context, and (3) conducting predictive tasks independently using downstream models. Extensive evaluations are performed across four structurally diverse e-commerce datasets and three representative predictive tasks, including purchase prediction, churn prediction, and click prediction. Various input modalities, such as URL-level touchpoints and product identifiers, are examined, revealing that the granularity of input data significantly affects embedding quality and predictive accuracy. These findings validated the predictive strength and real-time applicability of the proposed decoupled embeddings relative to both task-specific and state-of-the-art baseline models.

The second research question is addressed through the development of Time Extended Embedding (TEE), which augments UCR embeddings by incorporating temporal context, such as minute of hour, hour of day, day of week, and day of year, into the self-supervised learning process. Empirical evaluation demonstrated that embedding temporal signals leads to substantial performance gains, particularly in cases where interaction patterns are sparse or semantically limited. A trade-off between predictive performance and inference latency is observed: while the full TEE model attained the highest accuracy, it incurred additional computational cost. Conversely, a simplified variant using only the minute of hour feature preserved most performance improvements while significantly lowering inference time, thereby achieving an effective balance between accuracy and operational efficiency.

In response to the third research question, Lifelong Learning Embedding (LLE) is proposed to support continuous adaptation and incremental updates of customer behavior embeddings. The LLE method incorporates mechanisms such as incremental token integration for new interactions, adaptive dimensionality resizing, regularization-based CL to prevent forgetting, and optional pruning of obsolete tokens. Experimental validations on dynamic e-commerce scenarios demonstrated that LLE consistently outperforms static retraining approaches. The principal driver of these gains is attributed to the effective reuse of prior embedding knowledge, while dimensional adaptation and CL regularization contributed to the robustness and stability of the embeddings under evolving conditions.

The open research question explored in this thesis concerns the transferability of the proposed embedding approach to domains beyond e-commerce that are likewise characterized by behavioral sequence data. For such transferability to be feasible, three structural prerequisites are identified: (1) the presence of symbolic interaction sequences, (2) inherent temporal ordering of events, and (3) semantic coherence among interactions. A literature review across domains such as healthcare, finance, education, and cybersecurity indicates that these structural conditions are commonly fulfilled, thereby suggesting strong potential for cross-domain application of UCR embeddings. Nevertheless, domain-specific challenges, such as data sparsity, symbolic heterogeneity, and irregular temporal patterns remain, defining important directions for future research.

To better classify the contribution of the proposed work, a critical reflection on its limitations is provided. It is emphasized that the proposed UCR methodology is not intended as a universal replacement for high-capacity end-to-end DL systems. Rather, it is positioned as a resource-efficient, modular, and privacy-compliant alternative, well-suited for deployment in practical scenarios where data protection constraints and operational efficiency are paramount.

Several promising directions for future research have been outlined, including privacy-preserving extensions based on differential privacy and secure computation techniques, adaptive temporal modeling through multi-scale architectures, and the enrichment of symbolic representations using product metadata. Further research is also recommended on improved strategies for embedding pruning, advanced dimensionality adaptation, and the establishment of standardized benchmarks for privacy-compliant learning systems. Moreover, decentralized implementations of UCR through customer-governed data ecosystems are proposed as a pathway toward ethical and customer-centric personalization.

In conclusion, this thesis successfully establishes a generalized, scalable, and privacy-preserving methodology for modeling customer behavior using self-supervised embeddings. The resulting UCR approach addresses critical operational requirements such as privacy compliance, computational efficiency, and adaptability, providing a robust foundation for intelligent, ethical, and scalable personalization across diverse e-commerce applications and potentially broader operational contexts.

Bibliography

1. Adlin, T., and Pruitt, J. Putting personas to work: Using data-driven personas to focus product planning, design, and development. In *Human-Computer Interaction.* CRC Press, 2009, pp. 111–136.
2. Ahmed, M. S., et al. Predicting chronic wasting disease in white-tailed deer at the county scale using machine learning. *Scientific Reports 14* (2024), 14373.
3. Akiba, T., Sano, S., Yanase, T., Ohta, T., and Koyama, M. Optuna: A next-generation hyperparameter optimization framework. In *Proceedings of the 25th ACM SIGKDD International Conference on Knowledge Discovery and Data Mining* (2019).
4. Aljundi, R., Babiloni, F., Elhoseiny, M., Rohrbach, M., and Tuytelaars, T. Memory aware synapses: Learning what (not) to forget. In *Computer Vision – ECCV 2018: 15th European Conference, Munich, Germany, September 8–14, 2018, Proceedings, Part III* (Berlin, Heidelberg, 2018), Springer-Verlag, p. 144–161. https://doi.org/10.1007/978-3-030-01219-9_9.
5. Alves Gomes, M., Meisen, P., and Meisen, T. Towards lifelong learning embeddings: An algorithmic approach to dynamically extend embeddings. In *3rd Workshop on End-End Customer Journey Optimization at KDD2024* (2024). https://arxiv.org/abs/2408.14118.
6. Alves Gomes, M., Meisen, P., and Meisen, T. Efficient personalization in e-commerce: Leveraging universal customer representations with embeddings. *Journal of Theoretical and Applied Electronic Commerce Research 20*, 1 (2025). https://www.mdpi.com/0718-1876/20/1/12.
7. Alves Gomes, M., and Meisen, T. A review on customer segmentation methods for personalized customer targeting in e-commerce use cases. *Information Systems and e-Business Management 21*, 3 (2023), 527–570.
8. Alves Gomes, M., Meslem, D., Meisen, P., and Meisen, T. Lifelong-learning embeddings: Continual representation learning for dynamic e-commerce trends. In *Submitted to 34st ACM International Conference on Information and Knowledge Management* (2025).
9. Alves Gomes, M., Meyes, R., Meisen, P., and Meisen, T. Will this online shopping session succeed? predicting customer's purchase intention using embeddings. In *Proceedings of the 31st ACM International Conference on Information and Knowledge Management* (New York, NY, USA, 2022), CIKM'22, Association for Computing Machinery, pp. 2873–2882. https://doi.org/10.1145/3511808.3557127.

M. Alves Gomes, *Utilizing Embeddings to Learn a Universal Customer Behavior Representation in E-Commerce*, https://doi.org/10.1007/978-3-658-50781-7

10. Alves Gomes, M., Meyes, R., Meisen, P., and Meisen, T. It's not always about wide and deep models: Click-through rate prediction with a customer behavior-embedding representation. *Journal of Theoretical and Applied Electronic Commerce Research 19*, 1 (2024), 135–151. https://www.mdpi.com/0718-1876/19/1/8.
11. Alves Gomes, M., Tercan, H., Bodnar, T., Meisen, P., and Meisen, T. A filter is better than none: Improving deep learning-based product recommendation models by using a user preference filter. In *2021 IEEE 23rd Int Conf on High Performance Computing & Communications; 7th Int Conf on Data Science & Systems; 19th Int Conf on Smart City; 7th Int Conf on Dependability in Sensor, Cloud & Big Data Systems & Application (HPCC/DSS/SmartCity/DependSys)* (2021), pp. 1278–1285. https://doi.org/10.1109/HPCC-DSS-SmartCity-DependSys53884.2021.00195.
12. Alves Gomes, M., Wönkhaus, M., Meisen, P., and Meisen, T. Tee: Real-time purchase prediction using time extended embeddings for representing customer behavior. *Journal of Theoretical and Applied Electronic Commerce Research 18*, 3 (2023), 1404–1418. https://www.mdpi.com/0718-1876/18/3/70.
13. Amruthnath, N., and Gupta, T. A research study on unsupervised machine learning algorithms for early fault detection in predictive maintenance. In *5th International Conference on Industrial Engineering and Applications (ICIEA)* (2018), IEEE, pp. 355–361.
14. Apichottanakul, A., Goto, M., Piewthongngam, K., and Pathumnakul, S. Customer behaviour analysis based on buying-data sparsity for multi-category products in pork industry: A hybrid approach. *Cogent Engineering 8*, 1 (2021).
15. Aryafar, K., Guillory, D., and Hong, L. An ensemble-based approach to click-through rate prediction for promoted listings at etsy. In *Proceedings of the ADKDD'17* (2017), pp. 1–6.
16. Asad, M., Shaukat, S., Javanmardi, E., Nakazato, J., and Tsukada, M. A comprehensive survey on privacy-preserving techniques in federated recommendation systems. *Applied Sciences 13*, 10 (2023). https://www.mdpi.com/2076-3417/13/10/6201.
17. Asare, K. O., Terhorst, Y., Vega, J., Peltonen, E., Lagerspetz, E., and Ferreira, D. Predicting depression from smartphone behavioral markers using machine learning methods, hyperparameter optimization, and feature importance analysis. *JMIR mHealth and uHealth 9*, 7 (2021), e26540.
18. Balyemah, A. J., Weamie, S. J., Bin, J., Janda, K. V., and Joshua, F. J. Predicting purchasing behavior on e-commerce platforms: A regression model approach for understanding user features that lead to purchasing. *International Journal of Communications, Network and System Sciences 17*, 6 (2024), 81–103.
19. Bamler, R., and Mandt, S. Dynamic word embeddings. In *International conference on Machine learning* (2017), PMLR, pp. 380–389. https://doi.org/10.48550/arXiv.1702.08359.
20. Beaumont, C. D., Berry, D., and Ricketts, J. Technology has empowered the consumer, but marketing communications need to catch-up: An approach to fast-forward the future. *Businesses 2*, 2 (2022), 246–272. https://www.mdpi.com/2673-7116/2/2/17.
21. Bengio, Y., Courville, A., and Vincent, P. Representation learning: A review and new perspectives. *IEEE Transactions on Pattern Analysis and Machine Intelligence 35*, 8 (2013), 1798–1828.

22. Berger, P., and Kompan, M. User modeling for churn prediction in e-commerce. *IEEE Intelligent Systems 34*, 2 (2019), 44–52.
23. Berry, M. J. A., and Linoff, G. S.*Data Mining Techniques: For Marketing, Sales, and Customer Relationship Management*. John Wiley & Sons, Inc., Hoboken, NJ, USA, 2004.
24. Bertrand, J. H., Gargano, J. P., Mombaerts, L., and Taws, J. Autoencoder-based general purpose representation learning for customer embedding. *arXiv preprint* arXiv:2402.18164 (2024).
25. Beyari, H., and Garamoun, H. The effect of artificial intelligence on end-user online purchasing decisions: Toward an integrated conceptual framework. *Sustainability 14*, 15 (2022). https://www.mdpi.com/2071-1050/14/15/9637.
26. Bielak, P., Tagowski, K., Falkiewicz, M., Kajdanowicz, T., and Chawla, N. V. Fildne: A framework for incremental learning of dynamic networks embeddings. *Knowledge-Based Systems 236* (2022), 107453. https://www.sciencedirect.com/science/article/pii/S0950705121007152.
27. Bin Sarhan, B., and Altwaijry, N. Insider threat detection using machine learning approach. *Applied Sciences 13*, 1 (2023), 259.
28. Birtolo, C., Diessa, V., De Chiara, D., and Ritrovato, P. Customer churn detection system: Identifying customers who wish to leave a merchant. In *International Conference on Industrial, Engineering and Other Applications of Applied Intelligent Systems* (2013), Springer, pp. 411–420.
29. Brown, T., Mann, B., Ryder, N., Subbiah, M., Kaplan, J. D., Dhariwal, P., Neelakantan, A., Shyam, P., Sastry, G., Askell, A., Agarwal, S., Herbert-Voss, A., Krueger, G., Henighan, T., Child, R., Ramesh, A., Ziegler, D., Wu, J., Winter, C., Hesse, C., Chen, M., Sigler, E., Litwin, M., Gray, S., Chess, B., Clark, J., Berner, C., McCandlish, S., Radford, A., Sutskever, I., and Amodei, D. Language models are few-shot learners. In *Advances in Neural Information Processing Systems* (2020), H. Larochelle, M. Ranzato, R. Hadsell, M. Balcan, and H. Lin, Eds., vol. 33, Curran Associates, Inc., pp. 1877–1901. https://proceedings.neurips.cc/paper_files/paper/2020/file/1457c0d6bfcb4967418bfb8ac142f64a-Paper.pdf.
30. Browning, E., Bolton, M., Owen, E., Shoji, A., Guilford, T., and Freeman, R. Predicting animal behaviour using deep learning: GPS data alone accurately predict diving in seabirds. *Methods in Ecology and Evolution 9*, 3 (2018), 681–692.
31. Burri, M., and Schär, R. The reform of the eu data protection framework: outlining key changes and assessing their fitness for a data-driven economy. *Journal of Information Policy 6*, 1 (2016), 479–511.
32. Cai, J. Research on the influencing factors of consumer buying behavior. *Highlights in Science, Engineering and Technology 61* (Jul. 2023), 119–127. https://drpress.org/ojs/index.php/HSET/article/view/10281.
33. Card, S. K., Robertson, G. G., and Mackinlay, J. D. The information visualizer, an information workspace. In *Proceedings of the SIGCHI Conference on Human Factors in Computing Systems* (New York, NY, USA, 1991), CHI '91, Association for Computing Machinery, p. 181–186. https://doi.org/10.1145/108844.108874.
34. Carmel, D., Haramaty, E., Lazerson, A., and Lewin-Eytan, L. Multi-objective ranking optimization for product search using stochastic label aggregation. In *Proceedings of The Web Conference 2020* (New York, NY, USA, 2020), WWW '20,

Association for Computing Machinery, p. 373–383. https://doi.org/10.1145/3366423.3380122.

35. Celik, E., and Ilhan Omurca, S. Skip-gram and transformer model for session-based recommendation. *Applied Sciences 14*, 14 (2024). https://www.mdpi.com/2076-3417/14/14/6353.
36. Chandra, S., and Verma, S. Personalized recommendation during customer shopping journey. In *The Palgrave Handbook of Interactive Marketing*. Springer, 2023, ch. Chapter 32, pp. 729–752. https://EconPapers.repec.org/RePEc:spr:sprchp:978-3-031-14961-0_32.
37. Chang, H.- C., and Tsai, H.- P. Group rfm analysis as a novel framework to discover better customer consumption behavior. *Expert Systems With Applications 38*, 12 (2011), 14499–14513.
38. Chang, V., Sivakulasingam, S., Wang, H., and Wong, S. T. Credit risk prediction using machine learning and deep learning: A study on credit card customers. *Risks 12*, 11 (2024), 174.
39. Chaudhuri, N., Gupta, G., Vamsi, V., and Bose, I. On the platform but will they buy? predicting customers' purchase behavior using deep learning. *Decision Support Systems 149* (2021), 113622. https://www.sciencedirect.com/science/article/pii/S0167923621001329.
40. Chawla, N. V., Bowyer, K. W., Hall, L. O., and Kegelmeyer, W. P. Smote: synthetic minority over-sampling technique. *Journal of artificial intelligence research 16* (2002), 321–357.
41. Chen, C., Chen, H., Zhao, K., Zhou, J., He, L., Deng, H., Xu, J., Zheng, B., Zhang, Y., and Xing, C. Extr: Click-through rate prediction with externalities in e-commerce sponsored search. In *Proceedings of the 28th ACM SIGKDD Conference on Knowledge Discovery and Data Mining* (New York, NY, USA, 2022), Association for Computing Machinery, pp. 2732–2740.
42. Chen, Q., Zhang, M., and Xue, B. Feature selection to improve generalization of genetic programming for high-dimensional symbolic regression. *IEEE Transactions on Evolutionary Computation 21*, 5 (2017), 792–806.
43. Chen, T., Kornblith, S., Norouzi, M., and Hinton, G. A simple framework for contrastive learning of visual representations. In *Proceedings of the 37th International Conference on Machine Learning* (2020), ICML'20, JMLR.org.
44. Chen, X., Fang, Y., Yang, M., Nie, F., Zhao, Z., and Huang, J. Z. Purtreeclust: A clustering algorithm for customer segmentation from massive customer transaction data. *IEEE Transactions on Knowledge and Data Engineering 30*, 3 (2018), 559–572.
45. Cheng, H.- T., Koc, L., Harmsen, J., Shaked, T., Chandra, T., Aradhye, H., Anderson, G., Corrado, G., Chai, W., Ispir, M., Anil, R., Haque, Z., Hong, L., Jain, V., Liu, X., and Shah, H. Wide & deep learning for recommender systems. In *Proceedings of the 1st Workshop on Deep Learning for Recommender Systems* (New York, NY, USA, 2016), DLRS 2016, Association for Computing Machinery, p. 7–10. https://doi.org/10.1145/2988450.2988454.
46. Chou, Y.- C., and Chuang, H. H.- C. A predictive investigation of first-time customer retention in online reservation services. *Service Business 12* (2018), 685–699.
47. Chowdhury, A., Rosenthal, J., Waring, J., and Umeton, R. Applying self-supervised learning to medicine: Review of the state of the art and medical implementations. *Informatics 8*, 3 (2021). https://www.mdpi.com/2227-9709/8/3/59.

48. COCKBURN, I. M., HENDERSON, R., AND STERN, S. The impact of artificial intelligence on innovation: An exploratory analysis. In *The economics of artificial intelligence: An agenda*. University of Chicago Press, 2018, pp. 115–146.
49. CONNEAU, A., KIELA, D., SCHWENK, H., BARRAULT, L., AND BORDES, A. Supervised learning of universal sentence representations from natural language inference data. In *Proceedings of the 2017 Conference on Empirical Methods in Natural Language Processing* (Copenhagen, Denmark, Sept. 2017), M. Palmer, R. Hwa, and S. Riedel, Eds., Association for Computational Linguistics, pp. 670–680. https://aclanthology.org/D17-1070/.
50. COOPER, H. M. Organizing knowledge syntheses: A taxonomy of literature reviews. *Knowledge in Society 1*, 1 (1988), 104–126.
51. CRISCI, C., GHATTAS, B., AND PERERA, G. A review of supervised machine learning algorithms and their applications to ecological data. *Ecological Modelling 240* (2012), 113–122. https://www.sciencedirect.com/science/article/pii/S0304380012001081.
52. DARUNA, A., GUPTA, M., SRIDHARAN, M., AND CHERNOVA, S. Continual learning of knowledge graph embeddings. *IEEE Robotics and Automation Letters 6*, 2 (2021), 1128–1135.
53. DE HOUWER, J., BARNES-HOLMES, D., AND MOORS, A. What is learning? on the nature and merits of a functional definition of learning. *Psychonomic bulletin & review 20* (2013), 631–642.
54. DE LA LLAVE MONTIEL, M. A., AND LÓPEZ, F. Spatial models for online retail churn: Evidence from an online grocery delivery service in madrid. *Papers in Regional Science 99*, 6 (2020), 1643–1665.
55. DE LANGE, M., ALJUNDI, R., MASANA, M., PARISOT, S., JIA, X., LEONARDIS, A., SLABAUGH, G., AND TUYTELAARS, T. A continual learning survey: Defying forgetting in classification tasks. *IEEE Transactions on Pattern Analysis and Machine Intelligence 44*, 7 (2022), 3366–3385.
56. DE MARCO, M., FANTOZZI, P., FORNARO, C., LAURA, L., AND MILOSO, A. Cognitive analytics management of the customer lifetime value: an artificial neural network approach. *Journal of Enterprise Information Management 34*, 2, SI (2021), 679–696.
57. DEL BONIFRO, F., GABBRIELLI, M., LISANTI, G., AND ZINGARO, S. P. Student dropout prediction. In *Artificial Intelligence in Education, Proc. 21st Int. Conf. (AIED 2020)* (2020), vol. 12163 of *Lecture Notes in Computer Science*, Springer, pp. 129–140.
58. DENG, C., JI, X., RAINEY, C., ZHANG, J., AND LU, W. Integrating machine learning with human knowledge. *Iscience 23*, 11 (2020).
59. DESAI, D. Hyper-personalization: an ai-enabled personalization for customer-centric marketing. In *Adoption and Implementation of AI in Customer Relationship Management*. IGI Global, 2022, pp. 40–53.
60. DEVLIN, J., CHANG, M.-W., LEE, K., AND TOUTANOVA, K. Bert: Pre-training of deep bidirectional transformers for language understanding. *arXiv preprint* arXiv:1810.04805 (2018).
61. DONG, G., AND LIU, H. *Feature Engineering for Machine Learning and Data Analytics*, 1st ed. CRC Press, Inc., USA, 2018.
62. DORKIN, A., PURASON, T., AND SIRTS, K. Prune or retrain: Optimizing the vocabulary of multilingual models for Estonian. In *Proceedings of the 9th International*

Workshop on Computational Linguistics for Uralic Languages (Helsinki, Finland, Nov. 2024), M. Hämäläinen, F. Pirinen, M. Macias, and M. Crespo Avila, Eds., Association for Computational Linguistics, pp. 104–108. https://aclanthology.org/2024.iwclul-1.13/.

63. Douillard, A., Ramé, A., Couairon, G., and Cord, M. Dytox: Transformers for continual learning with dynamic token expansion. *CoRR abs/2111.11326* (2021). https://arxiv.org/abs/2111.11326.
64. Dzulfikar, M. F., Purwandari, B., Sensuse, D. I., Lusa, J. S., Solichah, I., Prima, P., and Wilarso, I. Personalization features on business-to-consumer e-commerce: Review and future directions. In *2018 4th International Conference on Information Management (ICIM)* (2018), pp. 220–224.
65. Ehsani, F., and Hosseini, M. Customer churn prediction using a novel meta-classifier: an investigation on transaction, telecommunication and customer churn datasets. *Journal of Combinatorial Optimization 48*, 1 (2024), 1–31.
66. Esmeli, R., Bader-El-Den, M., and Abdullahi, H. Using word2vec recommendation for improved purchase prediction. In *2020 International Joint Conference on Neural Networks (IJCNN)* (2020), pp. 1–8.
67. Esmeli, R., Bader-El-Den, M., and Abdullahi, H. Towards early purchase intention prediction in online session based retailing systems. *Electronic Markets 31*, 3 (2021), 697–715.
68. Esmeli, R., Bader-El-Den, M., and Abdullahi, H. An analyses of the effect of using contextual and loyalty features on early purchase prediction of shoppers in e-commerce domain. *Journal of Business Research 147* (2022), 420–434. https://www.sciencedirect.com/science/article/pii/S0148296322003393.
69. European-Parliament. Regulation (eu) 2016/679 of the european parliament and of the council, 2016. https://eur-lex.europa.eu/legal-content/EN/TXT/PDF/?uri=CELEX:32016R0679, accessed 2024–10–11.
70. Fabra, J., Álvarez, P., and Ezpeleta, J. Log-based session profiling and online behavioral prediction in e–commerce websites. *IEEE Access 8* (2020), 171834–171850.
71. Fan, Z., Liu, Z., Zhang, J., Xiong, Y., Zheng, L., and Yu, P. S. Continuous-time sequential recommendation with temporal graph collaborative transformer. In *Proceedings of the 30th ACM International Conference on Information & Knowledge Management* (New York, NY, USA, 2021), CIKM '21, Association for Computing Machinery, pp. 433–442. https://doi.org/10.1145/3459637.3482242.
72. Fan, Z., Ou, D., Gu, Y., Fu, B., Li, X., Bao, W., Dai, X.-Y., Zeng, X., Zhuang, T., and Liu, Q. Modeling users' contextualized page-wise feedback for click-through rate prediction in e-commerce search. In *Proceedings of the Fifteenth ACM International Conference on Web Search and Data Mining* (New York, NY, USA, 2022), Association for Computing Machinery, pp. 262–270.
73. Fang, Q., Zhou, Z., Barbieri, F., Liu, Y., Neves, L., Nguyen, D., Oberski, D., Bos, M., and Dotsch, R. General-purpose user modeling with behavioral logs: A snapchat case study. In *Proceedings of the 47th International ACM SIGIR Conference on Research and Development in Information Retrieval* (New York, NY, USA, 2024), Sigir '24, Association for Computing Machinery, p. 2431–2436. https://doi.org/10.1145/3626772.3657908.
74. Farayola, O. A., Olorunfemi, O. L., and Shoetan, P. O. Data privacy and security in it: A review of techniques and challenges. *Computer Science & IT Research Journal 5*, 3 (03 2024), 606–615. https://fepbl.com/index.php/csitrj/article/view/909.

75. FATHALLA, A., SALAH, A., AND ALI, A. A novel price prediction service for e-commerce categorical data. *Mathematics 11*, 8 (2023). https://www.mdpi.com/2227-7390/11/8/1938.
76. FAWCETT, T. An introduction to roc analysis. *Pattern Recognition Letters 27*, 8 (2006), 861–874. ROC Analysis in Pattern Recognition. https://www.sciencedirect.com/science/article/pii/S016786550500303X.
77. FENG, J., LI, Y., YANG, Z., QIU, Q., AND JIN, D. Predicting human mobility with semantic motivation via multi-task attentional recurrent networks. *IEEE Transactions on Knowledge and Data Engineering* (2020). Early Access.
78. FENG, W., CAO, Y., CHEN, Y., WANG, Y., HU, N., JIA, Y., AND GU, Z. Multi-granularity user anomalous behavior detection. *Applied Sciences 15*, 1 (2025), 128.
79. FENG, Y., LV, F., HU, B., SUN, F., KUANG, K., LIU, Y., LIU, Q., AND OU, W. Mtbrn: Multiplex target-behavior relation enhanced network for click-through rate prediction. In *Proceedings of the 29th ACM International Conference on Information & Knowledge Management* (New York, NY, USA, 2020), CIKM '20, Association for Computing Machinery, p. 2421–2428. https://doi.org/10.1145/3340531.3412729.
80. FERRERA, C., AND KESSEDJIAN, E. Evolution of e-commerce and global marketing. *International Journal of Technology for Business (IJTB) 1*, 1 (2019), 33–38.
81. FERRI, C., HERNÁNDEZ- ORALLO, J., AND MODROIU, R. An experimental comparison of performance measures for classification. *Pattern Recognition Letters 30*, 1 (2009), 27–38. https://www.sciencedirect.com/science/article/pii/S0167865508002687.
82. FREDDI, D. Digitalisation and employment in manufacturing: Pace of the digitalisation process and impact on employment in advanced italian manufacturing companies. *Ai & Society 33*, 3 (2018), 393–403.
83. FRIDRICH, M., AND DOSTAL, P. User churn model in e-commerce retail. *Sci. Pap. Univ. Pardubic. Ser. D Fac. Econ. Adm 30* (04 2022), 1478.
84. FUTOMA, J., SENDAK, M., CAMERON, C. B., AND HELLER, K. Predicting disease progression with a model for multivariate longitudinal clinical data. In *Proceedings of the Machine Learning for Healthcare Conference (MLHC)* (2016), vol. 56 of *Proceedings of Machine Learning Research*, pp. 42–54.
85. GAO, C., ZHAO, Z., HU, S., SHAO, L., AND LIU, T. Collaborative contrastive network for click-through rate prediction, 2024. https://arxiv.org/abs/2411.11508.
86. GAO, T., YAO, X., AND CHEN, D. SimCSE: Simple contrastive learning of sentence embeddings. In *Proceedings of the 2021 Conference on Empirical Methods in Natural Language Processing* (Online and Punta Cana, Dominican Republic, Nov. 2021), M.-F. Moens, X. Huang, L. Specia, and S. W.-t. Yih, Eds., Association for Computational Linguistics, pp. 6894–6910. https://aclanthology.org/2021.emnlp-main.552/.
87. GARINE, R. Enhanced e-commerce demand prediction through ensemble models and optuna-based hyperparameter optimization. In *2024 2nd DMIHER International Conference on Artificial Intelligence in Healthcare, Education and Industry (IDICAIEI)* (2024), pp. 1–7.
88. GE, T., ZHAO, L., ZHOU, G., CHEN, K., LIU, S., YI, H., HU, Z., LIU, B., SUN, P., LIU, H., YI, P., HUANG, S., ZHANG, Z., ZHU, X., ZHANG, Y., AND GAI, K. Image matters: Visually modeling user behaviors using advanced model server. In *Proceedings of the 27th ACM International Conference on Information and Knowledge Management* (2018), pp. 2087–2095.

89. Gelß, P., Klus, S., Schuster, I., and Schütte, C. Feature space approximation for kernel-based supervised learning. *Knowledge-Based Systems 221* (2021), 106935. https://www.sciencedirect.com/science/article/pii/S0950705121001982.
90. Geng, B., Huan, Z., Zhang, X., He, Y., Zhang, L., Yuan, F., Zhou, J., and Mo, L. Breaking the length barrier: Llm-enhanced ctr prediction in long textual user behaviors, 2024. https://arxiv.org/abs/2403.19347.
91. Goldberger, A., Amaral, L., Glass, L., Hausdorff, J., Ivanov, P., Mark, R., and Stanley, H. Physiobank, physiotoolkit, and physionet: Components of a new research resource for complex physiologic signals. *Circulation 101*, 23 (2000), e215–e220.
92. Goodfellow, I. J., Mirza, M., Xiao, D., Courville, A., and Bengio, Y. An empirical investigation of catastrophic forgetting in gradient-based neural networks, 2015. https://arxiv.org/abs/1312.6211.
93. Grandini, M., Bagli, E., and Visani, G. Metrics for multi-class classification: an overview, 2020. https://arxiv.org/abs/2008.05756.
94. Grave, É., Joulin, A., Cissé, M., Grangier, D., and Jégou, H. Efficient softmax approximation for GPUs. In *Proceedings of the 34th International Conference on Machine Learning* (06–11 Aug 2017), D. Precup and Y. W. Teh, Eds., vol. 70 of *Proceedings of Machine Learning Research*, PMLR, pp. 1302–1310. https://proceedings.mlr.press/v70/grave17a.html.
95. Gu, J., Wang, F., Sun, Q., Ye, Z., Xu, X., Chen, J., and Zhang, J. Exploiting behavioral consistence for universal user representation. In *Proceedings of the AAAI Conference on Artificial Intelligence* (2021), vol. 35, pp. 4063–4071.
96. Gu, Y., Zalkikar, A., Liu, M., Kelly, L., Hall, A., Daly, K., and Ward, T. Predicting medication adherence using ensemble learning and deep learning models with large scale healthcare data. *Scientific Reports 11* (2021), 18961.
97. Gui, J., Chen, T., Zhang, J., Cao, Q., Sun, Z., Luo, H., and Tao, D. A survey on self-supervised learning: Algorithms, applications, and future trends. *IEEE Transactions on Pattern Analysis and Machine Intelligence 46*, 12 (2024), 9052–9071.
98. Guo, W., Zhang, C., He, Z., Qin, J., Guo, H., Chen, B., Tang, R., He, X., and Zhang, R. Miss: Multi-interest self-supervised learning framework for click-through rate prediction. In *2022 IEEE 38th International Conference on Data Engineering (ICDE)* (2022), pp. 727–740.
99. Haresamudram, H., Beedu, A., Agrawal, V., Grady, P. L., Essa, I., Hoffman, J., and Plötz, T. Masked reconstruction based self-supervision for human activity recognition. In *Proceedings of the 2020 ACM International Symposium on Wearable Computers* (New York, NY, USA, 2020), ISWC '20, Association for Computing Machinery, pp. 45–49. https://doi.org/10.1145/3410531.3414306.
100. Higham, C. F., and Higham, D. J. Deep learning: An introduction for applied mathematicians. *SIAM Review 61*, 4 (2019), 860–891.
101. Hinton, G., Vinyals, O., and Dean, J. Distilling the knowledge in a neural network, 2015. https://arxiv.org/abs/1503.02531.
102. Hochreiter, S., and Schmidhuber, J. Long short-term memory. *Neural Computation 9*, 8 (11 1997), 1735–1780. https://doi.org/10.1162/neco.1997.9.8.1735.
103. Holmlund, M., van Vaerenbergh, Y., Ciuchita, R., Ravald, A., Sarantopoulos, P., Ordenes, F. V., and Zaki, M. Customer experience management in the age of big data analytics: A strategic framework. *Journal of Business Research 116* (2020), 356–365.

104. HOMBURG, C., JOZIĆ, D., AND KUEHNL, C. Customer experience management: toward implementing an evolving marketing concept. *Journal of the Academy of Marketing Science 45*, 3 (2017), 377–401.
105. HONG, T., AND KIM, E. Segmenting customers in online stores based on factors that affect the customer's intention to purchase. *Expert Systems with Applications 39*, 2 (2012), 2127–2131.
106. HOO, Z. H., CANDLISH, J., AND TEARE, D. What is an roc curve?, June 2017. https://emj.bmj.com/content/emermed/34/6/357.full.pdf.
107. HOSSIN, M., AND SULAIMAN, M. N. A review on evaluation metrics for data classification evaluations. *International journal of data mining & knowledge management process 5*, 2 (2015), 1. https://doi.org/10.5121/ijdkp.2015.5201.
108. HOU, Y., MU, S., ZHAO, W. X., LI, Y., DING, B., AND WEN, J.- R. Towards universal sequence representation learning for recommender systems. In *Proceedings of the 28th ACM SIGKDD Conference on Knowledge Discovery and Data Mining* (New York, NY, USA, 2022), Kdd '22, Association for Computing Machinery, p. 585–593. https://doi.org/10.1145/3534678.3539381.
109. HOWARD, T. Journey mapping: a brief overview. *Commun. Des. Q. Rev 2*, 3 (2014), 10–13. https://doi.org/10.1145/2644448.2644451.
110. HUANG, C., WU, X., ZHANG, X., ZHANG, C., ZHAO, J., YIN, D., AND CHAWLA, N. V. Online purchase prediction via multi-scale modeling of behavior dynamics. In *Proceedings of the 25th ACM SIGKDD International Conference on Knowledge Discovery & Data Mining* (New York, NY, USA, 2019), KDD '19, Association for Computing Machinery, pp. 2613–2622. https://doi.org/10.1145/3292500.3330790.
111. HUANG, G., CHEN, Q., AND DENG, C. A new click-through rates prediction model based on deep&cross network. *Algorithms 13*, 12 (2020), 342.
112. HUGHES, A. M. Strategic database marketing: the masterplan for starting and managing a profitable. *Customer-Based Marketing Program, Irwin Professional* (1994).
113. HÜTTEN, N., ALVES GOMES, M., HÖLKEN, F., ANDRICEVIC, K., MEYES, R., AND MEISEN, T. Deep learning for automated visual inspection in manufacturing and maintenance: A survey of open- access papers. *Applied System Innovation 7*, 1 (2024). https://www.mdpi.com/2571-5577/7/1/11.
114. INC., B. Breinify - ai-powered personalization, 2025. Accessed: 2025–03–11. https://home.breinify.ai/.
115. JANSEN, B. J., SALMINEN, J., JUNG, S.- G., AND GUAN, K.*Data-driven personas*. Springer Nature, 2022. https://doi.org/10.1007/978-3-031-02231-9.
116. JARRAHI, M. H. Artificial intelligence and the future of work: Human-ai symbiosis in organizational decision making. *Business Horizons 61*, 4 (2018), 577–586. https://www.sciencedirect.com/science/article/pii/S0007681318300387.
117. JING, C., QIU, L., SUN, C., AND YANG, Q. Ice-den: A click-through rate prediction method based on interest contribution extraction of dynamic attention intensity. *KNOWLEDGE-BASED SYSTEMS 250* (2022), 109135.
118. JOHNSON, A., BULGARELLI, L., POLLARD, T., GOW, B., MOODY, B., HORNG, S., CELI, L., AND MARK, R. Mimic-iv (version 3.1). *PhysioNet* (2024).
119. JOHNSON, A., BULGARELLI, L., SHEN, L., AND ET AL. Mimic-iv, a freely accessible electronic health record dataset. *Scientific Data 10* (2023).
120. KALIFA, D., SINGER, U., GUY, I., ROSIN, G. D., AND RADINSKY, K. Leveraging world events to predict e-commerce consumer demand under anomaly. In *Proceedings*

of the Fifteenth ACM International Conference on Web Search and Data Mining (New York, NY, USA, 2022), WSDM '22, Association for Computing Machinery, pp. 430–438. https://doi.org/10.1145/3488560.3498452.

121. KARINGULA, S. R., RAMANAN, N., TAHMASBI, R., AMJADI, M., JUNG, D., SI, R., THIMMISETTY, C., POLANIA, L. F., SAYER, M., TAYLOR, J., ET AL. Boosted embeddings for time-series forecasting. In *Machine Learning, Optimization, and Data Science: 7th International Conference, LOD 2021, Grasmere, UK, October 4–8, 2021, Revised Selected Papers, Part II* (2022), Springer, pp. 1–14.
122. KAZEMI, S. M., GOEL, R., EGHBALI, S., RAMANAN, J., SAHOTA, J., THAKUR, S., WU, S., SMYTH, C., POUPART, P., AND BRUBAKER, M. Time2vec: Learning a vector representation of time. *arXiv preprint* arXiv:1907.05321 (2019).
123. KIM, B., AND LEE, J.- G. Continuous-time linear positional embedding for irregular time series forecasting, 2024. https://arxiv.org/abs/2409.20092.
124. KIM, K. J., AND AHN, H. Using a clustering genetic algorithm to support customer segmentation for personalized recommender systems. In *Artificial Intelligence and Simulation* (2004), T. G. Kim, Ed., vol. 3397 of *Lecture Notes in Computer Science*, pp. 409–415.
125. KIM, Y., LEE, Y., YUAN, J., LEE, A., AND LEE, Y. A temporal graph network framework for dynamic recommendation. In *Workshop on Recommendation Ecosystems: Modeling, Optimization and Incentive Design* (2024). https://openreview.net/forum?id=t9sKJcr3tW.
126. KINGMA, D. P., AND BA, J. Adam: A method for stochastic optimization. *arXiv preprint* arXiv:1412.6980 (2014).
127. KIRA, K., AND RENDELL, L. A. A practical approach to feature selection. In *Machine Learning Proceedings 1992*, D. Sleeman and P. Edwards, Eds. Morgan Kaufmann, San Francisco (CA), 1992, pp. 249–256. https://www.sciencedirect.com/science/article/pii/B9781558602472500371.
128. KIRKPATRICK, J., PASCANU, R., RABINOWITZ, N., VENESS, J., DESJARDINS, G., RUSU, A. A., MILAN, K., QUAN, J., RAMALHO, T., GRABSKA- BARWINSKA, A., HASSABIS, D., CLOPATH, C., KUMARAN, D., AND HADSELL, R. Overcoming catastrophic forgetting in neural networks. *Proceedings of the National Academy of Sciences 114*, 13 (2017), 3521–3526. https://www.pnas.org/doi/abs/10.1073/pnas.1611835114.
129. KOZAL, J., LEŚ, M., ZYBLEWSKI, P., KSIENIEWICZ, P., AND WOŹNIAK, M. Feature integration strategies for multilingual fake news classification. In *2022 IEEE International Conference on Big Data (Big Data)* (2022), pp. 5049–5058.
130. KRISHNAN, C., AND MARIAPPAN, J. The ai revolution in e-commerce: Personalization and predictive analytics. In *Role of Explainable Artificial Intelligence in E-Commerce*. Springer, 2024, pp. 53–64.
131. KUMAR, V., AND PATRA, S. K. *Feature Engineering for Machine Learning and Deep Learning Assisted Wireless Communication*. Springer International Publishing, Cham, 2021, pp. 77–95. https://doi.org/10.1007/978-3-030-70542-8_4.
132. KUMAR, V., VENKATESAN, R., AND REINARTZ, W. Performance implications of adopting a customer-focused sales campaign. *Journal of Marketing 72*, 5 (2008), 50–68.
133. LEE, N.- T., LEE, H.- C., HSIN, J., AND FANG, S.- H. Prediction of customer behavior changing via a hybrid approach. *IEEE Open Journal of the Computer Society 5* (2024), 27–38.

134. Leeflang, P. S., Verhoef, P. C., Dahlström, P., and Freundt, T. Challenges and solutions for marketing in a digital era. *European Management Journal 32*, 1 (2014), 1–12. https://www.sciencedirect.com/science/article/pii/S0263237313001576.
135. Lemon, K. N., and Verhoef, P. C. Understanding customer experience throughout the customer journey. *Journal of Marketing 80*, 6 (2016), 69–96.
136. Li, C., Yi, K., Fei, M., Zhou, W., Wu, X., and Chen, Y. Multiple-structure attentional network for click-through prediction in recommendation system. In *2021 IEEE International Conference on Recent Advances in Systems Science and Engineering (RASSE)* (2021), pp. 1–6.
137. Li, F., Chen, Z., Wang, P., Ren, Y., Di Zhang, and Zhu, X. Graph intention network for click-through rate prediction in sponsored search. In *Proceedings of the 42nd International ACM SIGIR Conference on Research and Development in Information Retrieval* (2019), pp. 961–964.
138. Li, Q., Gu, M., Zhou, K., and Sun, X. Multi-classes feature engineering with sliding window for purchase prediction in mobile commerce. In *2015 IEEE International Conference on Data Mining Workshop (ICDMW)* (New York, NY, USA, 2015), IEEE, IEEE, pp. 1048–1054.
139. Li, X., and Li, Z. A hybrid prediction model for e-commerce customer churn based on logistic regression and extreme gradient boosting algorithm. *Ingénierie des Systèmes d'Information 24*, 5 (2019).
140. Li, X., Wang, C., Tan, J., Zeng, X., Ou, D., and Zheng, B. Adversarial multimodal representation learning for click-through rate prediction. In *Proceedings of The Web Conference 2020* (2020), pp. 827–836.
141. Li, X., Wang, C., Tong, B., Tan, J., Zeng, X., and Zhuang, T. Deep time-aware item evolution network for click-through rate prediction. In *Proceedings of the 29th ACM International Conference on Information & Knowledge Management* (New York, NY, USA, 2020), Association for Computing Machinery, pp. 785–794.
142. Li, Y., Wang, J., Dai, T., Zhu, J., Yuan, J., Zhang, R., and Xia, S.-T. Rat: Retrieval-augmented transformer for click-through rate prediction. In *Companion Proceedings of the ACM Web Conference 2024* (New York, NY, USA, 2024), WWW '24, Association for Computing Machinery, p. 867–870. https://doi.org/10.1145/3589335.3651550.
143. Li, Z., and Hoiem, D. Learning without forgetting. In *Computer Vision – ECCV 2016* (Cham, 2016), B. Leibe, J. Matas, N. Sebe, and M. Welling, Eds., Springer International Publishing, pp. 614–629.
144. Lika, B., Kolomvatsos, K., and Hadjiefthymiades, S. Facing the cold start problem in recommender systems. *Expert Systems with Applications 41*, 4, Part 2 (2014), 2065–2073. https://www.sciencedirect.com/science/article/pii/S0957417413007240.
145. Lin, S., Li, C.-T., and Kot, A. C. Multi-domain adversarial feature generalization for person re-identification. *IEEE Transactions on Image Processing 30* (2020), 1596–1607.
146. Lin, W., Milic-Frayling, N., Zhou, K., and Ch'ng, E. Predicting outcomes of active sessions using multi-action motifs. In *IEEE/WIC/ACM International Conference on Web Intelligence* (New York, NY, USA, 2019), WI '19, Association for Computing Machinery, p. 9–17. https://doi.org/10.1145/3350546.3352495.
147. Liu, H., Huang, Y., Wang, Z., Liu, K., Hu, X., and Wang, W. Personality or value: A comparative study of psychographic segmentation based on an online review

enhanced recommender system. *Applied Sciences 9*, 10 (2019). https://www.mdpi.com/2076-3417/9/10/1992.

148. Liu, H., Lu, J., Yang, H., Zhao, X., Xu, S., Peng, H., Zhang, Z., Niu, W., Zhu, X., Bao, Y., and Yan, W. Category-specific cnn for visual-aware ctr prediction at jd.com. In *Proceedings of the 26th ACM SIGKDD International Conference on Knowledge Discovery & Data Mining* (2020), pp. 2686–2696.
149. Liu, Y., Ott, M., Goyal, N., Du, J., Joshi, M., Chen, D., Levy, O., Lewis, M., Zettlemoyer, L., and Stoyanov, V. Roberta: A robustly optimized bert pretraining approach. *arXiv preprint* arXiv:1907.11692 (2019).
150. Liu, Z., Song, Q., Li, L., Choi, S.- H., Chen, R., and Hu, X. Pme: pruning-based multi-size embedding for recommender systems. *Frontiers in big Data 6* (2023), 1195742. https://doi.org/10.3389/fdata.2023.1195742.
151. Lo, C., Frankowski, D., and Leskovec, J. Understanding behaviors that lead to purchasing: A case study of pinterest. In *Proceedings of the 22nd ACM SIGKDD International Conference on Knowledge Discovery and Data Mining* (New York, NY, USA, 2016), KDD '16, Association for Computing Machinery, pp. 531–540. https://doi.org/10.1145/2939672.2939729.
152. Logeswaran, L., and Lee, H. An efficient framework for learning sentence representations. In *Proceedings of the 6th International Conference on Learning Representations (ICLR)* (2018).
153. Lu, J., Long, Y., Li, X., Shen, Y., and Wang, X. Hybrid model integration of lightgbm, deepfm, and din for enhanced purchase prediction on the elo dataset. In *2024 IEEE 7th International Conference on Information Systems and Computer Aided Education (ICISCAE)* (2024), pp. 16–20.
154. Lu, Q. E-commerce big data processing based on an improved rbf model. *Journal of Intelligent Systems 33*, 1 (2024), 20230131. https://doi.org/10.1515/jisys-2023-0131.
155. Malik, V., Mittal, R., Chaudhry, R., and Yadav, S. A. Predicting purchases and personalizing the customer journey with artificial intelligence. In *2024 11th International Conference on Reliability, Infocom Technologies and Optimization (Trends and Future Directions)(ICRITO)* (2024), IEEE, pp. 1–5.
156. Martínez, A., Schmuck, C., Pereverzyev, S., Pirker, C., and Haltmeier, M. A machine learning framework for customer purchase prediction in the non-contractual setting. *European Journal of Operational Research 281*, 3 (2020), 588–596. Featured Cluster: Business Analytics: Defining the field and identifying a research agenda. https://www.sciencedirect.com/science/article/pii/S0377221718303370.
157. Matz, S. C., Bukow, C. S., Peters, H., Deacons, C., Dinu, A., and Stachl, C. Using machine learning to predict student retention from socio-demographic characteristics and app-based engagement metrics. *Scientific Reports 13* (2023), 5705.
158. McNee, S. M., Riedl, J., and Konstan, J. A. Being accurate is not enough: how accuracy metrics have hurt recommender systems. In *CHI '06 Extended Abstracts on Human Factors in Computing Systems* (New York, NY, USA, 2006), CHI EA '06, Association for Computing Machinery, pp. 1097–1101. https://doi.org/10.1145/1125451.1125659.
159. Mermillod, M., Bugaiska, A., and BONIN, P. The stability-plasticity dilemma: investigating the continuum from catastrophic forgetting to age-limited learning effects. *Frontiers in Psychology Volume 4–2013* (2013). https://www.frontiersin.org/journals/psychology/articles/10.3389/fpsyg.2013.00504.

160. MIECH, A., ALAYRAC, J.- B., SMAIRA, L., LAPTEV, I., SIVIC, J., AND ZISSERMAN, A. End-to-end learning of visual representations from uncurated instructional videos. In *Proceedings of the IEEE/CVF Conference on Computer Vision and Pattern Recognition (CVPR)* (June 2020).
161. MIKOLOV, T., SUTSKEVER, I., CHEN, K., CORRADO, G. S., AND DEAN, J. Distributed representations of words and phrases and their compositionality. *Advances in neural information processing systems 26* (2013).
162. MILLER, R. B. Response time in man-computer conversational transactions. In *Proceedings of the December 9–11, 1968, fall joint computer conference, part I* (New York, NY, USA, 1968), AFIPS '68 (Fall, part I), Association for Computing Machinery, p. 267–277. https://doi.org/10.1145/1476589.1476628.
163. MOKRYN, O., BOGINA, V., AND KUFLIK, T. Will this session end with a purchase? inferring current purchase intent of anonymous visitors. *Electronic Commerce Research and Applications 34* (2019), 100836. https://www.sciencedirect.com/science/article/pii/S1567422319300134.
164. MORTAZ, E. Imbalance accuracy metric for model selection in multi-class imbalance classification problems. *Knowledge-Based Systems 210* (2020), 106490. https://www.sciencedirect.com/science/article/pii/S0950705120306195.
165. MORWITZ, V. G., STECKEL, J. H., AND GUPTA, A. When do purchase intentions predict sales? *International Journal of Forecasting 23*, 3 (2007), 347–364. https://www.sciencedirect.com/science/article/pii/S0169207007000799.
166. MULHERN, F. J. Customer profitability analysis: Measurement, concentration, and research directions. *Journal of Interactive Marketing 13*, 1 (1999), 25–40.
167. MURTHY, M. Y. B., MASTANBI, S., SUJITHA, B., AND BABU, K. R. Evaluating deep learning algorithms for natural language processing. In *Proceedings of International Conference on Communication and Computational Technologies* (Singapore, 2023), S. Kumar, S. Hiranwal, S. D. Purohit, and M. Prasad, Eds., Springer Nature Singapore, pp. 709–720.
168. NAKANO, S., AND KONDO, F. N. Customer segmentation with purchase channels and media touchpoints using single source panel data. *Journal of Retailing and Consumer Services 41* (2018), 142–152.
169. NALMPANTIS, C., AND VRAKAS, D. Signal2vec: Time series embedding representation. In *Engineering Applications of Neural Networks: 20th International Conference, EANN 2019, Xersonisos, Crete, Greece, May 24–26, 2019, Proceedings* (2019), Springer, pp. 80–90.
170. NGUYEN, S. P. Deep customer segmentation with applications to a vietnamese supermarkets' data. *Soft Computing 25*, 12, SI (2021), 7785–7793.
171. NI, J., LI, J., AND MCAULEY, J. Justifying recommendations using distantly-labeled reviews and fine-grained aspects. In *Proceedings of the 2019 conference on empirical methods in natural language processing and the 9th international joint conference on natural language processing (EMNLP-IJCNLP)* (2019), pp. 188–197.
172. NI, Y., OU, D., LIU, S., LI, X., OU, W., ZENG, A., AND SI, L. Perceive your users in depth: Learning universal user representations from multiple e-commerce tasks. In *Proceedings of the 24th ACM SIGKDD International Conference on Knowledge Discovery &; Data Mining* (New York, NY, USA, 2018), Kdd '18, Association for Computing Machinery, pp. 596–605. https://doi.org/10.1145/3219819.3219828.

173. OSISANWO, F., AKINSOLA, J., AWODELE, O., HINMIKAIYE, J., OLAKANMI, O., AKINJOBI, J., ET AL. Supervised machine learning algorithms: classification and comparison. *International Journal of Computer Trends and Technology (IJCTT) 48*, 3 (2017), 128–138. https://doi.org/10.14445/22312803/IJCTT-V48P126.
174. PADILLA, R., NETTO, S. L., AND DA SILVA, E. A. B. A survey on performance metrics for object-detection algorithms. In *2020 International Conference on Systems, Signals and Image Processing (IWSSIP)* (2020), pp. 237–242.
175. PAGLIARDINI, M., GUPTA, P., AND JAGGI, M. Unsupervised learning of sentence embeddings using compositional n-gram features. In *Proceedings of the 2018 Conference of the North American Chapter of the Association for Computational Linguistics: Human Language Technologies, Volume 1 (Long Papers)* (New Orleans, Louisiana, June 2018), M. Walker, H. Ji, and A. Stent, Eds., Association for Computational Linguistics, pp. 528–540. https://aclanthology.org/N18-1049/.
176. PAN, Z., CHEN, E., LIU, Q., XU, T., MA, H., AND LIN, H. Sparse factorization machines for click-through rate prediction. In *2016 IEEE 16th International Conference on Data Mining (ICDM)* (2016), pp. 400–409.
177. PARK, C., KIM, D., OH, J., AND YU, H. Predicting user purchase in e-commerce by comprehensive feature engineering and decision boundary focused under-sampling. In *Proceedings of the 2015 International ACM Recommender Systems Challenge* (New York, NY, USA, 2015), RecSys '15 Challenge, Association for Computing Machinery. https://doi.org/10.1145/2813448.2813517.
178. PERISIC, A., AND PAHOR, M. Rfm-lir feature framework for churn prediction in the mobile games market. *IEEE Transactions on Games 14*, 2 (2022), 126–137.
179. PFEIFER, P. E. The optimal ratio of acquisition and retention costs. *Journal of targeting, measurement and analysis for marketing 13* (2005), 179–188.
180. PI, Q., BIAN, W., ZHOU, G., ZHU, X., AND GAI, K. Practice on long sequential user behavior modeling for click-through rate prediction. In *Proceedings of the 25th ACM SIGKDD International Conference on Knowledge Discovery & Data Mining* (New York, NY, USA, 2019), KDD '19, Association for Computing Machinery, p. 2671–2679. https://doi.org/10.1145/3292500.3330666.
181. PIRES, P. B., SANTOS, J. D., BRITO, P. Q. D., AND MARQUES, D. N. Connecting digital channels to consumers' purchase decision-making process in online stores. *Sustainability 14*, 21 (2022). https://www.mdpi.com/2071-1050/14/21/14392.
182. PITCHBOOK. Breinify company profile—pitchbook, 2025. Accessed: 2025–03–11. https://pitchbook.com/profiles/company/161565-94.
183. POLLARD, T., JOHNSON, A., RAFFA, J., CELI, L., BADAWI, O., AND MARK, R. The eicu collaborative research database, a freely available multi-center database for critical care research. *Scientific Data 5* (2018).
184. POLLARD, T., JOHNSON, A., RAFFA, J., CELI, L., BADAWI, O., AND MARK, R. eicu collaborative research database (version 2.0). *PhysioNet* (2019).
185. POWERS, D. M. W. Evaluation: from precision, recall and f-measure to roc, informedness, markedness and correlation. *CoRR abs/2010.16061* (2020). https://arxiv.org/abs/2010.16061.
186. PRAPAS, I., DERAKHSHAN, B., MAHDIRAJI, A. R., AND MARKL, V. Continuous training and deployment of deep learning models. *Datenbank-Spektrum 21*, 3 (2021), 203–212. https://doi.org/10.1007/s13222-021-00386-8.

187. Rachid, A. D., Abdellah, A., Belaid, B., and Rachid, L. Clustering prediction techniques in defining and predicting customers defection: The case of e-commerce context. *International Journal of Electrical and Computer Engineering 8*, 4 (2018), 2367.
188. Radford, A., and Narasimhan, K. Improving language understanding by generative pre-training, 2018.
189. Radford, A., Wu, J., Child, R., Luan, D., Amodei, D., and Sutskever, I. Language models are unsupervised multitask learners, 2019.
190. Rahman, M. S., Hossain, M. A., Zaman, M. H., and Mannan, M. E-service quality and trust on customer's patronage intention: moderation effect of adoption of advanced technologies. *Journal of Global Information Management (JGIM) 28*, 1 (2020), 39–55.
191. Rai, S., Gupta, A., Anand, A., Trivedi, A., and Bhadauria, S. Demand prediction for e-commerce advertisements: A comparative study using state-of-the-art machine learning methods. In *2019 10th International Conference on Computing, Communication and Networking Technologies (ICCCNT)* (2019), pp. 1–6.
192. Raji, M. A., Olodo, H. B., Oke, T. T., Addy, W. A., Ofodile, O. C., and Oyewole, A. T. E-commerce and consumer behavior: A review of ai-powered personalization and market trends. *GSC Advanced Research and Reviews 18*, 3 (2024), 066–077.
193. Raza, H. Understanding consumers buying behaviour analyzing nestle's television advertising strategies. *Journalism, Politics and Society 1*, 01 (Mar. 2023), 1–9. https://www.jpolas.com/index.php/Journal/article/view/2.
194. Razzaghi, P., Abbasi, K., and Ghasemi, J. B. Chapter 3—multivariate pattern recognition by machine learning methods. In *Machine Learning and Pattern Recognition Methods in Chemistry from Multivariate and Data Driven Modeling*, J. B. Ghasemi, Ed. Elsevier, 2023, pp. 47–72. https://www.sciencedirect.com/science/article/pii/B9780323904087000022.
195. REES46. OpenCDP E-Commerce Benchmark Dataset. https://rees46.com/. Accessed: 2025–06–30.
196. Ren, K., Zhang, W., Rong, Y., Zhang, H., Yu, Y., and Wang, J. User response learning for directly optimizing campaign performance in display advertising. In *Proceedings of the 25th ACM International on Conference on Information and Knowledge Management* (2016), pp. 679–688.
197. Ren, M., Triantafillou, E., Ravi, S., Snell, J., Swersky, K., Tenenbaum, J. B., Larochelle, H., and Zemel, R. S. Meta-learning for semi-supervised few-shot classification. *arXiv preprint* arXiv:1803.00676 (2018).
198. Romov, P., and Sokolov, E. Recsys challenge 2015: Ensemble learning with categorical features. In *Proceedings of the 2015 International ACM Recommender Systems Challenge* (New York, NY, USA, 2015), RecSys '15 Challenge, Association for Computing Machinery. https://doi.org/10.1145/2813448.2813510.
199. Rosenbloom, B.*Marketing channels: A management view*. South-Western, Cengage Learning, 2013.
200. Rudolph, M., and Blei, D. Dynamic embeddings for language evolution. In *Proceedings of the 2018 World Wide Web Conference* (Republic and Canton of Geneva, CHE, 2018), WWW '18, International World Wide Web Conferences Steering Committee, p. 1003–1011. https://doi.org/10.1145/3178876.3185999.

201. Santos, S., and Gonçalves, H. M. The consumer decision journey: A literature review of the foundational models and theories and a future perspective. *Technological Forecasting and Social Change 173* (2021), 121117.
202. Scherr, F., Guo, Q., and Moraitis, T. Self-supervised learning through efference copies. In *Advances in Neural Information Processing Systems* (2022), S. Koyejo, S. Mohamed, A. Agarwal, D. Belgrave, K. Cho, and A. Oh, Eds., vol. 35, Curran Associates, Inc., pp. 4543–4557. https://proceedings.neurips.cc/paper_files/paper/2022/file/1d1cea122b9ec9f78acc21510659e500-Paper-Conference.pdf.
203. Senel, L. K., Utlu, I., Yücesoy, V., Koç, A., and Çukur, T. Semantic structure and interpretability of word embeddings. *IEEE/ACM Transactions on Audio, Speech, and Language Processing 26*, 10 (2018), 1769–1779.
204. Sennrich, R., Haddow, B., and Birch, A. Neural machine translation of rare words with subword units. *arXiv preprint* arXiv:1508.07909 (2015).
205. Shalev- Shwartz, S., and Ben- David, S.*Understanding machine learning: From theory to algorithms*. Cambridge university press, 2014.
206. Sheil, H., Rana, O., and Reilly, R. Predicting purchasing intent: automatic feature learning using recurrent neural networks, 2018. http://arxiv.org/abs/1807.08207.
207. Shen, W. Deepctr: Easy-to-use, modular and extendible package of deep-learning based ctr models. https://github.com/shenweichen/deepctr, 2017.
208. Shin, H., Lee, J. K., Kim, J., and Kim, J. Continual learning with deep generative replay. In *Proceedings of the 31st International Conference on Neural Information Processing Systems* (Red Hook, NY, USA, 2017), NIPS'17, Curran Associates Inc., p. 2994–3003.
209. Shin, K., Kwak, H., Kim, S. Y., Ramström, M. N., Jeong, J., Ha, J.- W., and Kim, K.- M. Scaling law for recommendation models: towards general-purpose user representations. In *Proceedings of the Thirty-Seventh AAAI Conference on Artificial Intelligence and Thirty-Fifth Conference on Innovative Applications of Artificial Intelligence and Thirteenth Symposium on Educational Advances in Artificial Intelligence* (2023), Aaai'23/iaai'23/eaai'23, AAAI Press. https://doi.org/10.1609/aaai.v37i4.25582.
210. Siricharoen, W. V. Using empathy mapping in design thinking process for personas discovering. In *Context-Aware Systems and Applications, and Nature of Computation and Communication* (Cham, 2021), P. C. Vinh and A. Rakib, Eds., Springer International Publishing, pp. 182–191.
211. Sismeiro, C., and Bucklin, R. E. Modeling purchase behavior at an e-commerce web site: A task-completion approach. *Journal of Marketing Research 41*, 3 (2004), 306–323. https://doi.org/10.1509/jmkr.41.3.306.35985.
212. Sokol, O., and Holy, V. The role of shopping mission in retail customer segmentation. *Iternational Journal of Market Research 63*, 4 (2021), 454–470.
213. Soni, N., Sharma, E. K., Singh, N., and Kapoor, A. Artificial intelligence in business: from research and innovation to market deployment. *Procedia Computer Science 167* (2020), 2200–2210.
214. Srilakshmi, M., Chowdhury, G., and Sarkar, S. Two-stage system using item features for next-item recommendation. *Intelligent Systems With Applications 14* (2022), 200070. https://www.sciencedirect.com/science/article/pii/S2667305322000114.
215. State of California Department of Justice. California consumer privacy act (ccpa), 2018. https://oag.ca.gov/privacy/ccpa, accessed 2024–10–11.

216. STATISTA. ecommerce—worldwide, 2024. Retrieved October 07, 2024, from https://www.statista.com/outlook/emo/ecommerce/worldwide. https://www.statista.com/outlook/emo/ecommerce/worldwide.
217. STATISTA RESEARCH DEPARTMENT. Global digital population and eu e-commerce share as of 2024. https://www.statista.com/topics/871/online-shopping/, 2024. Accessed: 2025–06–30.
218. STORMI, K., LINDHOLM, A., LAINE, T., AND KORHONEN, T. Rfm customer analysis for product-oriented services and service business development: an interventionist case study of two machinery manufacturers. *Journal of Management & Governance 24*, 3, SI (2020), 623–653.
219. SUBROTO, C. A. M., AND AKBAR, S. The effect of preprocessing techniques on stacked generalization and stand-alone method for e-commerce demand prediction. In *2022 9th International Conference on Advanced Informatics: Concepts, Theory and Applications (ICAICTA)* (2022), pp. 1–6.
220. SUDIRMAN, I. D., SHARIF, O. O., RAHMATILLAH, I., AND DEWI, C. K. Customer purchase prediction using optimized decision tree with particle swarm optimization. In *2024 International Conference on Data Science and Its Applications (ICoDSA)* (2024), pp. 58–63.
221. SUN, F., LIU, J., WU, J., PEI, C., LIN, X., OU, W., AND JIANG, P. Bert4rec: Sequential recommendation with bidirectional encoder representations from transformer. In *Proceedings of the 28th ACM International Conference on Information and Knowledge Management* (New York, NY, USA, 2019), CIKM '19, Association for Computing Machinery, p. 1441–1450. https://doi.org/10.1145/3357384.3357895.
222. SUTSKEVER, I., VINYALS, O., AND LE, Q. V. Sequence to sequence learning with neural networks. In *Proceedings of the 27th International Conference on Neural Information Processing Systems—Volume 2* (Cambridge, MA, USA, 2014), NIPS'14, MIT Press, p. 3104–3112.
223. SUTTON, R. S., AND BARTO, A. G. *Reinforcement learning: An introduction.* MIT press, 2018.
224. TAM, K. Y., AND HO, S. Y. Understanding the impact of web personalization on user information processing and decision outcomes. *MIS Q. 30*, 4 (2006), 865–890.
225. TENDLE, A., AND HASAN, M. R. A study of the generalizability of self-supervised representations. *Machine Learning with Applications 6* (2021), 100124. https://www.sciencedirect.com/science/article/pii/S2666827021000621.
226. TERCAN, H., BITTER, C., BODNAR, T., MEISEN, P., AND MEISEN, T. Evaluating a session-based recommender system using prod2vec in a commercial application. In *Proceedings of the 23rd International Conference on Enterprise Information Systems - Volume 1: ICEIS,* (2021), INSTICC, SciTePress, pp. 610–617.
227. TIEN, J.- B., JOYCENV, AND CHAPELLE, O. Display advertising challenge. https://kaggle.com/competitions/criteo-display-ad-challenge, 2014. Kaggle.
228. TO, M. L., AND NGAI, E. W. Predicting the organisational adoption of b2c e-commerce: an empirical study. *Industrial Management & Data Systems 106*, 8 (2006), 1133–1147.
229. TOUSSIDE, B., FROCHTE, J., AND MEISEN, T. Dynamic capacity expansion in continual learning: The esecl approach. In *Agents and Artificial Intelligence* (Cham, 2025), A. P. Rocha, L. Steels, and J. van den Herik, Eds., Springer Nature Switzerland, pp. 272–291.

230. TSENG, K.- K., LIN, R. F.- Y., ZHOU, H., KURNIAJAYA, K. J., AND LI, Q. Price prediction of e-commerce products through internet sentiment analysis. *Electronic commerce research 18* (2018), 65–88.
231. TSCHANNEN, M., BACHEM, O., AND LUCIC, M. Recent advances in autoencoder-based representation learning. *CoRR abs/1812.05069* (2018). http://arxiv.org/abs/1812.05069.
232. URIBARRI, G., AND MINDLIN, G. B. Dynamical time series embeddings in recurrent neural networks. *Chaos, Solitons & Fractals 154* (2022), 111612. https://www.sciencedirect.com/science/article/pii/S0960077921009668.
233. U. S. DEPARTMENT OF JUSTICE. Electronic communications privacy act of 1986 (ecpa), 1986. https://bja.ojp.gov/program/it/privacy-civil-liberties/authorities/statutes/1285, accessed 2024–10–11.
234. VAN NGUYEN, A. T., MCCLELLAND, R., AND THUAN, N. H. Omni–channel customer segmentation: A personalized customer journey perspective. *Journal of Consumer Behaviour* (2024).
235. VAN RIJSBERGEN, C. J. Information retrieval. 2nd. newton, ma, 1979.
236. VASILE, F., SMIRNOVA, E., AND CONNEAU, A. Meta-prod2vec: Product embeddings using side-information for recommendation. In *Proceedings of the 10th ACM Conference on Recommender Systems* (New York, NY, USA, 2016), Association for Computing Machinery, pp. 225–232.
237. VASWANI, A., SHAZEER, N., PARMAR, N., USZKOREIT, J., JONES, L., GOMEZ, A. N., KAISER, L., AND POLOSUKHIN, I. Attention is all you need. *Advances in neural information processing systems 30* (2017).
238. VOM BROCKE, J., SIMONS, A., RIEMER, K., NIEHAVES, B., PLATTFAUT, R., AND CLEVEN, A. Standing on the shoulders of giants: Challenges and recommendations of literature search in information systems research. *Communications of the Association for Information Systems 37*, 1 (2015), 9.
239. WANG, D., LIN, J., CUI, P., JIA, Q., WANG, Z., FANG, Y., YU, Q., ZHOU, J., YANG, S., AND QI, Y. A semi-supervised graph attentive network for financial fraud detection. In *2019 IEEE International Conference on Data Mining (ICDM)* (2019), IEEE, pp. 598–607.
240. WANG, F., AND ZHAO, L. A hybrid model for commercial brand marketing prediction based on multiple features with image processing. *SECURITY AND COMMUNICATION NETWORKS 2022* (2022), 1–10.
241. WANG, L. Application of deep learning based inventory optimization and intelligent demand prediction in e-commerce. In *2024 International Conference on Power, Electrical Engineering, Electronics and Control (PEEEC)* (2024), pp. 1150–1153.
242. WANG, R., FU, B., FU, G., AND WANG, M. Deep & cross network for ad click predictions. ADKDD'17, Association for Computing Machinery. https://doi.org/10.1145/3124749.3124754.
243. WANG, Y., XUE, Y., LIU, B., WEN, M., ZHAO, W., GUO, S., AND YU, P. S. Click-conversion multi-task model with position bias mitigation for sponsored search in ecommerce. In *Proceedings of the 46th International ACM SIGIR Conference on Research and Development in Information Retrieval* (New York, NY, USA, 2023), SIGIR '23, Association for Computing Machinery, p. 1884–1888. https://doi.org/10.1145/3539618.3591963.

244. WANG, Y., ZHANG, D., AND WULAMU, A. Multi-view improved sequence behavior with adaptive multi-task learning in ranking. *Applied Intelligence* (2022), 1–20.
245. WARDANA, M. A., MASLIARDI, A., AFIFAH, N., SAJILI, M., AND KUSNARA, H. P. Unlocking purchase preferences: Harnessing psychographic segmentation, promotion and location strategies. *Jurnal Informatika Ekonomi Bisnis 5*, 3 (Sep. 2023), 713–719. https://www.infeb.org/index.php/infeb/article/view/624.
246. WIEDMANN, K.-P., BUXEL, H., AND WALSH, G. Customer profiling in e-commerce: Methodological aspects and challenges. *Journal of Database Marketing & Customer Strategy Management 9* (2002), 170–184.
247. WONG, C.-M., FENG, F., ZHANG, W., VONG, C.-M., CHEN, H., ZHANG, Y., HE, P., CHEN, H., ZHAO, K., AND CHEN, H. Improving conversational recommender system by pretraining billion-scale knowledge graph. In *2021 IEEE 37th International Conference on Data Engineering (ICDE)* (2021), pp. 2607–2612.
248. WU, C., WU, F., QI, T., LIAN, J., HUANG, Y., AND XIE, X. Ptum: Pre-training user model from unlabeled user behaviors via self-supervision. *arXiv preprint* arXiv:2010.01494 (2020).
249. WU, C., AND YAN, M. Session-aware information embedding for e-commerce product recommendation. In *Proceedings of the 2017 ACM on Conference on Information and Knowledge Management* (New York, NY, USA, 2017), CIKM '17, Association for Computing Machinery, pp. 2379–2382. https://doi.org/10.1145/3132847.3133163.
250. WU, T., KHAN, A., YONG, M., QI, G., AND WANG, M. Efficiently embedding dynamic knowledge graphs. *Know.-Based Syst. 250*, C (Aug. 2022). https://doi.org/10.1016/j.knosys.2022.109124.
251. WU, W.-W. Segmenting and mining the erp users' perceived benefits using the rough set approach. *Expert Systems With Applications 38*, 6 (2011), 6940–6948.
252. WU, Z., PAN, S., CHEN, F., LONG, G., ZHANG, C., AND YU, P. S. A comprehensive survey on graph neural networks. *IEEE Transactions on Neural Networks and Learning Systems 32*, 1 (2021), 4–24.
253. WU, Z., PAN, S., LONG, G., JIANG, J., AND ZHANG, C. Graph wavenet for deep spatial-temporal graph modeling. In *Proceedings of the 28th International Joint Conference on Artificial Intelligence (IJCAI-19)* (2019), IJCAI/AAAI Press, pp. 1907–1913.
254. XIA, Z., MAO, S., BAI, J., GENG, X., AND YI, L. A novel integrated network with lightgbm for click-through rate prediction. *Research Square* (2021).
255. XIAHOU, X., AND HARADA, Y. B2c e-commerce customer churn prediction based on k-means and svm. *Journal of Theoretical and Applied Electronic Commerce Research 17*, 2 (2022), 458–475. https://www.mdpi.com/0718-1876/17/2/24.
256. XIAO, Y., HE, W., ZHU, Y., AND ZHU, J. A click-through rate model of e-commerce based on user interest and temporal behavior. *EXPERT SYSTEMS WITH APPLICATIONS 207* (2022), 117896.
257. XU, Y., WANG, Z., AND CHEN, H. A-wdl: An improved recommendation algorithm for wdl based on attentional mechanism adaptation. *Research Square* (2021).
258. XUE, T., LIN, Z., ZHANG, Z., GUO, L., CHEN, H., BAO, M., AND YAN, P. Large scale hierarchical user interest modeling for click-through rate prediction. In *Proceedings of the Recommender Systems Challenge 2024* (New York, NY, USA, 2024), RecSysChallenge '24, Association for Computing Machinery, p. 53–57. https://doi.org/10.1145/3687151.3687163.

259. YAN, S., XIE, J., AND HE, X. Der: Dynamically expandable representation for class incremental learning. In *2021 IEEE/CVF Conference on Computer Vision and Pattern Recognition (CVPR)* (2021), pp. 3013–3022.
260. YANG, B., GU, J., LIU, K., XU, X., XU, R., SUN, Q., AND LIU, H. Empowering general-purpose user representation with full-life cycle behavior modeling. In *Proceedings of the 29th ACM SIGKDD Conference on Knowledge Discovery and Data Mining* (New York, NY, USA, 2023), Kdd '23, Association for Computing Machinery, p. 2908–2917. https://doi.org/10.1145/3580305.3599331.
261. YANG, B., LIU, K., XU, X., XU, R., LIU, H., ET AL. Learning universal user representations via self-supervised lifelong behaviors modeling, 2021. https://openreview.net/forum?id=YTtMaJUN_uc.
262. YAO, S., TAN, J., CHEN, X., YANG, K., XIAO, R., DENG, H., AND WAN, X. Learning a product relevance model from click-through data in e-commerce. In *Proceedings of the Web Conference 2021* (2021), pp. 2890–2899.
263. YAO, Z., SUN, Y., DING, W., RAO, N., AND XIONG, H. Dynamic word embeddings for evolving semantic discovery. In *Proceedings of the Eleventh ACM International Conference on Web Search and Data Mining* (New York, NY, USA, 2018), WSDM '18, Association for Computing Machinery, p. 673–681. https://doi.org/10.1145/3159652.3159703.
264. YUAN, Q., ZHU, M., LI, Y., LIU, H., AND GUO, S. Feature-interaction-enhanced sequential transformer for click-through rate prediction. *Applied Sciences 14*, 7 (2024). https://www.mdpi.com/2076-3417/14/7/2760.
265. ZANKER, M., ROOK, L., AND JANNACH, D. Measuring the impact of online personalisation: Past, present and future. *International Journal of Human-Computer Studies 131* (2019), 160–168. 50 years of the International Journal of Human-Computer Studies. Reflections on the past, present and future of human-centred technologies. https://www.sciencedirect.com/science/article/pii/S107158191930076X.
266. ZEITHAML, V. A., RUST, R. T., AND LEMON, K. N. The customer pyramid: creating and serving profitable customers. *California Management Review 43*, 4 (2001), 118–142.
267. ZENG, F., LI, Y., XIAO, J., AND YANG, D. Ddhcn: Dual decoder hyperformer convolutional network for downstream-adaptable user representation learning on app usage. *Expert Syst. Appl. 237*, Pb (03 2024). https://doi.org/10.1016/j.eswa.2023.121564.
268. ZENG, J., CHEN, Y., ZHU, H., TIAN, F., MIAO, K., LIU, Y., AND ZHENG, Q. User sequential behavior classification for click-through rate prediction. In *Database Systems for Advanced Applications. DASFAA 2020 International Workshops*. Springer, Berlin/Heidelberg, Germany, 2020, pp. 267–280.
269. ZENG, M., CAO, H., CHEN, M., AND LI, Y. User behaviour modeling, recommendations, and purchase prediction during shopping festivals. *Electronic Markets 29* (2019), 263–274.
270. ZENG, X., PAN, Y., WANG, M., ZHANG, J., AND LIU, Y. Realistic face reenactment via self-supervised disentangling of identity and pose. *Proceedings of the AAAI Conference on Artificial Intelligence 34*, 07 (Apr. 2020), 12757–12764. https://ojs.aaai.org/index.php/AAAI/article/view/6970.
271. ZHANG, A., LIPTON, Z. C., LI, M., AND SMOLA, A. J. *Dive into Deep Learning*. Cambridge University Press, 2023. https://D2L.ai.

272. Zhang, H., Pan, J., Liu, D., Jiang, J., and Li, X. Deep pattern network for click-through rate prediction. In *Proceedings of the 47th International ACM SIGIR Conference on Research and Development in Information Retrieval* (New York, NY, USA, 2024), SIGIR '24, Association for Computing Machinery, p. 1189–1199. https://doi.org/10.1145/3626772.3657777.
273. Zhang, S., Ye, J., and Wang, Q. Spa-l transformer: Sparse-self attention model of long short-term memory positional encoding based on long text classification. In *2023 26th International Conference on Computer Supported Cooperative Work in Design (CSCWD)* (2023), pp. 618–623.
274. Zhang, W., Yang, L., Geng, S., and Hong, S. Self-supervised time series representation learning via cross reconstruction transformer. *IEEE Transactions on Neural Networks and Learning Systems 35*, 11 (2024), 16129–16138. https://doi.org/10.1109/TNNLS.2023.3292066.
275. Zhang, X., Wang, Z., Du, B., Wu, J., Zhang, X., and Meng, E. Deep session heterogeneity-aware network for click through rate prediction. *IEEE Transactions on Knowledge and Data Engineering 36*, 12 (2024), 7927–7939.
276. Zhang, Y., Chen, M., Chen, R., Zhao, C., Yuan, M., and Sun, Z. Bayesian attention-based user behaviour modelling for click-through rate prediction. *CAAI Transactions on Intelligence Technology 9*, 5 (2024), 1320–1330. https://ietresearch.onlinelibrary.wiley.com/doi/abs/10.1049/cit2.12343.
277. Zhang, Z. From artificial neural networks to deep learning: A research survey. *Journal of Physics: Conference Series 1576*, 1 (jun 2020), 012030. https://dx.doi.org/10.1088/1742-6596/1576/1/012030.
278. Zhou, C., Bai, J., Song, J., Liu, X., Zhao, Z., Chen, X., and Gao, J. Atrank: An attention-based user behavior modeling framework for recommendation. *Proceedings of the AAAI Conference on Artificial Intelligence 32*, 1 (4 2018). https://ojs.aaai.org/index.php/AAAI/article/view/11618.
279. Zhou, G., Mou, N., Fan, Y., Pi, Q., Bian, W., Zhou, C., Zhu, X., and Gai, K. Deep interest evolution network for click-through rate prediction. *Proceedings of the AAAI Conference on Artificial Intelligence 33* (2019), 5941–5948.
280. Zhou, G., Zhu, X., Song, C., Fan, Y., Zhu, H., Ma, X., Yan, Y., Jin, J., Li, H., and Gai, K. Deep interest network for click-through rate prediction. In *Proceedings of the 24th ACM SIGKDD International Conference on Knowledge Discovery & Data Mining* (New York, NY, USA, 2018), KDD '18, Association for Computing Machinery, p. 1059–1068. https://doi.org/10.1145/3219819.3219823.
281. Zhou, J., Gandomi, A. H., Chen, F., and Holzinger, A. Evaluating the quality of machine learning explanations: A survey on methods and metrics. *Electronics 10*, 5 (2021). https://www.mdpi.com/2079-9292/10/5/593.
282. Zhou, S., and Hudin, N. S. Advancing e-commerce user purchase prediction: Integration of time-series attention with event-based timestamp encoding and graph neural network-enhanced user profiling. *PLOS ONE 19*, 4 (04 2024), 1–26. https://doi.org/10.1371/journal.pone.0299087.

283. Zhou, Z.- H.*Machine learning*. Springer Nature, 2021. https://doi.org/10.1007/978-981-15-1967-3.

284. Zhu, H., Shen, C., Li, L., Wang, D., Huang, W., and Zhu, Z. Reserving embedding space for new fault types: A new continual learning method for bearing fault diagnosis. *Reliability Engineering & System Safety 252* (2024), 110433. https://www.sciencedirect.com/science/article/pii/S0951832024005052.

285. Zhu, X., Ye, Y., Zhao, L., and Shen, C. Mooc behavior analysis and academic performance prediction based on entropy. *Sensors 21*, 19 (2021), 6629.

MIX
Papier aus verantwortungsvollen Quellen
Paper from responsible sources
FSC® C105338

If you have any concerns about our products,
you can contact us on
ProductSafety@springernature.com

In case Publisher is established outside the EU,
the EU authorized representative is:
Springer Nature Customer Service Center GmbH
Europaplatz 3, 69115 Heidelberg, Germany

Printed by Libri Plureos GmbH
in Hamburg, Germany